COMPARATISTS AT WORK

A BLAISDELL BOOK IN COMPARATIVE LITERATURE

COMPARATISTS AT WORK

WORK

■   *Studies in Comparative Literature*

EDITED BY
STEPHEN G. NICHOLS, JR.
RICHARD B. VOWLES
UNIVERSITY OF WISCONSIN

Blaisdell Publishing Company

A DIVISION OF GINN AND COMPANY

WALTHAM, MASSACHUSETTS ■ TORONTO ■ LONDON

ACKNOWLEDGMENTS

The editors are grateful to the following individuals and publishers for their permission to reprint the articles used in this book:

HASKELL M. BLOCK and the University of Illinois Press for permission to reprint "The Alleged Parallel of Metaphysical and Symbolist Poetry" which appeared in *Comparative Literature Studies*, 4 (1967), 145–159.

WOLFGANG BERNARD FLEISCHMANN for permission to reprint "Christ and Epicurus"

GEORGE GIBIAN for permission to reprint "The Forms of Discontent in Dostoevsky and Tolstoy"

CLAUDIO GUILLÉN for permission to reprint "On the Concept and Metaphor of Perspective"

JEAN HAGSTRUM for permission to reprint "The Sister Arts: From Neoclassic to Romantic"

HARRY LEVIN and the Oxford University Press for permission to reprint "Shakespeare in the Light of Comparative Literature" from *Refractions: Essays in Comparative Literature*, New York and London, 1966. This essay first appeared in *A Garland for Mario Praz*, ed. Vittorio Gabrieli (Rome: Edizioni de Storia e Letteratura, 1966).

NEAL OXENHANDLER for permission to reprint "Character and Emotion in Balzac's Novels"

JOSEPH SZILI for permission to reprint "Recent Trends of Marxist Criticism in the Countries of Eastern Europe"

RENÉ WELLEK for permission to reprint "The Name and Nature of Comparative Literature"

THEODORE ZIOLKOWSKI for permission to reprint "The Crisis of the Thirty-Year-Old in Modern Fiction: Toward a Phenomenology of the Novel"

Preface

Although comparative literature continues to expand at a rather astonishing rate, it may safely be said that many people, and not only students, remain unclear as to the concept and nature of the discipline. Part of the confusion, of course, stems from the fact that, traditionally, the study of literature has been under the auspices of given language departments who accepted responsibility for the literature written in the languages they represented. The division was a purely mechanical one, fostered by the political and economic structure of higher institutions of learning. It had little basis in fact, for the mode of existence of literary works is not bound in a fatally deterministic way to the fortune of the language in which they are written.

Nevertheless, there remains a certain resistance to the notion that literature should be studied and taught by scholars who are not safely identified with a traditional language department. "Comparative literature is nothing but watered-down literature," complained one graduate student of English recently, as though the whole question were one of bonded spirits rather than intellectual endeavor. The student's scorn was prompted by the widespread misconception that comparative literature simply veils in elegant euphemism the venerable concept of literature-in-translation. That notion was and is a very democratic one, offering the possibility of acquaintance with the riches of world literature to those who have not had the advantage of language training. In no sense, however, can it be termed a discipline.

Comparative literature, on the other hand, *is* a discipline in the best sense of the term, and one that touches on all aspects of the study of literature. Professed by scholars and teachers who have had a thorough grounding in at least three languages and literatures, the discipline concerns itself particularly with aspects of literary criticism, literary theory, and literary history, with the interaction of literature and the other arts, and with the role of literature in the development of the great ideas that have motivated societies and individuals throughout history. One of the best theoretical expositions of the interconnected functions of literary criticism, theory, and history may be found in René Wellek's *Concepts of Criticism* (New Haven, Conn.: Yale Univ. Press, 1963), particularly in the first chapter. Roughly speaking, though, these branches of literary study comprehend such questions as structure, style, rhetoric, language, on the formal level; typology, themes, mythology, periodization, genre theory, and so forth, on the broader scale. Theoretical formulations suggest the topics for practical criticism, while the historical view helps to provide the proper perspective for evaluating both the literature and the concepts developed to study it. The primary purpose of comparative literature, however, remains what Harry Levin has felicitously called "comparing the literature."

This does not mean simply and baldly tracing the influence of the literature of one language or period upon another. Rather, Mr. Levin's phrase is a gentle reminder that theory, either literary or critical, is not an end in itself: the fundamental principle of the discipline remains the study of the concrete work of literature in all its aspects.

With this stricture in mind, the editors set out to demonstrate the nature of the discipline by showing how comparatists work. The thought was not to make a formal handbook, but to offer a sampler with a broad range of questions actively being explored by some of the leading scholars in the field. The questions raised, as well as the general rubrics under which they are placed, should thus in no way be taken as exhaustive. In a very real sense, our purpose was less to emphasize the methodology of the discipline than to stress how consistently it strives to elucidate the necessary relations between individual works, their literary traditions, and the audience responsible for keeping both alive. If the book succeeds, even the casual reader interested only in a single essay should come away with a sense of what Wellek, at the close of his essay, calls "the wide perspective which only comparative literature can give."

S. G. N., Jr.

Contents

I | CRITICAL THEORY

René Wellek

The Name and Nature
of Comparative Literature

The term "comparative literature" has given rise to so much discussion, has been interpreted so differently and misinterpreted so frequently that it might be useful to examine its history and to attempt to distinguish its meanings in the main languages. Only then can we hope to define its exact scope and content. Lexicography, "historical semantics," will be our starting point. Beyond it, a brief history of comparative studies should lead to conclusions of contemporary relevance. "Comparative literature" is still a controversial discipline and idea.

There seems no particular problem raised by our two words individually. "Comparative" occurs in Middle English, obviously derived from Latin *comparativus*, and it is used by Shakespeare, as when Falstaff denounces Prince Hal as "the most comparative, rascalliest, sweet young prince." [1] Francis Meres, as early as 1598, uses the term in the caption of "A Comparative Discourse of Our English Poets with the Greek, Latin and Italian Poets." [2] The adjective occurs in the titles of several seventeenth and eighteenth century books: in 1602 William Fulbecke published *A Comparative Discourse of the Laws*. I also find *A Comparative Anatomy of Brute Animals* in 1765. Its author, John Gregory, published *A Comparative View of the State and Faculties of Man with Those of the Animal World* in the very next year. Bishop Robert Lowth in his Latin *Lectures on the Sacred Poetry of the Hebrews* (1753) formulated the ideal of comparative study well enough: "We must see all things with their eyes [i.e., the ancient Hebrews]: estimate all things by their opinions; we must endeavour as much as possible to read Hebrew as the Hebrews would have read it. We must act as the Astronomers with regard to that branch of their science which is called comparative who, in order to form a more perfect idea of the general system and its different parts, conceive themselves as passing through, and surveying, the whole universe, migrating from one planet to another and becoming for a short time inhabitants of each." [3] In his pioneering *History of English Poetry*, Thomas

3

Warton announced in the Preface to the first volume that he would present "a comparative survey of the poetry of other nations." [4] George Ellis, in his *Specimens of Early English Poets* (1790) speaks of antiquaries whose "ingenuity has often been successful in detecting and extracting by comparative criticism many particulars respecting the state of society and the progress of arts and manners" from medieval chronicles.[5] In 1800, Charles Dibdin published, in five volumes, *A Complete History of the English Stage, Introduced by a Comparative and Comprehensive Review of the Asiatic, the Grecian, the Roman, the Spanish, the Italian, the Portuguese, the German, the French and other Theatres.* Here the main idea is fully formulated, but the combination "comparative literature" itself seems to occur for the first time only in a letter by Matthew Arnold in 1848 where he says: "How plain it is now, though an attention to the comparative literatures for the last fifty years might have instructed anyone of it, that England is in a certain sense far behind the Continent." But this was a private letter not published till 1895 and "comparative" means here hardly more than "comparable." In English, the decisive use was that of Hutcheson Macaulay Posnett, an Irish barrister who later became Professor of Classics and English Literature at University College, Auckland, New Zealand, who put the term on the title of his book in 1886. As part of Kegan Paul, Trench, and Trübner's International Scientific Series, the book aroused some attention and was, e.g., favorably reviewed by William Dean Howells.[7] Posnett, in an article, "The Science of Comparative Literature," claimed "to have first stated and illustrated the method and principles of the new science, and to have been the first to do so not only in the British Empire but in the world." [8] Obviously this is preposterous, even if we limit "comparative literature" to the specific meaning Posnett gave to it. The English term cannot be discussed in isolation from analogous terms in France and Germany.

The lateness of the English term can be explained if we realize that the combination "comparative literature" was resisted in English, because the term "literature" had lost its earlier meaning of "knowledge or study of literature" and had come to mean "literary production in general" or "the body of writings in a period, country, or region." That this long process is complete today is obvious from such a fact that, e.g., Professor Lane Cooper of Cornell University refused to call the department he headed in the twenties "Comparative Literature" and insisted on "The Comparative Study of Literature." He considered it a "bogus term" that "makes neither sense nor syntax." "You might as well permit yourself to say 'comparative potatoes' or 'comparative husks'." [9]   But in earlier English usage "literature" meant "learning" and "literary culture," particularly a knowledge of Latin. *The Tatler* reflects sagely in 1710: "It is in vain for folly to attempt to conceal itself by the refuge of learned languages. Literature does but make a man more eminently the thing which nature made him." [10]   Boswell says, for instance, that Baretti was an "Italian of considerable literature." [11]   This usage survived into the 19th century, when James Ingram gave an inaugural lecture on the *Utility of Anglo-Saxon Literature* (1807), meaning the "utility of our knowing Anglo-Saxon," or when J. Petherham wrote *An Historical Sketch of the Progress and Present State of Anglo-Saxon Literature in England* (1840), where "literature" obviously must mean the study of literature. But these were survivals; "literature" had assumed by then the present meaning of a body of writing. The *Oxford English Dictionary* gives the first occurrence in 1812, but this is far too late; rather, the modern usage penetrated in the later 18th century from France.

Actually, the meaning of "literature" as "literary production" or "a body of writings" revived a usage of late antiquity. Earlier *literatura* in Latin is simply a translation of the Greek *grammatike* and sometimes means a knowledge of reading and writing, or even an inscription or the alphabet itself. But Tertullian (who lived from about A.D. 160 to 240) and Cassian contrast secular literature with scriptural, pagan with Christian, *literatura* with *scriptura*.[12]

This use of the term reemerges only in the thirties of the 18th century in competition with the term *literae, lettres, letters*. An early example is François Granet's series, *Réflexions sur les ouvrages de littérature* (1736–1740). Voltaire in *Le Siècle de Louis XIV* (1751), under the chapter heading "des Beaux Arts," uses *littérature* with an uncertain reference alongside "eloquence, poets, and books of morals and amusement," and elsewhere in the book he speaks of "littérature légère" and "les genres de littérature" cultivated in Italy.[13]   In 1759 Lessing began to publish his *Briefe die neueste Literatur betreffend*, where literature clearly refers to a body of writings. That the usage was still unusual at that time may be illustrated from the fact that Nicolas Trublet's *Essais sur divers sujets de littérature et morale* (1735–1754) were translated into German as *Versuche über verschiedene Gegenstände der Sittenlehre und Gelehrsamkeit* (1776).[14]

This use of the word "literature" for all literary production, which is still one of our meanings, was in the 18th century soon nationalized and localized. It was applied to French, German, Italian, and Venetian literature, and almost simultaneously the term often lost its original inclusiveness and was narrowed down to mean what we would today call "imaginative literature," poetry, and imaginative, fictive prose. The first book which exemplifies this double change is, as far as I know, Carlo Denina's *Discorso sopra le vicende della letteratura* (1760).[15] Denina professes "not to speak of the progress of the sciences and arts, which are not properly a part of literature"; he will speak of works of learning only when they belong to "good taste, and to eloquence, that is to say, to literature." [16] The Preface of the French translator speaks of Italian, English, Greek and Latin literature. In 1774 there appeared an *Essai sur la littérature russe* by N. Novikov in Leghorn, and we have a sufficiently local reference in Mario Foscarini's *Storia della letteratura veneziana* (1752). The process of nationalization and, if I may use the term, aesthetization of the word is beautifully illustrated by A. de Giorgi-Bertòla's *Idea della letteratura alemanna* (Lucca, 1784), which is an expanded edition of the earlier *Idea della poesia alemanna* (Naples, 1779), where the change of title was forced by his inclusion of a report on German novels.[17] In German the term *Nationalliteratur* focuses on the nation as the unit of literature: it appears for the first time on the title of Leonhard Meister's *Beyträge zur Geschichte der teutschen Sprache und Nationalliteratur* (1777) and persists into the 19th century. Some of the best known German literary histories carry it on the title: Wachler, Koberstein, Gervinus in 1835, and later A. Vilmar, and R. Gottschall.[18]

But the aesthetic limitation of the term was for a long time strongly resented. Philarète Chasles, for example, comments in 1847: "I have little esteem for the word literature; it seems to me meaningless; it is a result of intellectual corruption." It seems to him tied to the Roman and Greek tradition of rhetoric. It is "something which is neither philosophy, nor history, nor erudition, nor criticism—something I know not what in being vague, ungraspable and elusive." [19] Chasles prefers "intellectual history" to "literary history."

In English the same process took place. Sometimes it is still difficult to distinguish between the old meaning of literature as literary culture and a reference to a body of writing. Thus, as early as 1755, Dr. Johnson wanted to found *Annals of Literature, Foreign as well as Domestick.* In 1761 George Colman, the elder, thought that "Shakespeare and Milton seem to stand alone, like first rate authors, amid the general wreck of old English Literature." [20] In 1767 Adam Ferguson included a chapter, "Of the History of Literature," in his *Essay on the History of Civil Society.* In 1774 Dr. Johnson, in a letter, wished that "what is undeservedly forgotten of our antiquated literature might be revived," [21] and John Berkenhout in 1777 subtitled his *Biographia Literaria, A Biographical History of Literature,* in which he proposed to give a "concise view of the rise and progress of literature." The Preface to De La Curme de Sainte-Palaye's *Literary History of the Trouba- dours*, translated in 1779 by Mrs. Susanna Dobson, speaks of the troubadours as "the fathers of modern literature" and James Beattie, in 1783, wants to trace the rise and progress of romance in order to shed light upon "the history and politics, the manners and the literature of these latter ages." [22] There were books such as William Rutherford's *A View of Ancient History, Including the Progress of Literature, and the Fine Arts* (1788), *Sketches of a History of Literature* by Robert Alves (1794), and *An Introduction to the Literary History of the 14th and 15th Centuries* (1798) by Andrew Philpot, which complains that "there is nothing more wanting in English literature" than "a history of the revival of letters." But we may be surprised to hear that the first book with the title *A History of English Language and Literature* was a little handbook by Robert Chambers in 1836 and that the first Professor of English Language and Literature was the Reverend Thomas Dale, at University College, London, in 1828. [23]

Thus the change in meaning of the term "literature" hindered in English the adoption of the term "comparative literature," while "com- parative politics," prominently advocated by the historian E. A. Free- man in 1873, [24] was quite acceptable, as was "comparative grammar," which appeared on the title page of a translation of Franz Bopp's *Comparative Grammar of Sanskrit, Zend, Greek, etc.* in 1844.

In France the story was different; there *littérature* for a long time preserved the meaning of literary study. Voltaire, in his unfinished article on *Littérature* for his *Dictionnaire philosophique* (1764–1772) defines literature as "a knowledge of the works of taste, a smattering of history, poetry, eloquence and criticism," and he distinguishes it from "la belle littérature" which relates to "objects of beauty, to poetry, eloquence and well-written history." [25] Voltaire's follower, Jean-François Marmontel, who wrote the main literary articles for the great *Encyclopédie* which were collected as *Eléments de littérature* (1787), clearly uses *littérature* as meaning "a knowledge of *belles lettres*" which he contrasts with erudition. "With wit, talent and taste," he avows, "one can produce ingenious works, without any erudi- tion, and with little literature." [26] Thus it was possible early in the 19th century to form the combination *littérature comparée*, which was apparently suggested by Cuvier's famous *Anatomie comparée* (1800) or Dégerando's *Histoire comparée des systèmes de philosophie* (1804). In 1816 two compilers, Noël and Laplace, published a series of anthologies from French, classical, and English literature with the otherwise unused and unexplained title page: *Cours de littérature comparée.*[27] Charles

Pougens in *Lettres philosophiques à Madame xxx sur divers sujets de morale et littérature* (1826) complained that there is no work on the principles of literature he can recommend: "un cours de littérature comme je l'entends, c'est-à-dire, un cours de littérature comparée." [28]

The man, however, who gave the term currency in France was undoubtedly Abel-François Villemain, whose course in 18th century literature was a tremendous success at the Sorbonne in the late twenties. It was published in 1828–1829 as *Tableau de la littérature française au XVIIIe siècle* in 4 volumes, with even the flattering reactions of the audience inserted ("Vifs applaudissements. On rit."). There he uses several times *tableau comparé, études comparées, histoire comparée,* but also *littérature comparée* in praising the Chancelier d'Agnesseau for his "vastes études de philosophie, d'histoire, de littérature comparée." [29] In the second lecture series, *Tableau de la littérature au moyen âge en France, en Italie, en Espagne et en Angleterre* (2 vols., 1830), he speaks again of "amateurs de la littérature comparée," and in the Preface to the new edition in 1840, Villemain, not incorrectly, boasts that here for the first time in a French university an attempt at an "analyse comparée" of several modern literatures was made.[30]

After Villemain the term was used fairly frequently. Philarète Chasles delivered an inaugural lecture at the Athénée in 1835: in the printed version in the *Revue de Paris,* the course is called "Littérature étrangère comparée." [31] Adolphe-Louis de Puibusque wrote a two-volume *Histoire comparée de la littérature française et espagnole* (1843) where he quotes Villemain, the perpetual Secretary of the French Academy, as settling the question. The term *comparative,* however, seems to have for a time competed with *comparée.* J.–J. Ampère, in his *Discours sur l'histoire de la poésie* (1830), speaks of "l'histoire comparative des arts et de la littérature" [32] but later also uses the other term in the title of his *Histoire de la littérature française au moyen âge comparée aux littératures étrangères* (1841). The decisive text in favor of the term *littérature comparée* is in Sainte-Beuve's very late article, an obituary of Ampère, in the *Revue des Deux Mondes* in 1868.[33]

In Germany the word "comparative" was translated *vergleichend* in scientific contexts. Goethe in 1795 wrote "Erster Entwurf einer allgemeinen Einleitung in die vergleichende Anatomie." [34] *Vergleichende Grammatik* was used by August Wilhelm Schlegel in a review in 1803,[35] and Friedrich Schlegel's pioneering book, *Über Sprache und Weisheit der Inder* (1808), used *vergleichende Grammatik* [36] prominently as a program of a new science expressly recalling the model of "vergleichende Anatomie." The adjective becomes common in Germany for ethnology, and later psychology, historiography, and poetics. But for the very same reason as in English, it had difficulty making its way with the word "literature." As far as I know, Moriz Carriere in 1854 in a book, *Das Wesen und die Formen der Poesie,* uses the term *vergleichende Literaturgeschichte* for the first time.[37] The term *vergleichende Literatur* occurs surprisingly as the title of a forgotten periodical edited by Hugo von Meltzl, in the remote city of Klausenburg (now Cluj in Rumania): his *Zeitschrift für vergleichende Literatur* ran from 1877–1888. In 1886 Max Koch, at the University of Breslau, founded a *Zeitschrift für vergleichende Literaturgeschichte,* which survived till 1910. Von Meltzl emphasized that his conception of comparative literature was not confined to history and, in the last numbers of his periodical, changed the title to *Zeitschrift für vergleichende Literaturwissenschaft.*[38] A fairly new term in German, *Literaturwissenschaft,* was adopted early in the 20th century for what we usually call "literary criticism," or "theory of literature." The new German periodical *Arcadia* is called *Zeitschrift für vergleichende Literaturwissenschaft.*

There is no need to enter into a history of the terms elsewhere: In Italian *letteratura comparata* is clearly and easily formed on the French model. The great critic Francesco De Sanctis occupied a chair called *Della letteratura comparata* at Naples, from 1872 till his death in 1883.[39] Arturo Graf became the holder of such a chair at Turin in 1876. In Spanish the term *literatura comparada* seems even more recent.

I am not sure when the term is used first in the Slavic languages; Alexander Veselovsky, the greatest Russian *comparatiste* does not use the term in his inaugural lecture as Professor of General Literature at St. Petersburg in 1870, but he reviewed Koch's new periodical in 1887 and uses there the term *sravitelnoe literaturovedenie,* which is closely modeled on *vergleichende Literaturwissenschaft.*[40] At the University of Prague a chair called *srovnávací literatura* was created in 1911.

In its detail incomplete or even slightly. incorrect, this history of the terms in the main languages could become more meaningful if treated in the context of competition with rival terms. "Comparative literature" occurs in what semanticists have called "a field of meaning." We have alluded to "learning," "letters," and *"belles lettres,"* as rival terms for "literature." "Universal literature," "international literature," "general literature," and "world literature" are the competitors of "comparative literature." "Universal literature" occurs in the 18th century and is used rather widely in German: there is an article in 1776 discussing *eine Universalgeschichte der Dichtkunst,* and in 1859 a reviewer proposed *eine Universalgeschichte der modernen Littera-tur*.[41] "General literature" exists in English: e.g., James Montgomery gave *Lectures on General Literature, Poetry,* etc. (1833), where "general literature" means what we would call "theory of literature" or "principles of criticism." The Rev. Thomas Dale in 1831 became Professor of English Literature and History in the Department of General Literature and Science at King's College, London.[42] In Germany J. G. Eichhorn edited a whole series of books called *Allgemeine Geschichte der Literatur* (1788ff). There were similar compilations: Johann David Hartmann, *Versuch einer allgemeinen Geschichte der Poesie* (2 vols., 1797 and 1798), and Ludwig Wachler, *Versuch einer allgemeinen Geschichte der Literatur* in 4 volumes, (1793–1801), and Johann George Grässe's *Lehrbuch einer allgemeinen Literärgeschichte* (1837–1857), an enormous bibliographical compilation.

The term "world literature," *Weltliteratur,* was used by Goethe in 1827 commenting on a translation of his drama *Tasso* into French and then several times, sometimes in slightly different senses: he thought mainly of a single unified world literature in which differences between the individual literatures would disappear, though he knew that this would be quite remote. In a draft, Goethe equates "European" with "world literature," surely provisionally.[43] There is a well-known poem by Goethe, "Weltliteratur," (1827), which rehearses rather the delights of folk poetry and actually got its title erroneously from the editor of the 1840 posthumous edition.[44] The history of the concept has been studied well.[45] Today world literature may mean simply all literature, as in the title of many books, such as Otto Hauser's, or it may mean a canon of excellent works from many languages, as when you say that this or that book or author belongs to world literature: Ibsen belongs to world literature, while Jonas Lie does not. Swift belongs to world literature, while Thomas Hardy does not.

Just as the exact use of "world literature" is still debatable, the use of "comparative literature" has given rise to disputes as to its exact scope and methods which are not yet resolved. It is useless to be dogmatic about such matters, as words have the meaning authors assign to them and neither a knowledge of history nor common usage can prevent changes and even complete distortions of the original meaning. Still, clarity on such matters avoids mental confusion, while excessive ambiguity or arbitrariness leads into intellectual dangers which may not be as serious as calling hot, cold, or communism, democracy, but which still hamper agreement and communication. One can distinguish, first, a strict, narrow definition; Van Tieghem, for example, defines it thus: "The object of comparative literature is essentially the study of diverse literatures in their relations with one another." [46]   Guyard in his handbook, which follows Van Tieghem closely in doctrine and contents, calls comparative literature succinctly "the history of international literary relations," [47] and J.–M. Carré in his Preface to Guyard calls it "a branch of literary history; it is the study of spiritual international relations, of factual contacts which took place between Byron and Pushkin, Goethe and Carlyle, Walter Scott and Vigny, between the works, the inspirations and even the lives of writers belonging to several literatures." [48]   Similar formulations can be found elsewhere: e.g., in the volume on comparative literature of Momigliano's series *Problemi ed orientamenti* (1948), where Anna Saita Ravignes speaks of comparative literature as "a modern science which centers on research into the problems connected with the influences exercised reciprocally by various literatures." [49]   Fernand Baldensperger, the recognized leader of the French school, in the programmatic article introducing the first number of the *Revue de littérature comparée* (1921) does not attempt a definition but agrees with one implied limitation of the concept: he has no use for comparisons which do not involve "a real encounter" which has "created a dependence." [50] But his article does discuss many wider problems excluded by his followers.

In a wider sense "comparative literature" includes what Van Tieghem calls "general literature."   He confines "comparative literature" to "binary" relations, between two elements, while "general literature" concerns research into "the facts common to several literatures." [51]   It can, however, be argued that it is impossible to draw a line between comparative literature and general literature, between, say, the influence of Walter Scott in France and the rise of the historical novel.   Besides, the term "general literature" lends itself to confusion: it has been understood to mean literary theory, poetics, the principles of literature. Comparative literature in the narrow sense of binary relations cannot make a meaningful discipline, as it would have to deal only with the "foreign trade" between literatures and hence with fragments of the literary production.   It would not allow handling the individual work of art.   It would be (as apparently Carré is content to think) a strictly auxiliary discipline of literary history with a fragmentary, scattered subject matter and with no peculiar method of its own.   The study of the influence, say, of Byron in England cannot, methodologically, differ from a study of the influence of Byron in France or from a study of European Byronism.   The method of comparison is not peculiar to comparative literature; it is ubiquitous in all literary study and in all sciences, social and natural.   Nor does literary study, even in the practice of the most orthodox comparative scholars, proceed by the method of comparison alone. Any literary scholar will not only compare but reproduce, analyze, interpret, evoke, evaluate, generalize, etc., all on one page.

There are other attempts to define the scope of comparative literature by adding something specific to the narrow definition. Thus Carré and Guyard include the study of national illusions, the ideas which nations have of each other. M. Carré has written an interesting book on *Les Ecrivains français et le mirage allemand* (1947), which is national psychology or sociology drawn from literary sources but hardly literary history. A book such as Guyard's *La Grande Bretagne dans le roman français: 1914–1940* (1954) is slightly disguised *Stoffgeschichte:* an account of the English clergymen, diplomats, writers, chorus girls, businessmen, etc., appearing in French novels of a certain time.

Less arbitrary and more ambitious is the recent attempt by H. H. Remak to expand the definition of comparative literature. He calls it "the study of literature beyond the confines of one particular country, and the study of the relationships between literature on the one hand and the other areas of knowledge and belief, such as the arts, philosophy, history, the social sciences, the sciences, religion, etc., on the other hand." [52] But Mr. Remak is forced to make artificial and untenable distinctions: e.g., between a study of Hawthorne's relation to Calvinism, labeled "comparative," and a study of his concepts of guilt, sin, and expiation, reserved for "American" literature. The whole scheme strikes one as devised for purely practical purposes in an American graduate school where you may have to justify a thesis topic as "comparative literature" before unsympathetic colleagues resenting incursions into their particular fields of competence. But as a definition it cannot survive closer scrutiny.

At one time in history, the time decisive for the establishment of the term in English, comparative literature was understood to mean something both very specific and very wide-ranging. In Posnett's book it means "the general theory of literary evolution, the idea that literature passes through stages of inception, culmination and decline." [53] Comparative literature is set into a universal social history of mankind, "the gradual expansion of social life, from clan to city, from city to nation, from both of these to cosmopolitan humanity." [54] Posnett and his followers are dependent on the evolutionary philosophy of Herbert Spencer, which today is almost forgotten in literary studies.

Finally, the view has been propounded that comparative literature can be best defended and defined by its perspective and spirit, rather than by any circumscribed partition within literature. It will study all literature from an international perspective, with a consciousness of the unity of all literary creation and experience. In this conception (which is also mine) comparative literature is identical with the study of literature independent of linguistic, ethnic, and political boundaries. It cannot be confined to a single method: Description, characterization, interpretation, narration, explanation, evaluation are used in its discourse just as much as comparison. Nor can comparison be confined to actual historical contacts. There may be, as the experience of recent linguistics should teach literary scholars, as much value in comparing phenomena such as languages or genres historically unrelated as in studying influences discoverable from evidence of reading or parallels. A study of Chinese, Korean, Burmese, and Persian narrative methods or lyrical forms is surely as justified as the study of the casual contacts with the East exemplified by Voltaire's *Orphelin de Chine*. Nor can comparative literature be confined to literary history to the exclusion of criticism and contemporary literature. Criticism, as I have argued many times, cannot be divorced from history, as there are no neutral facts in literature. The mere act of selecting from millions of printed books is a critical act, and the selection of the traits or aspects under which a book may be treated is equally an act of criticism and judgment. The attempt to erect precise barriers between the study of literary history and contemporary literature is doomed to failure: Why should a specified date or even the death of an author constitute a sudden lifting of a taboo? Such limits may be possible to enforce in the centralized system of French education, but elsewhere they are unreal. Nor can the historical approach be considered the only possible method even for the study of the dim past. Works of literature are monuments and not documents. They are immediately accessible to us today; they challenge us to seek an understanding in which knowledge of the historical setting or the place in a literary tradition may figure, but not exclusively or exhaustively. The three main branches of literary study—history, theory, and criticism—involve each other, just as the study of a national literature cannot be divorced from the study of the totality of literature, at least in idea. Comparative literature can and will flourish only if it shakes off artificial limitations and becomes simply the study of literature.

The meaning and the origin of these distinctions and issues will become clearer if we glance at the history of comparative studies without regard to the name or to definitions. H. H. Remak in a lecture at the Fribourg Congress in 1964 rightly said that there is "no more urgent task than the writing and publication of a thorough history of our discipline." [55]   I obviously cannot pretend to fulfill this demand in such a short space, but as I wrote the first and only history of English literary historiography twenty-five years ago [56] and paid constant attention to writings on literary history in the four volumes of my *History of Modern Criticism,* I can sketch the main stages of the development of comparative and general literature with some assurance.

If we glance at antiquity, it will be obvious that the Greeks could not have been comparative students in the early period, as they lived in a closed world to which all the other nations were barbarians. But the Romans were highly conscious of their dependence on the Greeks. In Tacitus' *Dialogue on Orators,* for example, there is an elaborate parallel between Greek and Roman orators where the individual writers are matched or contrasted with some care. In Quintilian's *Institutio* a whole sketch of the history of Greek and Roman literature is provided which consistently pays attention to the Greek models of the Romans. Longinus, or whoever wrote the treatise usually called *On the Sublime,* compares the style of Cicero and Demosthenes briefly and gives as an example of the Grand Style the passage from *Genesis:* " 'Let there be light'; and there was light." [57]   Macrobius, in the much later *Saturnalia,* has a long discussion of Virgil's imitations of Greek poets. Though the experience of the variety of literature in antiquity was limited and though much of their scholarship was lost—during the Middle Ages it must have been considered ephemeral or local and thus not worth copying—we should not underrate the scope and the intensity of literary scholarship in classical antiquity, particularly in Alexandria and Rome. There was much textual criticism, stylistic observation, and even something which might please a modern comparatist: An elaborate comparison of the treatment of the Philoctetes theme by Aeschylus, Sophocles, and Euripides has been preserved.[58]

The Renaissance revived literary scholarship on a very large scale. There is a clear historical consciousness in the very idea of the revival of learning and the break with the intellectual traditions of the Middle Ages, even though the break was not as complete or sudden as it has been assumed in the 19th century. Still, looking for forerunners of comparative methods or perspectives yields little in that time. The authority of antiquity often rather stifled the concrete variety of the literary traditions of the Middle Ages and imposed, at least in theory, a certain uniformity. Scaliger in his *Poetics* (1561) devotes a whole book, "Criticus" (a new term then), to a series of comparisons of Homer with Virgil, Virgil with Greeks other than Homer, Horace and Ovid with Greeks, always asserting the superiority of the Romans over the Greeks, using passages on the same subjects from different poets.[59] Scaliger is mainly interested in the game of ranking and is motivated by an odd kind of Latin nationalism interested in denigrating everything that is Greek. Etienne Pasquier (1529–1615) uses the same method in comparing a passage from Virgil with one from Ronsard.[60] To give an English example for the widespread method of rhetorical comparisons: Francis Meres in "A Comparative Discourse of Our English Poets with the Greek, Latin and Italian Poets," which I have mentioned, quite perfunctorily ranked Shakespeare with Ovid, Plautus, and Seneca.[61] The motivation of most Renaissance scholarship was patriotic: Englishmen compiled lists of writers in order to prove their glorious achievements in all subjects of learning; Frenchmen, Italians, and Germans did exactly the same.

There was also a very occasional awareness of the existence of literature outside of the Western tradition. Samuel Daniel's remarkable *Defence of Rime* (1607) shows that he knew that Turks and Arabs, Slavs and Hungarians use rhyme. For him Greece and Rome are no absolute authority, since even barbarians are "children of nature as well as they." "There is but one learning, which *omnes gentes habent in cordibus suis,* one and the self-same spirit that worketh in all." [62] But this tolerance and universality in Daniel is still completely unhistorical: men are everywhere and at any time the same.

About the same time a new conception of literary history was propounded by Francis Bacon, in his *Advancement of Learning* (1603). Literary history was to be a "history of the flourishings, decays, depressions, removes" of schools, sects, and traditions. "Without it the history of the world seemeth to me as the *statua* of Polyphemus with his eye out; that part being wanting which doth most show the spirit and life of the person." [63] In the later Latin version (1623) Bacon adds the proposal that from "taste and observation of the argument, style and method" of the best books, "the learned spirit of an age, as by a kind of charm, should be awaked and raised from the dead." [64] Bacon, of course, did not conceive of literary history as primarily a history of imaginative literature: it was rather a history of learning which included poetry.[65] Still, Bacon's proposal went far beyond the dull lists of authors, collections of lives of authors, and the bibliographical repertories which were being assembled at that time in most Western countries.

It took a long time before Bacon's program was carried out in practice. In Germany, for example, Peter Lambeck (1628–1680) compiled a *Podromus historiae literariae* (1659) which reprints the passage from Bacon as a kind of epigraph, but the contents show that Lambeck had not understood the idea of Bacon's universal intellectual history at all.

He begins with the creation of the world, Biblical history, describes the teachings of Zoroaster, compiles data on Greek philosophers, etc. It all remains a mass of inert and undigested uncritical learning.[66] If we want to feel proud about progress in our studies, I recommend looking into Jakob Friederich Reimann's *Versuch einer Einleitung in die historiam literariam antediluvianam d.h. in die Geschichte der Gelehrsamkeit und derer Gelehrten vor der Sündflut* (1727), a display of childish pedantry which shows no sense of evidence or chronology beyond that which can be extracted from the Old Testament accounts.[67]

The accumulation of storehouses of bibliographical and biographical information reached enormous proportions in the 18th century. In France the Benedictines started an *Histoire littéraire de la France* (12 vols., 1733–1762) which, in the 18th century, barely reached the 12th century. Girolamo Tiraboschi's *Storia della letteratura italiana* (14 vols., 1772–1781) is still admired for its accuracy and wealth of information. A Spanish Jesuit, Juan Andres, compiled in Italian one of the most impressive repertories of all literatures, *Dell'origine, progresso e stato attuale d'ogni letteratura* (1782–1799), in seven large volumes, where the whole world of books is divided up by genres, disciplines, nations, and centuries with no sense of narrative flow and little of continuity. The English work in literary history which is comparable to those Continental achievements, Thomas Warton's *History of English Poetry* (3 vols., 1774–1781), while in the main a repertory of extracts, an account of manuscripts and biographical notices, is, however, permeated by a new spirit. It could not have been written without the idea of progress, without the new tolerant interest in the Middle Ages, and without an idea (however schematic) of literary development.[68]

The idea of progress, also in literature, triumphed in the *Querelle des Anciens et Modernes*, which in English is usually called The Battle of Books. Charles Perrault's *Parallèle des anciens et des modernes* (1688–1697) argues by contrasting and comparing the funeral orations of Pericles, Lysias, and Isocrates with those of Bossuet, Flechier, and Bourdaloue, or the panegyric of Pliny on the Emperor Trajan with the eulogy of Voiture on Richelieu, or the letters of Pliny and Cicero with those of Guez de Balzac—always preferring the French to the ancients.[69] Progress, in literature as in other spheres, became the obsessive theme of the whole century, though it is not always naively conceived as unilateral and allows for relapses. To give English examples: even the conservative Dr. Johnson conceives of the history of English poetry as a steady advance from the barbaric roughness of Chaucer to the perfect smoothness of Pope, which could not be improved on even in the future; Warton, who had a genuine liking for Chaucer and Spenser, always prefers his own time's ideas of discrimination, propriety, correctness, and good taste to the irregular charms of the Elizabethans.[70] Still, Warton shows a new tolerance for the variety of literature and a curiosity for its origins and derivations. He belongs to a whole group of scholars in the 18th century who were interested in the institution of chivalry, in courtly love, and in their literary analogues, the romance and the courtly lyric. But the new interest in the non-Latin literary tradition was still halfhearted. Men like Warton, Bishop Percy, and Bishop Hurd held a point of view which exalted the age of Queen Elizabeth as the golden age of English literature but at the same time allowed them to applaud the triumph of reason in their own "polite" literature. They believed in the progress of civilization and even modern good taste, but regretted the decay of "a world of fine fabling" which they studied as antiquaries pursuing a fascinating hobby. They were animated by a truly historical spirit of tolerance but also remained detached and uninvolved and thus strangely sterile in their eclecticism.[71]

In Warton and his contemporaries another trend had won out which had been preparing for a long time. Literature was conceived in the main as *belles lettres*, as imaginative literature, and not merely as a branch of learning on the same footing as astronomy or jurisprudence. This process of specialization is connected with the whole rise of the modern system of arts and their clear distinction from the sciences and crafts, and with the formulation of the whole enterprise of aesthetics.[72] Aesthetics as a term comes from Germany and was invented by Baumgarten in 1735, but the singling out of poetry and imaginative prose had been accomplished before in connection with the problem of taste, good taste, or *belles lettres*, "elegant," "polite" arts or however they might call it then.[73] With the emphasis on what we would call the art of literature came also the emphasis on nationality, for poetry was deeply embedded in a national language, and the increasing resistance to the cultural leveling accomplished by the Enlightenment brought about a new turn toward the past, which inevitably was medieval or at the most very early modern. The English and Scottish critics of the 18th century prepared the way, but it was in Germany that the ideal of literary history on these new terms was stated and carried out most consistently. The decisive figure was Johann Gottfried Herder (1744–1803), who conceived of literary history as a totality in which "the origin, the growth, the changes and the decay of literature with the divers styles of regions, periods, and poets" [74] would be shown and in which the individual national literatures would make up the basic entities which he wanted to defend in their purity and originality. Herder's first important book, *Über die neuere deutsche Literatur: Fragmente* (1767), attacks imitation, particularly of French and Latin literature, and points to the regenerative powers of folk poetry. Herder recommends collecting it not only among Germans but among "Scythians and Slavs, Wends and Bohemians, Russians, Swedes and Poles." [75] Thus the fervent German nationalism led, paradoxically, to a wide expansion of the literary horizon: Every nation does or should take part with its characteristic voice in the great concert of poetry. While Herder sketched a new ideal, which was fulfilled only by the Romantics, he was still steeped in the concepts of his time. The literary process is seen by him most often in terms of a rather naive determinism of climate, landscape, race, and social conditions. Madame de Staël's book, *De la littérature* (1800), with its simple-minded trust in perfectibility and in the contrast between the gay and sunny South with the dark and gloomy North, even in literature, belongs still to the schematic history of the Enlightenment.

Only the two Schlegels developed the forward-looking suggestions of Herder's sketches and became the first literary historians who, on a broad scale and with considerable concrete knowledge, carried out the idea of a universal narrative literary history in a historical context. While they were understandably preoccupied with Western Europe, they extended, at least on occasion, their interest to Eastern Europe and became pioneers in the study of Sanskrit literature. Friedrich Schlegel's *Über Sprache und Weisheit der Inder* (1808) was a bold program which was later carried out in part by A. W. Schlegel with his editions of the Indian epics. For Friedrich Schlegel literature forms "a great, completely coherent and evenly organized whole, comprehending in its unity many worlds of art and itself forming a peculiar work of art," [76] but this "universal progressive poetry" is conceived as being based on national literature as an organism, as epitome of a nation's history: "the essence of all intellectual faculties and productions of a nation." [77] Unfortunately Friedrich Schlegel's *Geschichte der alten und neuen Literatur* (1815) was written after his conversion to Roman Catholicism, in the atmosphere of the Vienna of 1812, and is thus colored strongly with the spirit of the anti-Napoleonic Restoration. A. W. Schlegel's early Berlin lectures (1803–1804), which sketch the whole history of Western literature with the dichotomy of classical versus romantic as an organizing principle, were not published till 1884,[78] and his *Lectures on Dramatic Art and Literature* (1809–1811) are limited to one genre and are strongly polemical. Still, they carried, in French, English, and Italian translation, the message of German Romanticism to the rest of Europe.[79] The Schlegels' concept of literature, which is definitely comparative both in the narrow and in a wide sense, seems to me still true and meaningful in spite of the deficiencies of their information, the limitations of their taste, and the bias of their nationalism.

Schlegelian literary history was written throughout the 19th century in many lands. It penetrated with Sismondi to France, where Villemain, Ampère and Chasles attempt it. In Italy Emiliani-Guidici, in Denmark Brandes (with his very different politics), and in England Carlyle share their concept. When Carlyle says "the History of a nation's Poetry is the essence of its History, political, economic, scientific, religious" and when he calls literature "the truest emblem of the national spirit and manner of existence," [80] he echoes the Schlegels and Herder. Surprising though this may appear, even Taine shares their basic insight. Works of art "furnish documents because they are monuments." [81]

The Schlegelian concept of literary history must be distinguished from the concept I would call peculiarly "Romantic": the view based on the idea of pre-history, a kind of reservoir of themes from which all modern literature is derived and to whose glories it compares only as a dim artificial light to the sun. This view was stimulated by the new study of mythology, comparative religion and philology. The Brothers Grimm are its main exponents, the early practitioners of comparative research into the migration of fairy tales, legends, and sagas. Jacob Grimm believed in natural poetry as composing itself far in the dim past and as gradually deteriorating with the distance from the divine source of revelation. His patriotism is Pan-Teutonic, but his taste embraces all folk poetry wherever found: old Spanish romances, French *chansons de geste,* Serbian heroic epics, Arabic and Indian folk tales.[82] The Grimms stimulated everywhere the study of what later was called *Stoffgeschichte.* It is worth looking at Richard Price's Preface to the new edition of Warton's *History of English Poetry* (1824) to see the changed conception. He pleads for "general literature" as a huge treasure house of themes which spread, multiply, and migrate according to laws similar to those established for language by the new comparative philology. Price believes that "popular fiction is in its nature traditive" and represents an age-old symbolic wisdom.[83] In England scholars such as Sir Francis Palgrave and Thomas Wright pursued these studies systematically with great erudition. In France Claude Fauriel, who had translated Greek folk songs, is a comparable figure, except that what in the Grimms was a dim Teutonic past is by him traced back to his own homeland: southern France, Provence.

Around 1850 the atmosphere changed completely. Romantic conceptions fell into discredit, and ideals imported from the natural sciences became victorious, even in the writing of literary history. One must, however, distinguish what might be called "factualism," the enormous proliferation of research into facts or supposed facts, from "scientism," which appealed mainly to the concept of biological evolution and envisaged an ideal of literary history in which the laws of literary production and change would be discovered. The transition can be illustrated strikingly from Renan's *L'Avenir de la science*. Renan looks back to Herder, to the new mythology and the study of primitive poetry. "The comparative study of literature," he tells us, has shown that Homer is a collective poet; it has brought out his *"mythisme,"* the primitive legend behind him. The progress of literary history is entirely due to its search for origins and hence its attention to exotic literatures. The use of the comparative method, that "grand instrument of criticism," is the turning point.[84] Renan, at the same time, is almost intoxicated with hope for the future of the science of philology, which will establish the history of the human mind. But he is still wary (and became more so in his later life) of all attempts to establish laws in literature and history as they were sought for by Comte, Mill, Buckle, and many others before Darwin or Spencer.

The idea of laws, of regularities in literature, goes back to antiquity and was restated in 18th century speculative schemes, but it becomes a dominant concern with the victory of comparative philology, its idea of development, continuity, and derivation. Darwinism and similar philosophical schemes, particularly Spencer's, gave a new impetus to the idea of evolution and genre, conceived on the analogy of a biological species in literary history.[85] In Germany Moriz Haupt advocated a "comparative poetics," particularly a natural history of the epic. He studied the analogical development of the epic in Greece, France, Scandinavia, Germany, Serbia, and Finland.[86] Haupt inspired Wilhelm Scherer, who conceived of literary history as a morphology of poetic forms.[87] Many of these ideas grew out of a Berlin circle around Steinthal, who founded the *Zeitschrift für Völkerpsychologie* in 1864. This circle provided the inspiration for Alexander Veselovsky who, after his return to Russia in 1870, put out a steady stream of studies on the migration of themes and plots, ranging all over the Western and Eastern world, from the dimmest antiquity to Romantic literature. He aimed at a "historical poetics," a universal evolutionary history of poetry, a collective approach which would approximate the ideal of a "history without names." [88] In England the influence of Spencer was felt somewhat differently. John Addington Symonds applied a strictly biological analogy to Elizabethan drama and Italian painting and defended the "application of evolutionary principles" to art and literature also theoretically: Each genre runs a fateful course of germination, expansion, efflorescence, and decay. We should be able to predict the future of literature.[89] Posnett's book, which was crucial for the establishment of the term "comparative literature," is another application of Spencer's scheme of a social development from communal to individual life. There are many now forgotten books, some by Americans, which follow this trend. Francis Gummere's *Beginnings of Poetry* (1901) and A. S. Mackenzie's *The Evolution of Literature* (1911) may serve as examples.

In France Ferdinand Brunetière was the theorist and practitioner of evolutionism. He treated genres as biological species and wrote histories of French criticism, drama, and lyrical poetry according to this scheme. Though he limited himself to French subjects, his theory led him logically to a concept of universal literature and to a defense of comparative literature. When in 1900, in connection with the World Exhibition in Paris, a Congress of Historical Studies was held, a whole section (sparsely attended) was reserved for "Histoire comparée des littératures." Brunetière opened it with an address on "European literature" which appealed not only to the model of the Schlegels and Ampère but also to J. A. Symonds. Brunetière was followed as speaker by Gaston Paris, the great French medievalist.[90] He expounded, in a dramatic clash of viewpoints, the older conception of comparative literature: i.e., the folklore concept, the idea of the migration of themes and motifs all over the world. Somewhat later this study received new impetus from Finnish folklore research and has expanded into an almost independent branch of learning related to ethnology and anthropology. In this country it is now rarely identified with comparative literature; but older 19th century literary journals are filled with such topics, and in the Slavic countries "comparative literature" often means just such a study of international themes and motifs.

With the decline of evolutionism and the criticism launched against its mechanistic application by Bergson, Croce, and others, and with the predominance of late 19th century aestheticism and impressionism, which stressed again the individual creator, the unique work of art, and highly sophisticated literature, these concepts of comparative literature were either abandoned or were pushed to the margin of literary studies.

What reemerged was largely the factualism inherited from the general tradition of empiricism and positivism supported by the ideal of scientific objectivity and causal explanation. The organized enterprise of comparative literature in France accomplished mainly an enormous accumulation of evidence about literary relations, particularly on the history of reputations, the intermediaries between nations —travelers, translators, and propagandists. The unexamined assumption in such research is the existence of a neutral fact which is supposed to be connected as if by a thread with other preceding facts. But the whole conception of a "cause" in literary study is singularly uncritical; nobody has ever been able to show that a work of art was "caused" by another work of art, even though parallels and similarities can be accumulated. A later work of art may not have been possible without a preceding one, but it cannot be shown to have been caused by it. The whole concept of literature in these researches is external and often vitiated by narrow nationalism: by a computing of cultural riches, a credit and debit calculus in matters of the mind.

I am not alone in criticizing the sterility of this conception. Still, my paper on "The Crisis of Comparative Literature," given at the second Congress of the International Association of Comparative Literature in Chapel Hill in 1958, seemed to have crystallized the opposition.[91] It formulated the objections to the factualism of the theories and the practices: its failure to delineate a subject matter and a specific methodology. The paper gave rise to endless polemics and, I am afraid, to endless misunderstandings.[92] Particularly distressing is the attempt to create an issue between a supposed American and a French conception of comparative literature. I was, of course, not arguing against a nation or even a local school of scholars. I was arguing against a method, not for myself or the United States, and not with new and personal arguments; I simply stated what follows from an insight into the totality of literature, that the distinction between comparative and general literature is artificial and that not much can be accomplished by the method of causal explanation except an infinite regress. What I, and many others, advocate is a turning away from the mechanistic, factualistic concepts inherited from the 19th century in favor of true criticism. Criticism means a concern for values and qualities, for an understanding of texts which incorporates their historicity, and thus requires the history of criticism for such an understanding, and finally it means an international perspective which envisages a distant ideal of universal literary history and scholarship. Comparative literature surely wants to overcome national prejudices and provincialisms but does not therefore ignore or minimize the existence and vitality of the different national traditions. We must beware of false and unnecessary choices: We need both national and general literature, we need both literary history and criticism, and we need the wide perspective which only comparative literature can give.

NOTES

1. *Henry IV, I*, ii, 90.
2. *Elizabethan Critical Essays*, ed. Gregory Smith (Oxford, 1904), *II*, 314.
3. Trans. G. Gregory (London, 1787), *I*, 113–114.
4. (London, 1774), *I*, iv.
5. 2nd ed. (London, 1801), *I*, 58.
6. *Letters*, ed. G. W. E. Russell (London, 1895), *I*, 8.
7. In *Harper's Magazine, 73* (1886), 318.
8. *The Contemporary Review, 79* (1901), 870.
9. *Experiments in Education* (Ithaca, N. Y., 1942), p. 75.
10. *Tatler*, No. 197 (July 13, 1710).
11. *Life of Samuel Johnson*, ed. G. B. Hill, revised L. F. Powell (Oxford, 1934), *I*, 302.
12. Eduard Wölfflin, in *Zeitschrift für lateinische Lexikographie, V* (1888), 49.
13. Ed. René Groos (Paris, 1947), *II*, 113: "Mais, dans l'éloquence, dans la poésie, dans la littérature, dans les livres de morale et d'agrément." Cf. *II*, 132, 145.
14. Reviewed by Herder, *Sämtliche Werke* (Berlin, 1877), ed. Suphan *I*, 123.
15. Turin, 1760. Paris, 1776. Glasgow, 1771, 1784. The connection with Glasgow is due to the fact that Denina knew Lady Elizabeth Mackenzie, the daughter of the Duke of Argyle, when her husband was the British Minister at Turin.
16. P. 6: "Non parleremo . . . dei progressi delle scienze e delle arti, che propriamente non sono parte di letteratura . . . al buon gusto, ed alla eloquenza, vale a dire alla letteratura."
17. Naples, 1779. Lucca, 1784.
18. Ludwig Wachler, *Vorlesungen über die Geschichte der teutschen Nationallitteratur* (1818; 2nd ed., 1834). A. Koberstein, *Grundriss der Geschichte der deutschen Nationalliteratur* (1827). Georg Gottfried Gervinus, *Geschichte der poetischen Nationalliteratur der Deutschen* (5 volumes, 1835–1842). A. Vilmar, *Vorlesungen über die Geschichte der deutschen Nationalliteratur* (1845). R. Gottschall, *Die deutsche Nationalliteratur des 19. Jahrhunderts* (1881). This term seems to have later disappeared, though note G. Könnecke, *Bilderatlas zur Geschichte der deutschen Nationalliteratur* (1886).
19. *Etudes sur l'antiquité* (Paris, 1846), p. 28: "J'ai peu d'estime pour le mot littérature. Ce mot me parait dénué de sens; il est éclos d'une dépravation intellectuelle." P. 30: "quelque chose qui n'est ni la Philosophie, ni

l'histoire, ni l'Erudition, ni la Critique;—je ne sais de quoi de vague, d'insaisissable et d'élastique."

20. *Critical Reflections on the Old English Dramatick Writers. Extracted from a Prefatory Discourse to the New Edition of Massinger's Works* (London, 1761).

21. Dr. Johnson's Letter to the Rev. Dr. Horne, April 30, 1774, in *Catalogue of the Johnsonian Collection of R. B. Adams* (Buffalo, 1921).

22. James Beattie, *Dissertations, Moral and Critical* (London, 1783), p. 518.

23. On Dale see D. J. Palmer, *The Rise of English Studies* (London, 1965), pp. 18ff.

24. (London, 1873). See *The Unity of History* (Cambridge, 1872), praising the comparative method as "a stage at least as great and memorable as the revival of Greek and Latin learning."

25. Not published till 1819. *Oeuvres*, ed. Moland. (Paris, 1877–1885), *XIX*, 590–592: "Une connaissance des ouvrages de goût, une teinture d'histoire, de poésie, d'éloquence, de critique . . . objets qui ont de la beauté, à la poésie, à l'histoire bien écrite."

26. Marmontel (Paris, 1856 reprint), II, 335: "La littérature est la connaissance de belles-lettres . . . avec de l'esprit, de talent et de goût, il peut produire des ouvrages ingénieux, sans aucune érudition, et avec peu de littérature."

27. The Bibliothèque Nationale lists *Leçons françaises de littérature et de morale*, 2 vols. (1816), and *Leçons latines de littérature et de morale*, 2 vols. (1816). *Leçons anglaises de littérature et de morale*, 2 vols. (1817–1819), has another co-author, Mr. Chapsal.

28. (Paris), p. 149.

29. New ed., 4 vols. (Paris, 1873), *I*, 2, 24; *II*, 45; *I*, 225.

30. New ed., 2 vols. (Paris, 1875), *I* 187; *I* 1.

31. Second Series, *13* (1835), ii, 238–262. In revised version introducing *Etudes sur l'antiquité* (1840), Chasles does not use the term. See Claude Pichois, *Philarète Chasles et la vie littéraire au temps du romantisme* (Paris, 1965), *I*, 483.

32. Originally Marseille, 1830. Reprinted in *Mélanges d'histoire littéraire* (Paris, 1867), *I*, 3.

33. Reprinted in *Nouveaux Lundis* (Paris, 1870), *XIII*, 183ff.

34. *Sämtliche Werke*, Jubiläumsausgabe (Stuttgart, 1902–1907), *XXXIX*, 137ff.

35. Of Bernhardi's *Sprachlehre, Sämtliche Werke*, ed. Böcking, *XII*, 152.

36. *Sämtliche Werke*, 2nd ed. (Vienna, 1846), *VIII*, 291, 318.

37. In a section entitled: "Grundzüge und Winke zur vergleichenden Literaturgeschichte des Dramas." A new edition (Leipzig, 1884) is renamed: *Die Poesie: Ihr Wesen und ihre Formen mit Grundzügen der vergleichenden Literaturgeschichte*.

38. See A. Berczik, "Eine ungarische Konzeption der Weltliteratur (Hugo von Meltzls vergleichende Literaturtheorie)," *Acta Literaria Academiae Scientiarum Hungaricae, 5* (1962), 287–293.

39. The chair was created in 1861 and reserved for the German poet Georg Herwegh, who never occupied it.

40. *Sobranie sochinenii* (St. Petersburg, 1913), *I*, 18–29. Veselovsky uses the term *sravnitelnoe izuchenie* (comparative study) as early as 1868, see *ibid., XVI*, 1.

41. "Über die Hauptperioden in der Geschichte der Dichtkunst," *Gothaisches Magazin der Künste und Wissenschaften, 1* (1776), 21ff., 199ff. A review of Albert Lacroix, *Histoire de l'influence de Shakespeare sur le théâtre français, Jahrbuch für romanische und englische Literatur, 1* (1859), 3.

42. See note 22.

43. Goethe, Jubiläumsausgabe, *XXXVIII*, 97, 137, 170, 278. Cf. discussion and collection of passages in Fritz Strich, *Goethe und die Weltliteratur* (Bern, 1946), pp. 393–400.

44. Jubiläumsausgabe, *III*, 243. Cf. p. 373 for title.

45. Cf. Else Beil, *Zur Entwicklung des Begriffs der Weltliteratur* (Leipzig, 1915); J. C. Brandt Corstius, "De Ontwikkeling van het begrif wereld-literatuur," *De Vlaamse Gids, 41* (1957), 582–600; Helmut Bender and Ulrich Melzer, "Zur Geschichte des Begriffes 'Weltliteratur'," *Saeculum, 9* (1958), 113–122.

46. *La Littérature comparée* (Paris, 1931), p. 57: "L'object de la littérature comparée est essentiellement d'étudier les oeuvres des diverses littératures dans leurs rapports les unes avec les autres."

47. *La Littérature comparée* (Paris, 1951), p. 7: "l'histoire des relations littéraires internationales."

48. *Ibid.*, p. 5: "Une branche de l'histoire littéraire; elle est l'étude des relations spirituelles internationales, des rapports de fait qui ont existé entre Byron et Pouchkine, Goethe et Carlyle, Walter Scott et Vigny, entre les oeuvres, les inspirations, voire les vies d'écrivains appartenant à plusieurs littératures."

49. *Problemi ed orientamenti: Notizie introduttive* (Milano, 1948), p. 430: "Una scienza moderna appunto ad indagare i problemi connessi e ogni influssi esercitati reciprocamente dalle varie letterature."

50. "Littérature comparée: le mot et la chose," *Revue de littérature comparée, 1* (1921), 1–29. P. 7: "Une recontre réelle . . . créé une dépendance."

51. Van Tieghem, *La Littérature comparée*, p. 170: "rapports binaires—entre deux éléments seulement." P. 174: "les faits communs à plusieurs littératures."

52. *Comparative Literature: Method and Perspective*, ed. Newton P. Stallknecht and Horst Frenz (Carbondale, Illinois, 1961), p. 3.

53. Charles Mills Gayley and Fred Newton Scott, *An Introduction to the Methods and Materials of Literary Criticism* (Boston, 1899), p. 248, summarizing Posnett.

54. H. M. Posnett, *Comparative Literature* (London, 1886), p. 86.

55. "The Impact of Nationalism and Cosmopolitism on Comparative Literature from the 1880's to the Post World War II Period," *Proceedings of the Fourth Congress of the International Comparative Literature Association* (The Hague, 1966), p. 391.

56. *The Rise of English Literary History* (Chapel Hill, 1941) (new ed., New York, 1966).

57. On Longinus, see Allan H. Gilbert, *Literary Criticism: Plato to Dryden* (New York, 1940), pp. 157, 162.

58. From J. W. Atkins, *Literary Criticism in Antiquity* (London, 1924), *II*, 187, 331. The treatise on Philoctetes is ascribed to either Dio of Prusa (A.D. 40–120) or Dio Chrysostomos.

59. (Geneva, 1561), Book V.

60. *Recherches de la France* (Paris, 1643), *VII*, XI.

61. See note 2.

62. *Elizabethan Critical Essays, II*, 359, 372.

63. *Works*, ed. J. Spedding, Ellis, et al. (London, 1857), *III*, 329.

64. *Ibid., I*, 502–504.

65. Cf. Ewald Flügel, "Bacon's Historia Literaria," *Anglia, 21* (1899), 259–288.

66. I have seen the Leipzig and Frankfurt 1710 edition. After the passage from Bacon he prints similar statements from Christopher Mylius, *De Scribenda Universitatis Historia* and from C. J. Vossius, *De Philologia*.

67. (Halle, 1727).

68. See Giovanni Getto, *Storia delle storie letterarie* (Milano, 1924) and my *Rise of English Literary History* for comments on Warton.

69. Ed. H. R. Jauss (Munich, 1964), e.g., 256ff., 269ff., 279.

70. Cf. my *Rise of English Literary History*, pp. 139, 180ff.

71. Cf. my *History of Modern Criticism* (New Haven, 1955), *I*, 131–132.

72. See Paul Oskar Kristeller, "The Modern System of the Arts," *Renaissance Thought II* (New York, 1965), pp. 163–227.

73. On aesthetics and taste see, besides general histories of aesthetics, Alfred Bäumler, *Kants Kritik der Urteilskraft* (Halle, 1923), *I*, and J. E. Spingarn's introduction to *Critical Essays of the Seventeenth Century* (Oxford, 1908), *I*.

74. *Sämtliche Werke, I*, 294: "Den Ursprung, das Wachstum, die Veränderungen und den Fall derselben nebst dem verschiedenen Stil der Gegenden, Zeiten und Dichter lehren."

75. *Ibid.*, I, 266: "Scythen und Slaven, Wenden und Böhmen, Russen, Schweden und Polen."

76. *Lessings Geist aus seinen Schriften*, 3 vols. (1804), *I*, 13: "ein grosses, durchaus zusammenhängendes und gleich organisirtes, in ihrer Einheit viele Kunstwelten umfassendes Ganzes und einiges Kunstwerk."

77. *Sämtliche Werke, I,* 11: "Der Inbegriff aller intellectuellen Fähigkeiten und Hervorbringungen einer Nation."

78. *Vorlesungen über schöne Literatur und Kunst,* ed. Jakob Minor (Stuttgart, 1884).

79. Josef Körner, *Die Botschaft der deutschen Romantik an Europa* (Augsburg, 1929).

80. *Works,* centenary edition (London, 1896–1899); *Essays II,* 341–342; *Unfinished History of German Literature,* ed. Hill Shine (Lexington, Ky., 1951), p. 6.

81. *Histoire de la littérature anglaise,* 2nd ed. (Paris, 1866), *I,* xvii: "Si elles fournissent des documents, c'est qu'elles sont des monuments."

82. See my *History of Modern Criticism, II,* 283ff.

83. Reprinted in Warton, *History of English Poetry,* ed. W. C. Hazlitt (London, 1871), *I,* 32–33.

84. (Paris, 1890), p. 297: "L'étude comparée des littératures." P. 296: "le grand instrument de la critique."

85. Cf. my "The Concept of Evolution in Literary History" (1956), *Concepts of Criticism* (New Haven, 1963), pp. 37–53.

86. See Christian Belger, *Moriz Haupt als akademischer Lehrer* (Berlin, 1879), p. 323, for review in 1835. See also W. Scherer, *Kleine Schriften,* ed. K. Burdach and E. Schmidt (Berlin, 1893), *I,* 120, 123, 130.

87. On Scherer, particularly his *Poetik* (1888), see my *History of Modern Criticism, IV* (1965), 297ff.

88. On Veselovsky, see *ibid.,* pp. 278–280, and V. Zhirmunsky, "Introduction," *Istoricheskaya poetika* (Leningrad, 1940).

89. See my *History, IV,* 400–407. Cf. Symonds' "On the Application of Evolutionary Principles to Art and Literature," *Essays Speculative and Suggestive,* 2 vols. (London, 1890), *I,* 52–83.

90. "La Littérature européenne," *Annales internationales d'histoire Congrès de Paris 1900* (Paris, 1901), *VI,* 5–28; "Résumé de l'allocution de M. Gaston Paris," *ibid.,* pp. 39–41.

91. Reprinted in my *Concepts of Criticism,* pp. 282–295.

92. Some of these are discussed in R. Wellek's "Comparative Literature Today," *Comparative Literature, 17* (1965), 325–337.

Claudio Guillén

On the Concept and Metaphor
of Perspective

In the fourth chapter of their *Theory of Literature* (1949), René
Wellek and Austin Warren discussed the fallacies of "relativism" and
"absolutism" as critical approaches to literature. Relativism, by referring the work exclusively to the values of its own time, ignores its
continuing identity and forfeits any effective instrument of valuation.
Absolutism disdains all relations between literature and history, or submits them to doctrinaire preconceptions. The answer to both, the
authors proposed, was "perspectivism," an intermediate attitude signifying "that we recognize that there is one poetry, one literature,
comparable in all ages, developing, changing, full of possibilities." [1]
Poetic works should be referred to the values of their own time *and* of
subsequent periods. Their meaning results from a process of temporal
accretion which is like an accumulation of critical perspectives. Perspectives, then, are both critical (they are illuminations of the work
of art) and historical (they belong to the process of literary history).
They combine the procedures of literary criticism with those of literary
history understood as a dynamic and temporal process, while avoiding
the extremes implicit in both: individualistic chaos (criticism) and
dogmatism (historicism). These ideas, I should recall, particularly
for the benefit of those few comparatists who have no Spanish, are related to a general attitude in 20th century thought of which José Ortega y Gasset was the most eloquent spokesman. Actually, in an
earlier version of the same chapter, René Wellek made clear his acquaintance with Ortega's uses of the term.[2]

My own concern with perspectivism was awakened many years ago
by my reading of Ortega y Gasset and René Wellek. The training of
a Hispanist-comparatist owed indeed, in my not untypical case, a
great deal to both. It made possible the following survey of the metaphor of perspective, which, I know full well, cannot do justice to either
the great range of the subject or the technical requirements of every
individual part. I propose it as a preliminary essay and an effort to

bring several approaches—several perspectives—to bear on a single metaphorical area which doubtless is still "developing, changing, full of possibilities."

I

Perspectiva, or *ars perspectiva,* derives from the Latin verb *perspicere,* meaning "to see clearly," "to examine," "to see through," and also "to regard mentally," "to ascertain." *Perspectiva* was a medieval Latin noun used to designate optics, the science of sight, which, as it rested on the application to vision of Euclidian laws, was considered a branch of geometry—"ancella," Dante calls it in the *Convivio (II,* 13)—and a part of the academic *quadrivium.* But Landino, in an early commentary to one of the passages in the *Divina Commedia* dealing with such optical phenomena as reflection and refraction, wrote that perspective "è parte di filosofia e parte di geometria" [3]—a significantly broader definition. The high esteem in which scholastic writers held optics is made clear particularly by Roger Bacon in his *Opus Majus* (1267), where it plays a central role. Bacon relies on the medieval tradition whose most original representatives had been the Arabic scientist Alhazen (Ibn al-Haitham, c. 965–1039), translated into Latin by Gerard of Cremona in the 12th century, and his follower, the 13th-century Polish writer Witelo. It was traditional for Bacon to affirm not only that sight was the noblest of all five senses, but that no other science could offer the beauty, sweetness, and usefulness of optics: "sed nulla tantam suavitatem et pulchritudinem utilitis habet." [4] Such was the prestige which optics enjoyed during the Middle Ages and which certain Florentine artists of the *Quattrocento* would bring to bear on the problem of projecting the three dimensions of space on the flat surfaces of painting.[5]

I have noted that the verb *perspicere* meant both "to see clearly" and, metaphorically, "to regard mentally," "to ascertain." It should be remembered at this point that the identification of light and the perception of light with divine or higher truths had been a continuing symbol in Mediterranean cultures since earliest historical times. Broad though the topic is, it needs to be kept in mind as a frame of reference for later uses of perspective as a cognitive metaphor. The Middle Ages had derived the conception of God as light from three main sources: Greek and Roman philosophy, the Bible (Psalms XXXVI, John 1:1–9, 8:12, James 1:17, etc.), and Judeo–Arabic thinkers like Ibn-Gabirol. Metaphysical speculations concerning the nature of light —an important feature of 13th-century scholasticism—revolved to a large extent around one question: that of the relationship between corporeal and spiritual light.[6] Two principal traditions were influential, the first of which affirmed that physical light was indivisible from spiritual light, as Augustine had stated;[7] while the other sustained that these were basically distinct entities, in agreement with Thomas Aquinas, who thought that to designate both by means of the same word was a verbal rather than a conceptual coincidence: "nihil enim prohibet unum nomen imponi rebus quantumcumque diversis."[8] Scholastic philosophers took a number of different positions. Yet these appear to share a common view of the universe as a ladder or as a hierarchy of light, and of light itself as a link—whatever its ontological status—between the spiritual and the physical orders. The *Divina Commedia* progresses, of course, from the visual aberrations occurring in the darkness of Hell to the illumination of Paradise, where the well-known optical phenomenon of *abbaglio* (a dazzling glare, as in the fact that a bright sun cannot be stared at) requires in the Thirtieth Canto the acquisition of "novella vista" by Dante the pilgrim.

Most relevant to our topic is the consistent use in this context—as the very notion of spiritual light implies—of visual events as vehicles of knowledge. In the Sixth Book of the *Republic* (*VI*, 508–509), Plato had stated analogically that the supreme Good makes the world intelligible even as the sun makes it visible. Among the Romans the Stoics were the first to utilize consistently the word *lumen* with regard to various forms of understanding.[9] And during the Middle Ages "it was common scholastic doctrine that sight shares knowing with the intellect and that thought had, when dealing with first principles, something of the immediacy of light."[10] As the light of the sun appears to stream downward in the direction of the Earth, the finite world was regarded as the will of God "above," and light as a universal bond inviting man to raise his thoughts to Him. Sight remained the dimension of cognitive ascent for Renaissance Neoplatonism, and Lorenzo the Magnificent experienced *abbaglio* most intensely when he dared to gaze on the sun-like beauty of his beloved.[11] During the 17th century reason would be called a "lumière naturelle" by Descartes and Leibniz,[12] while the traditional fusion of God with light would find perhaps its most eloquent expression in the famous incantation in Book III of *Paradise Lost* ("Hail, holy light, offspring of Heaven first-born!"). As Marjorie Nicolson has shown, it would remain for Newton to incorporate optics fully into the laws of nature, as far as both scientists and poets were concerned.[13]

The secularization of vision, and of its association with knowledge as well, in other words, is a process that spans the history of European culture. It cannot be understood without the crucial contribution of painting since the Renaissance. The fusion of vision with knowledge in general, in a secularized form, persists until the present day, as the itinerary of the metaphor of perspective, in its progress from optics to philosophy, from Alhazen and Roger Bacon to Ortega and Bertrand Russell, hopefully will demonstrate.

II

Art historians have devoted much study in recent years to the career of visual perspective since the Renaissance, often on a highly technical level, and I shall limit myself here to a commentary on, and an adaptation to our purpose, of some of the ideas developed by Panofsky, Krautheimer, Parronchi, Francastel, and others. The origins of artistic perspective are, for a layman, obscure. Illusionistic shapes can be found in Giotto, as Roberto Longhi has shown, but these are only fragments;[14] and, in general, the use by *Trecento* painters of isolated motifs like canopied buildings and square-tiled floors did not produce unified or centralized spaces. From the 1430's to the 1450's, certain Florentine artists discovered the applicability of the *perspectiva communis* (optics) to a *perspectiva artificialis* (in the visual arts), or, in Italian, *prospettiva*, by virtue of their exceptional gift for both artistic creation and the kind of scientific experimentalism which would culminate later in the work of Leonardo. Filippo Brunelleschi, fundamentally an architect, was familiar with the mathematics of construction, i.e., with the relevance of geometry to art. For the purpose of architectural surveys, he devised experimental paintings on wood, one of which, for example, represented the Piazza della Signoria and had its top cut out, so that an observer standing in the right place could look through the wood and find that its skyline coincided with that of the real buildings. This was hardly practical, as two preliminary drawings were needed, a ground plan and a vertical elevation.[15] A few years later Leon Battista Alberti, in his *Della Pittura* (1435–1436), succeeded in simplifying the discoveries of Brunelleschi and his followers, as well as in raising them to the level of an artistic theory.

"Chi mira una pittura, vede certa intersegazione d'una piramide": Alberti imagined that Euclid's visual pyramid, the apex of which is the observer's eye, was intersected by a flat plane as if it were made of glass ("non altrimenti, che se essa fosse di vetro tralucente"). This flat section became the surface of the painting, which no longer acted as such, but rather as an opening, an open window ("una finestra aperta") on the contents of the visual pyramid.[16] Thus the purpose of painting could be defined as the representation of things seen ("rappresentare cose vedute"),[17] a definition which Alberti the humanist associated with the myth of Narcissus: "che dirai tu essere dipingere altra cosa che simile abbracciare con arte, quella ivi superficie del fonte?"[18] This curious analogy supports Alberti's insistence on the idea that the artist finds individual self-achievement in his work, as it also suggests that realism in art amounts to a sort of narcissism on the part of all beings and things represented.[19] In three-dimensional terms—made possible by the laws of perspective—the canvas is an open window on the contents of a truncated pyramid, and in two-dimensional ones it is comparable to the reflection in a mirror. Finally, for practical goals Alberti devised an abbreviated perspective scheme based on a checkerboard system: the orthogonals composing the checkerboard floor or ground level were to converge on a vanishing point on the horizon, "and the problem of determining the gradual diminution of equidistant transversals was solved by the simple device of running an oblique line"—from an elevated point on the side, representing the eye-level of a person in the painting—"across the convergent orthogonals."[20]

Florentine perspective remained a fruitful artistic convention for four hundred years. It is generally recognized today, however, that "convention" also means in this case a limited and creatively limiting structure. That the perspective scheme was a conventional interpretation is made clear by the fact that it fell so short of being either faithful to the visual perception of men or "true to life" in a broader sense. This and other aspects of the subject were completely renovated in 1924 by Erwin Panofsky in a memorable article called (after Cassirer) "Die Perspektive als 'symbolische Form'." Panofsky showed that perspective is a significant and illusionistic form that does not coincide with the nature of perception. It is an abstraction of what we see. It does not distinguish between "visual images," where other sensory and psychological data are functional, and "retinal images," projected on the concave surface of the eye. The fact that images are projected not on a concave but on a flat surface causes the well-known effect of marginal aberration (also present in modern photography). Perspectives ignore both the real curvature of our field of vision and the three-dimensional effect of our having two eyes. Kepler, for example, noticed that the straight flight of a comet is perceived as curved by the observer and assumed that men were influenced by the new art of perspective in not realizing their error.[21]

I shall reduce, in order to clarify the rest of this essay, the principal assumptions of perspective to the following:

1. Painting is a mimetic fiction concerned with visual appearances —with Alberti's *cose vedute*. (A positive delight in *trompe l'oeil* will be especially noticeable in the 17th century, and as an example one may recall an entry in John Evelyn's *Diary* for February 27, 1644; Evelyn, while visiting Richelieu's villa in Rueil, admired a perspective painting of the Arch of Constantine and wrote later: "The sky and hills which seem to be between the arches, are so natural, that swallows and other birds, thinking to fly through, have dashed themselves against the wall. I was infinitely taken with this agreeable cheat.") [22]

2. The central projection and unified space of the painting are absolutely dependent on the fiction of the single beholder, i.e., on a unifying "point of view." It is not the thought of God—critics have said—or the cohesion of things as they really are on which the *system of the painting* rests, but the perception and understanding of the observing human being. Various beholders, various points of view, however, can serve as different but valid supports for several reproductions of a single scene.

3. The point of view is attached to both a single and an immobile eye. One of the perspective apparatuses proposed by Albrecht Dürer in his *Underweysung der Messung* (1525; revised edition, 1538) required a glass plate between the painter and the subject, as well as a device or chin-rest to keep the painter's head from moving (see Figure 1).[23] This fixed, monocular convention contradicts ordinary experience more than any other.

4. Objects are represented as having the same sizes and positions *in relation to one another* as they actually do when viewed by the single eye. Perspectives are relational.

5. These structures, or the connection between them as seen and their representation on the surface of the canvas, can be measured and are amenable to geometrical thinking. It was of course an aesthetic principle of the Italian Renaissance that beauty is a harmony of the parts with respect to the whole, and a mathematically correct system of relationships. This would make possible the rationalist theory which was developed during the 17th century and was called by Dilthey, with special reference to Leibniz, the natural system of aesthetic norms: "since . . . all harmonious relationships participated in the absolute order and harmony of the universe, there had to be, as the rationalist theorists believed, one and the same principle for beauty in the arts and in nature." [24] In this sense the geometrical connotations of perspective succeeded in bringing painting nearer to

*Dürer—An artist draws a sitting man on a glass grid by
looking through a moveable aperture.*

the status of music and the *artes liberales,* in turning it into a Pythagorean art.

6. The most important relational structure is distance, and things are seen in depth *with regard to the point of view,* that is to say, as more or less remote from the spectator. As Pierre Francastel suggests, it would be instructive to connect this view with the notion of "psychic distance" as wielded by anthropologists, who find it does not exist among primitive peoples who regard the world as an unbroken continuum.[25] The idea of perspective can be readily associated with a growing epistemological dualism, with a rigorous split between subject and object, as in the Cartesian distinction between mind and *res extensa.*[26]

I have just discussed the concept of perspective by isolating it—as most metaphors based on it will—from any individual use in any particular context. This should nearly suffice for the purposes of this essay. The historical view, nevertheless, cannot be lost sight of. The actual practice of perspective, as art historians show, varies a great deal not only from painter to painter or from period to period, but with regard to the very stress that the perspective scheme can be given. It can become a significant structure or stay in the background of the painting. It can be a "symbolical" and functional form or a mere preliminary, technical device. It can be a basic mimetic method, a formula for representing "things seen," or an aesthetic pattern within a set of patterns, an invitation (as in Paolo Uccello's famous *Battle of San Romano* [27]) to the formal beauties of geometry. I will now recall briefly, as illustrations, two individual works: a classic one from the *Quattrocento*—Donatello—and a 17th-century picture, not as widely known, by Zurbarán.

Donatello's bas-relief *The Miracle of the Healing of the Irascible Son* (for Sant'Antonio in Padua; see Figure 2) provides us with an early example of the enthusiastic application of linear perspective. The entire work depends on the convention of the truncated pyramid and on the controlling function of the point of view. The box-like pyramid, in the first place, stresses distance and depth. But it also makes clear the priority of space. Into the "container" of the area limited by the surrounding buildings, human figures have been *placed*, like landmarks or spatial indicators—and with all the difficulties implicit in the effort to fit life into mathematical coordinates. Space is a *continuum* previous to life. It separates one person from another and can only be covered in its entirety by the human eye. For the function of the point of view is such, in the second place, that objects and persons have been arranged in agreement with it. They have been located so as to be conveniently visible. Seeing actually "happens" in the work itself, and the observer feels invited to join the spectators *in* it, to lean on his own balustrade and watch the stagelike scene, to participate in the benefits of vision.

Zurbarán's *Viático de San Buenaventura* (Genoa, Galleria di Palazzo Bianco; see Figure 3) uses the perspective scheme as an occasion for symbolical form. The visual pyramid is extended into the distance, as the crowded foreground, occupied by no less than ten human figures, is mysteriously followed by the empty spaces in the back. Everything happens as if the lines of the perspective scheme had been continued, through sheer technical routine, beyond the area where the action occurs. Yet one soon notices that Zurbarán's preoccupation with perspective is neither an afterthought nor a fortuitous matter. The foreground prepares carefully the presence of the empty room behind it,

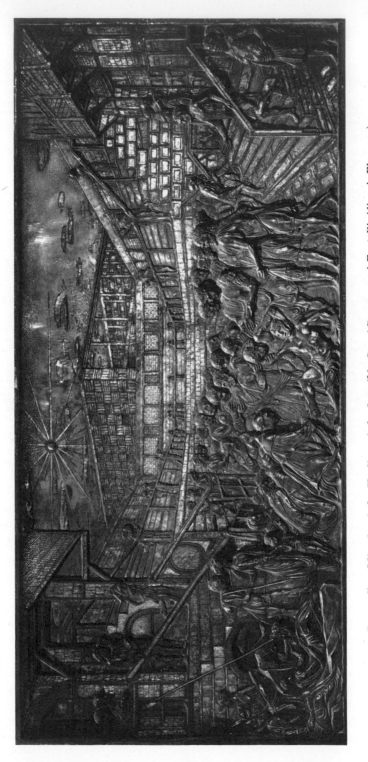

Donatello—Miracle of the Healing of the Irascible Son (Courtesy of Fratelli Alinari, Florence)

Francesco Zurbarán—Viático di San Bonaventura (Galleria di Palazzo Bianco, Genoa)

through the lines of the canopy over the bed, the carpet on the floor, the very arrangement of the bed and of the figures in the front. Thus we are led to observe the empty room, of which two features stand out: the book-lined walls and the light filling the void, falling from a high window. St. Bonaventura was of course an illustrious theologian and writer. Light, the most incorporeal of material phenomena, supplies his viaticum with a transition between one world and another, between the dying man and his Maker. The consolations of theology coincide, on this occasion, with the metaphysics of light that I discussed earlier. St. Bonaventura had believed—in J. A. Mazzeo's words—that "God is the true light, and that light is more properly to be predicated of spiritual than corporeal things. . . . For Bonaventura, light was not only the hierarchical principle and the principle of continuity in the corporeal universe, but he also accepted the Augustinian view that light is that by which the body is united to the soul and by which the soul rules the body. Its status as the corporeal substance most like spirit made it a kind of connecting link between the spiritual and corporeal orders." [28] Zurbarán's light rays not only signify but actually represent a ladder awaiting the ascent of the dying saint's soul.

When Dürer traveled from Venice to Bologna in 1506 in order to study *die Kunst der Messung*, which he, like other Northern painters, had approached in an empirical fashion, he was seeking a proficiency which only an elite of artists and theorists had attained. A set of practical rules had been collected by Johannes Viator (Jean Pélerin) in his *De artificiali perspectiva* (1505; 2nd edition, 1509). But the true theory or "art" of perspective was developed later, by a series of 16th-century publications, such as Dürer's own *Underweysung der Messung* (1525, 1538) and the works of H. Rodler (1531), A. Hirschvogel (1543), S. Serlio (1547), W. Jamnitzer (1548), F. Commandino (1558), D. Barbaro (1559), Jean Cousin the Younger (1565), J. Androuet (1576), J. B. Vignola (1583), L. Sirigatti (1599), G. Ubaldi del Monte (1600), and several others.[29] Many of these writers were geometricians, architects, or engineers. Venice, Nuremberg, and Holland, particularly, would publish treatises on perspective during the 16th and 17th centuries and make it possible for a specialized science to become common knowledge and a crucial influence on general visual habits.

Daniello Barbaro, in *La prattica della prospettiva* (1559), was one of the first to write concerning "anamorphoses," i.e., enigmatic pictures so contrived as to make sense only when seen obliquely or from a certain angle: for example, Erhard Schön's *Vexierbilder*, the signature in Holbein's *The Ambassadors* (1533), or the anamorphic picture, after Holbein, of Edward VI (1543) (see Figure 4). This vexing sort of visual trickery was but an extension of the illusionistic power implicit in perspective, and of the notion that the characteristics of vision could control the visible contents of the painting. An important affinity would develop between the possibilities of perspective and the so-called Baroque styles in the arts—a subject too complex and too well-known to be more than alluded to here. I need only recall the fondness for fiction and *trompe l'oeil* in the 17th-century Baroque theater, its perspective backcloths and curtains (like the curtain described by Calderón in the Prologue to *Fieras afemina amor:* "era su perspectiva de color de cielo, hermoseado de nubes y celajes" [30]), the crowding of illusions into the truncated pyramid of the stage—now seen from the front only, as through a larger version of Alberti's *finestra aperta*, by the immobile spectator. The Baroque builders of palaces and gardens, and their followers—the architects of Versailles, the

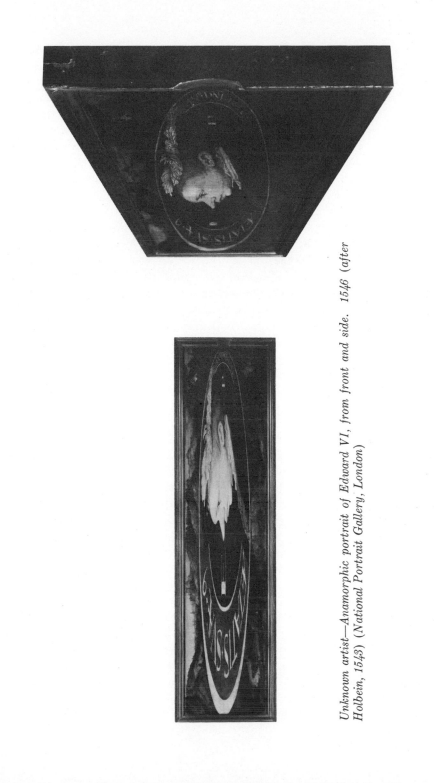

Unknown artist—Anamorphic portrait of Edward VI, from front and side. 1546 (after Holbein, 1543) (National Portrait Gallery, London)

Tuileries, St. Petersburg—converted into stone, tree-lined alleys or panoramic avenues the structural requirements of the point of view.[31] In an excellent essay Richard Alewyn has explained that the "impatient culture" of the age did not easily tolerate emptiness in either time or space. Of this he finds a symbol in the elaborate fetes and courtly celebrations of the later 17th century, and in the love of decorative make-believe: human bodies seemed in need of splendid costumes, human crowds of dances and masquerades, sentences of conceits and metaphors, and blank walls of perspective frescoes—capable, like mirrors, of enlarging or transcending the limited spaces at hand.[32]

During the same period the geometrical premises of perspective theory were being extended considerably by such scientists as G. Desargues, whose interest in the subject led him to formulate the general theory of conic projections (*Pratique de la perspective*, 1636). While the notion of perspective became common knowledge, its mathematical support was being developed on its own, and ultimately grew so elaborate as increasingly to confuse both the ordinary reader and the ordinary artist. It seems clear from the bric-a-brac of a book like Burton's *Anatomy of Melancholy* that many a layman was puzzled and had trouble distinguishing between the miracles of magic and those of optics.[33] Indeed, in 1635 Father Jean–François Niceron, O.M., published a treatise called *La Perspective curieuse, ou Magie artificielle des effets merveilleux de l'optique*. In their useful survey of the topic, A. Flocon and R. Taton have commented upon the divorce between painters and perspectivists toward the end of the 17th century. One might add that the alienated parties actually were mathematics and art, whose earlier collaboration had sustained the discoveries of the *Quattrocento*. It was a memorable day when the engraver Abraham Bosse (1611–1678), who had tried to teach his students the geometrical views of Desargues, quarreled with the fashionable Lebrun and was expelled from the Académie de Peinture.[34] Approximately at this time, as we shall see later, the concept of perspective was turned into a philosophical metaphor by the mathematically trained Leibniz.

III

Turning to the uses of the term in literature, it is not surprising to notice that the analogy or the metaphor of perspective arises first in Tuscany. A persuasive testimony of this is its appearance not only in cultured writing (as in Giovan Maria Cecchi, 1518–1587) [35] but in the markedly popular and lusty songs that were sung in Florence during carnival celebrations. One of these *canti carnacialeschi* is the "Canto de' Simulatori," one stanza of which reads:

> Se la ricchezza, sapïenza e fede
> di fuor falsa il colore,
> dunque, chi al vestir di costor crede,
> fa più degli altri errore;
> perchè la lingua, l'intelletto e'l cuore
> hanno pien di dispetti,
> e l'esser puri e netti
> vi danno indizio; e questo sol deriva
> ché'l mondo è tutto fatto in prospettiva.[36]

The Dissemblers are familiar with perspective as a sign of deceit. Though the entire world may be "fatto in prospettiva," this truth becomes an error for those who unmask it and look beyond externals, like the humble author of this popular song, who expresses an instinctive distrust of the visual as the conveyer of true knowledge. This derogatory meaning appears to have been central among early applications of the idea of perspective, either figurative or literal.

Metaphors based on perspective in painting—*perspectiva artificialis* —do not take hold, outside of Italy, until the early 17th century. Previous usage proceeds from the medieval *perspectiva* or optical science and designates instruments that improve or modify vision, like magnifying lenses or spyglasses. This meaning persists until the 19th century, and we still encounter it in Goethe, Gottfried Keller, or Browning, who exclaims in *Asolando* (1889):

> What would I give for the perspective glass
> At home, to make out if 't is really so! [37]

Browning speaks of the instrument with confidence, almost as a scientist might. Similarly, students of optics during the Middle Ages and the Renaissance often referred to their subject with admiration or respect: for example, Rabelais, who, concerning the phenomenon of *abbaglio*, which I discussed earlier, mentions the tradition of the "perspectifz" [38] (Alhazen, Witelo, Roger Bacon, etc.).

But a number of texts from the Renaissance and the Middle Ages throw a different light on the topic. They tend to stress that the image seen through the perspective glass is a distorted or ambiguous one, as if optical contrivances produced a kind of magic. The hero of Chaucer's *The Squire's Tale* receives from the King of Arabia a magical mirror where omens of future disasters may be read, and some of the curious bystanders advance the opinion that it consists

> Of anglis and sly reflexiouns

such as those that "Alocen and Vutulon" (Alhazen and Witelo) or other writers on optics had described when they wrote

Of queynte mirours and of perspectyues.[39]

For mirrors were associated for a long time with witchcraft, or the illusoriness of the senses. A Christian distrust of optics, besides, as a vain devotion to appearances, would be formulated in numerous sermons and in connection with comparisons or metaphors based on perspective—such as the characteristic words in William Drummond of Hawthornden's *Cypress Grove* (1623): "All we can set our eyes upon in these intricate mazes of Life is but Alchimie, vain Perspective, and deceiving Shadows, appearing far other ways afar off, than when enjoyed and looked upon at a near Distance." [40]

The notion of distance, or of a distant view brought closer to the beholder, was a common denominator of the image seen through the perspective glass and the illusion of the *perspectiva artificialis* in painting, so that it is difficult to tell from a text like William Drummond's whether one or the other kind of image is being indicated.[41] Toward the end of the 16th century and the beginning of the 17th, outside of Italy, we encounter an important turning point in the history of our metaphor. The original meanings of the word, referring to optical effects, appear to have been grafted on the newer frame of reference with which it was becoming associated. A certain significance or metaphorical purpose could be carried over from word to word even though the thing designated might have been different: in other terms, connotation persisted even though denotation changed.

Three texts from this period will illustrate my point. At one end of the spectrum, Ben Jonson—Drummond's good friend—alludes clearly to optics, magic, and pseudoscience in the *Alchemist* (1610). His hero, a rogue and *simulatore*, owns a glass for swindling:

> He'll show a perspective, where on one side
> You shall behold the faces and the persons
> Of all sufficient young heirs in town,
> Whose bonds are current for commodity. . . .[42]

But in Cervantes the association is less clear, and might also allude to painting. In the fourteenth chapter of the Second Part of *Don Quixote*, the Knight of the Mournful Countenance has just vanquished the Knight of the Mirrors when he raises the visor of his helmet in order to discover his victim's identity: "Vio, dice la historia, el rostro mismo, la misma figura, el mismo aspecto, la misma fisonomía, la misma efigie, la perspectiva misma del bachiller Sansón Carrasco." The more

Cervantes repeats *misma,* the greater the tension grows between identity and appearance. The accumulation of nouns signifying appearance suggests the reader's, and Don Quixote's, comic surprise, but it also builds a kind of visual *crescendo,* with an increasing reference to the *engaño a los ojos* and the entire problem of value-formation which surrounds, throughout the novel, the visual interpretation of single objects. The immediate context is visual—the verb *vio* is repeated four times within four sentences, and the stupendous nose of Sancho's counterpart, the squire Tomé Cecial, proves to be as illusory as the mirrors in his master's *nom de guerre.* The term *perspectiva* signifies here "aspect" in its most external and less reliable sense and could connote either painting—Cervantes might have read in Italy the theorists of perspective—or the persistent attacks of the enchanters' magic against Don Quixote's less superficial truth. At the other end of the spectrum, Francis Bacon refers undoubtedly to painting when he states in one of his *Essays* (1625), concerning the wrong use of judgment by false scholars: "It hath been an opinion that the French are wiser than they seem, and the Spaniards seem wiser than they are. . . . It is a ridiculous thing, and fit for a satire to persons of judgment, to see what shifts these formalists have, and what prospectives to make superficies to seem body that hath depth and bulk." [43]

This fusion of and confusion between the real and the representational aspects of optical phenomena may be found also in the plays of Shakespeare, where the term is used a number of times, generally, commentators tend to think, with regard to the perspective glass. [44] Not so in *Richard II,* where it seems clear in one passage that Shakespeare has in mind the anamorphoses—single-angle, deceitful pictures —of the kind that Daniello Barbaro had discussed in *La prattica della prospettiva* (1559). The passage where the simile occurs is not an isolated one from a thematic viewpoint. It seems indivisible, in fact, from the important theme I should like to recall: the visualization of grief.

Griefs and grievances, long-lasting and unresolved, haunt the stage of *Richard II.* Grief is universally present, not as a product but as an underlying condition of the action:

> Comfort's in heaven; and we are on the earth,
> Where nothing lives but crosses, cares and grief. (II, ii)

Looking toward the future, the exiled Bolingbroke knows himself doomed to be "a journeyman to grief" (I, iii), even as the deposed King can only remain the ruler of his sorrow:

> You may my glories and my state depose
> But not my griefs. Still am I king of those.   (IV, i)

Similarly, the king is aware of the special status of the grieving soul:

> O, that I were as great
> As is my grief, or lesser than my name!   (III, iii)

But it would hardly serve to illustrate here the general nature of grief. Its perception, its apprehension, is the problem that concerns us in *Richard II*. In order to observe in what ways grief becomes accessible or visible to other men it is necessary to indicate, however briefly, the relevance of images presenting hollowness, emptiness, or the relationship between a contained thing and its container. One may remember, for example, the comparison between the empty crown, the bucket, and the suffering soul:

> Now is this golden crown like a deep well,
> That owes two buckets, filling one another;
> The emptier ever dancing in the air,
> The other down, unseen, and full of water:
> That bucket down, and full of tears, am I,
> Drinking my griefs, whilst you mount up on high.   (IV, i)

In the Duchess of Gloucester's house at Plashy, which is temporarily empty, there is nothing to be seen:

> But empty lodgings and unfurnish'd walls,
> Unpeopled offices, untrodden stones. . . .   (I, ii)

As he approaches death, old John of Gaunt imagines his future grave:

> Gaunt am I for the grave, gaunt as a grave,
> Whose hollow womb inherits nought but bones.   (II, i)

Thus the spectator is prepared to visualize the fact that the soul is enclosed, enveloped, sealed off by the containing body:

> As if this flesh, which walls about our life,
> Were brass impregnable. . . .   (III, ii)

while the whole nation—"our sea-walled garden"—is like a fortress or a little world:

> England, bound in with the triumphant sea. . . .   (II, i)

Hollow objects can contain hidden substances, and a mobile, puzzling relationship can exist between container and contained. Also, between the traditionally divided soul and body. An important development of 16th-century literature is the increasing liberation of "inner man" from "outer man." Leo Spitzer has shown that in the medieval epic gestures revealed emotions—they were psycho-physical.[45] Lionel Friedman has explained further that the radical Christian division in the Middle Ages of "dual man" (*homo duplex*) into the physical and the spiritual (*homo exterior* and *homo interior*) was balanced by certain correspondences existing between the two. Though the soul's life was regarded as invisible and the heart as hidden (*occulta cordis*), a symbolical connection remained between body and soul, and facial expressions or other externals were a sign of this connection. Thus writers did not pretend, or feel the necessity, to portray inwardness independently from outer appearances.[46] This situation is modified by the Renaissance, of which one may recall two examples: the prose of Machiavelli; and the Spanish ancestors of the novel, such as *Lazarillo de Tormes* (whose hero is shaped above all by the teachings of his first master, the blindman, and by his uncanny ability to dispense with the visible). The unity of "dual man" is shattered in *Lazarillo* as it also will be in later novels, through their concentration on the "secret life" of the characters. There are many other Renaissance examples of the hero as lonely spirit, dissembler, or hypocrite. The challenge which Shakespeare faces in this sense is the portrayal of the *homo interior* by means of visible action on the stage.

Lies, confessions, accusations of untruth, the formulation of thoughts with regard to different strata of the inner or of the public personality as different situations arise, occupy many scenes of *Richard II* and emphasize its constant concern with treason: How does one unmask a traitor or discover a liar? Exile represents the banishment of the outer man, as the inner person and its latent treachery remain obscure or undisclosed:

> By this time, had the King permitted us,
> One of our souls had wand'red in the air,
> Banish'd this frail sepulchre of our flesh,
> As now our flesh is banish'd from this land.　　(I, iii)

A man's reputation or honor is in part the unseeing confidence of others in his inner integrity:

> . . . that away
> Men are but gilded loam or painted clay.　　(I, i)

And the political matter of the play involves the realization that righteous behavior can be controlled too closely by externals, i.e., by the letter rather than by the substance of the law.

Sorrow, of course, can be externally caused or feigned, as in the parting of Aumerle from Bolingbroke upon the latter's banishment. The wind makes Bolingbroke shed a tear, while Aumerle prefers not to counterfeit feeling:

K. RICH. What said our cousin when you parted with him?
AUM. Farewell:
And, for my heart disdained that my tongue
Should so profane the word, that taught me craft
To counterfeit oppression of such grief,
That words seem'd buried in my sorrow's grave. (I, iv)

Yet there are moments when inner grief can be *seen,* as when the King says to John of Gaunt:

Uncle, even in the glasses of thine eyes
I see thy grieved heart. (I, iii)

A closer reading of the play could show, in our terms, the varying conditions under which King Richard is reduced to acting as a mere *homo exterior* or surrenders to the outer glitter of language, while royalty is no more than an empty role. On those occasions the hero begins to lose sight of his own grief, his own inwardness, so that he is led, like a blind Narcissus, to question his face as if it could answer for the disappearing inner being. The famous scene of the breaking of the mirror implies such a level of self-reflection:

BOLING. The shadow of your sorrow hath destroy'd
The shadow of your face.
K. RICH.   Say that again.
The shadow of my sorrow? Ha! Let's see:
'Tis very true, my grief lies all within;
And these external manners of laments
Are merely shadows to the unseen grief
That swells with silence in the tortur'd soul;
There lies the substance. (IV, i)

Thus we can recognize the relevance, earlier in the play, of Bushy's anamorphic simile (see Figure 4) and its complex presentation of the visualization of grief:

Each substance of a grief hath twenty shadows,
Which shows like grief itself, but is not so;
For sorrow's eye, glazed with blinding tears,
Divides one thing entire to many objects,
Like perspectives, which rightly gaz'd upon
Show nothing but confusion—ey'd awry

> Distinguish form; so your sweet Majesty,
> Looking awry upon your lord's departure,
> Find shapes of grief, more than himself, to wail;
> Which, look'd on as it is, is nought but shadows
> Of what it is not.   (II, ii)

True perception requires, of course, what the dramatist Middleton calls "intellectual eyesight" [47]—or insight—through the "brass impregnable" of the flesh, or, in the words of the Earl of Salisbury in *Richard II*, "the eyes of heavy mind" (II, iv).

I have dwelt at length on Shakespeare's splendid perspective simile in order to show not that it is the most central in the play, but, conversely, how readily it fits into a larger and more significant intellectual framework. Optical error is also a fallacy of understanding in this and in other works where the metaphor of perspective appears. There is ultimately an important concentration not on the content of a given theme but on how it can be *known*. I have mentioned earlier that in a Donatello bas-relief the mechanics of vision control the nature of the visible. In Cervantes' narrative writing, the relationship between reality and the imagination becomes so basic as to bring sharply into focus the methods used for the presentation of fictional events. The artist in such cases is fundamentally concerned with how human experience can be perceived or known, and this in turn affects or enters the structure of the work of art. In *Richard II*, similarly, the career of grief seems no more problematic than its manifestation to the eyes of the characters and the spectators. This cognitive dimension based on vision surrounds and conditions the entire content of the tragedy on Shakespeare's stage.

During the later 17th century the term perspective will be applied with increasing frequency to the paintings themselves—sometimes called "perspective pieces" [48]—as well as to landscapes or vistas perceived in the same fashion. Thus the context of the poem, for example, is needed in order to clarify that Dryden is describing a *picture* when he writes in the "Elegy of Mrs. Anne Killigrew":

> Of lofty trees, with sacred shades,
> And perspectives of pleasant glades. . . .[49]

Dryden's line could also have designated a *real* landscape, as the laws of perspective were generally regarded as being true to life. A perspective began to signify "a view"—the contents of which are seen according to the Florentine pattern (distance, vanishing point, etc.). As the painter's device had become a generalized visual habit, the term could alternate with ease between art and life. I should add that I primarily have in mind in this essay the linear perspective of *Quattrocento* origin, from which metaphorical usage mainly has derived. The later development of aerial perspective (rendered by means of fading or contrasting colors, light effects, etc.) provided the painter with *additional* procedures. These could achieve precedence over the linear pattern in the works of some artists, but they did not contradict or nullify it. (A full study of the term perspective signifying "a view," however, would probably have to stress the Romantic period. I am referring to the fondness in certain writers for misty, dewy vistas, infinite distances, sunset hours—comparable to the softened hues of a landscape painted in aerial perspective—as when Wordsworth gazes, in "Descriptive Sketches," on a stormy twilight:

> Eastward, in long perspective glittering, shine
> The wood-crowned cliffs, that o'er the lake recline. . . .[50]

Or when Chateaubriand uses it metaphorically: "Les verités que contient le coeur sont du nombre de celles qui demandent le demi-jour et la perspective." [51])

The growth of the metaphor during the 17th century appears to have been founded principally on the notion of distance. The adverbial expression "in perspective" would come to signify "afar," "in the distance" (as the even more common "seeing things in perspective," "placing things in perspective," would allude not only to context but to the relation between what is near and what is far). We meet this meaning, for example, already in Lope de Vega's *Dorotea* (c. 1632). Fernando, Lope's hero, is always the poet and lover of words, beyond the mere activity of composing poems, and his changing identity is inseparable from the constantly inventive use of language. As Celia observes: "Ves ahí lo que te ha dejado don Fernando, versos, acotaciones y vocablos nuevos. . . ." (II, ii). One of these *vocablos neuvos* is *perspectiva*,[52] applied to land as seen from a distant boat:

> ¿En qué gavia descubres
> del árbol alta copa,
> la tierra en perspectiva,
> del mar incultas orlas?   (III, vii)

Nearly as soon the identical notion of distance was transferred metaphorically to *time*, usually with reference to the future. The most expressive instances I know of this—perspective as "mental view of the future," "outlook," "expectation"—are in the letters of Madame de Sévigné, whose imagination was capable of visualizing not only the past, as critics have stressed, but the future too. "Vous me donnez des

perspectives charmantes pour m'ôter l'horreur des séparations" [53]—
she writes to her daughter, who, needless to say, was the goal of her
heart despite and against every form of distance: "Du reste, je ne
vous dis point que vous êtes mon but, ma perspective, vous le
savez bien." [54] (Later on, with the growth of a sense of history, this
metaphorical usage—"seeing in perspective," "needing perspective," etc.—will refer not only to psychological but to *historical*
time.[55])

Most useful to our subject would be an investigation of the early
adaptation of the metaphor to the processes of knowledge. There is
evidence during the 17th century of the exact use by precise minds of
the perspective figure with all its scientific trappings (the point of
view, the visual pyramid, the vanishing point, etc.) with respect to
judgment. To be sure, the passage from a metaphor for illusion to a
metaphor for cognition had occurred earlier in individual cases, even
with reference to the perspective glass.[56] At that time, however,
mathematically educated minds brought their training to bear increasingly on the problems of human behavior. As there existed an exact
method for correct visual interpretation, why should analogous procedures not have been sought for the evaluation of moral situations?
This tempting parallel was likely to arise, especially in France, during
a period of growing rationalism. Even Pascal would mention with
admiration the virtues of the pictorial point of view: "Si on est trop
jeune, on ne juge pas bien; trop vieil, de même. . . . Ainsi les tableaux vus de trop loin—et de trop près; et il n'y a qu'un point indivisible qui soit le véritable lieu; les autres sont trop près, trop loin, trop
haut ou trop bas. La perspective l'assigne dans l'art de la peinture;
mais dans la vérité et dans la morale, qui l'assignera?" [57]

In this thought La Rochefoucauld, half a century later, will follow
substantially Pascal, though with the important omission of the question mark: "Les hommes et leurs affaires ont leur point de perspective:
il y en a qu'il faut voir de près, pour en bien juger; et d'autres dont on
ne juge jamais si bien que quand on en est éloigné." [58] The lucidity
called for by La Rochefoucauld implies that a man cannot see himself,
blinded as he is by self-love,[59] but can try to observe such other men
as have the advantage of being more or less remote, if only the appropriate distance can be previously selected: "Comme on doit garder les
distances pour voir les objets, il en faut garder aussi pour la société:
chacun a son point de vue, d'où il veut être regardé; on a raison, le
plus souvent, de ne vouloir pas être éclairé de trop près, et il n'y a
presque point d'homme qui veuille, en toutes choses, se laisser voir tel
qu'il est." [60] What La Rochefoucauld regards as right judgment, in

other words, provides us with an early psychological example of what is often called "seeing things in perspective."

The first condition of this attitude is distance. Men can thus be judged correctly and objectively, just as natural bodies are measured by the surveying eye. Man in La Rochefoucauld no longer towers aristocratically over nature, but is the object of far-off, perspective vision—as Paul Bénichou has explained: "Il était un *moi* au dessus des choses, et il devient une *chose* comme les autres."[61] Yet this cognitive posture requires a degree of mental sympathy, of "insight," that would not be necessary if human beings, unlike objects, did not offer more than external surfaces to the beholder's eye. Judgment, La Rochefoucauld writes, is like a penetrating, all-pervasive light: "Le jugement n'est que la grandeur de la lumière de l'esprit; cette lumière pénètre le fond des choses, elle y remarque tout ce qu'il faut remarquer, et aperçoit celles qui semblent imperceptibles."[62] The adequate choice of distance must be combined with the compensating effects of insight.

In his reflections concerning the *point de perspective* and the *point de vue*, what La Rochefoucauld means bears a direct relation, as in Pascal, to the differences between youth and old age. Youth is too impetuous to be able to judge wisely. Old men retire too far from the society of other men. This withdrawal results not only in excessive distance but in a rejection of the perils and difficulties of understanding. Old men specialize in things which they can submit to their wishes and are not likely to disappoint them. In fact, they deal with externals, with objects as mere objects: "Leur goût, détrompé des désirs inutiles, se tourne alors vers des objets muets et insensibles; les bâtiments, l'agriculture, l'économie, l'étude, toutes ces choses sont soumises à leur volonté."[63] The mature, superior mind—*le grand esprit*—on the contrary, controls a wide range of insights: "Il discerne les objets éloignés, comme s'ils étaient présents; il comprend, il imagine les plus grandes choses; il voit et connaît les plus petites."[64] The ability to see things and people in perspective demands a constant coordination of the various levels on which the observer's intellectual vision must function, and a selfless objectivity. A famous example is La Rochefoucauld's final evaluation in his *Mémoires* of Cardinal Richelieu—where he does not overestimate the resentments caused by the Cardinal's actions in particular areas and attempts to judge correctly, after all the evidence is in, the whole of his achievement. Thus the moralist's eye moves from external appearances to the intuition of inwardness, from the individual heart to the general manifestations of human passions and humors, from the detail to the totality of a man's life. Perspective vision, in this case too, is that of "the eyes of heavy mind." Beyond its earthly range, there is little to be seen, for in La Rochefoucauld the glare of *abbaglio,* the field where vision fails, applies no longer to God or to the loved woman, as in Dante or Lorenzo the Magnificent, but to death and its aftermath: "Le soleil ni la mort ne se peuvent regarder fixement." [65]

As we reach cognitive perspectives, we should take passing notice of the fact that the attendant metaphor of the point of view had also taken hold by La Rochefoucauld's time.[66] Actually, it seems that whereas the idea of perspective would remain a relatively cultured one, the point of view, perhaps because it appears simpler, would obtain greater acceptance in everyday speech. I will not attempt to deal here with this extension of our subject. But in this respect an important distinction needs to be made, which will be of use to us later. A point of view is not always individual, or subjective in an individual sense. It can also be ultra-personal. Dürer's perspective apparatus (Figure 1) did not set up necessarily a personal field of vision: a number of people could occupy the same position. This distinction becomes operative in the area of opinions or experiences collectively shared—such as politics, class prejudices, religion, etc. Thus Montesquieu's fictional Persian writes as an outsider about a *Christian* point of view: "Le mariage, chez toutes les nations du Monde, est un contrat susceptible de toutes les conventions, et on n'en a dû bannir que celles qui auraient pu en affaiblir l'objet. Mais les Chrétiens ne le regardent pas dans ce point de vue." [67] The ultra-individual point of view, as we shall see later, will play a role in the discussions of modern perspectivistic philosophers.[68]

IV

With Leibniz (1646–1716) the language of philosophy seizes upon the mathematical premises of perspective theory. Early in his career Leibniz occupied himself with optics and the methods of perspective measurement. These topics are mentioned in his correspondence, and we know that he found J. Michael's *De Visu* stimulating reading.[69] Like Spinoza, who ground lenses, and Huygens, who was concerned with the construction of telescopes, he combined a mathematical turn of mind with a practical interest in optical instruments. It has been said that the development of the microscope supported some of Leibniz's principal philosophical concepts.[70] On all these grounds the fact that he recurred to the perspective figure is not too startling.

It appears in a number of his writings, from the early *Letter to Thomasius* of 20–30 April, 1669, to the *Letter to the Electress Sophia of Hanover,* of February 6, 1706, the *Théodicée* (no. 357), and such important late works as the *Monadologie* (no. 57) and the *Principes de la Nature et de la Grâce, fondés en raison* (no. 3). There are good reasons for thinking that the figure of perspective is nearly as relevant to the core of Leibniz's imagination as that of the sphere, which he "had continually in mind"—H. W. Carr states—"and which served as the scheme of his system. . . . The center of the sphere is a point, but if you regard the center as belonging to the sphere and, so to speak, owning the waves which spread outwards, it is then a physical point, and it represents the unity of the whole sphere." [71] When asked by the Electress Sophia of Hanover to explain the relation between simple substances and the many, Leibniz replied that it is comparable to the manner in which numberless rays meet and form angles in the center of a sphere, though the center remains simple and indivisible. One may notice that the figure of perspective is an integral part of that of the sphere, for any portion of the latter can be considered as belonging to a perspective seen from the point of view of the center of the sphere, i.e., to one of the angles or of the visual cones spreading out from a central eye. Thus the image appears to be intimately associated with Leibniz's world view, and it would be impossible to present the former without doing full justice to the latter. Suffice it to indicate here the existence of such an association, as well as the originality and elegance of Leibniz's passage, in this context, from metaphor to metaphysics.

In Liebniz's writings between 1668 and 1671 the idea arises that the soul is like a mathematical point—i.e., nonextensive—on which all perceptions converge as perspective lines do on a point of view.[72] This joins his rejection of Descartes' notion of substance as *res extensa.* Leibniz seeks a unit of substance which is at once real and, unlike atoms, has no parts, is indivisible. This unit—the soul, later the monad—is, then, nonspatial, like a point. The question which this concept raises is that of the relationship between the soul and the rest of the world, between the one and the many. The nature of simple substances, Leibniz adds, is to have perceptions, and in these perceptions the universe is represented. In Carr's words:

> Perception is not an external relation, but an internal activity. To perceive is to *represent* composites. To represent the simple would be meaningless. We do not, in fact, perceive the simple substances which compose the universe, we perceive the world which is composed of them. Our perception is not the universe, it is the representation of the universe. In modern phrase we should say that knowledge, of which perception is a mode, is ideal or pictorial; it

gives us not the real itself, but a representation of the real. To Leibniz, this is the very meaning of individuality, because every representation of the world must be individual.[73]

This is no mere idealism. The soul perceives composites of which every simple part is real. The representation which the soul obtains is partial and insufficient—but also provisional and dynamic, as the soul is a growing activity moving from simple perception (*percevoir*) to developed "apperception" or consciousness (*s'apercevoir*). Each soul is a world in miniature that represents the larger world outside with greater or lesser distinctness, according to its individual nature, whereas God includes and knows all perfectly (*Letter to Sophia of Hanover*). Here our image becomes useful to Leibniz, who will identify the individual character of the soul, from which perception proceeds, with the "point of view," and the order imposed by the soul on representation, with "perspective." These figures imply a partial view of the whole by the single part, but they also show that the relations between perceiving units and perceived objects are at once different and "truthful," as the *Théodicée* states:

> Les projections de perspective, qui reviennent dans le cercle aux sections coniques, font voir qu'un même cercle peut être représenté par une ellipse, par une parabole, par une hyperbole, et même par un autre cercle et par une ligne droite, et par un point. Rien ne paraît si différent, ni si dissemblable, que ces figures; et cependant il y a un rapport exact de chaque point à chaque point. Aussi faut-il avouer que chaque âme se représente l'univers suivant son point de vue, et par un rapport qui lui est propre; mais une parfaite harmonie y subsiste toujours.[74]

The indivisible unit of being will become the monad, which is also connected with the rest of the world by means of perspectives, as Leibniz says in the classic example of the city in the *Monadologie:*

> Et comme une même ville regardée de différents côtés paraît tout autre et est comme multipliée perspectivement, il arrive de même que, par la multitude infinie de substances simples, il y a comme autant de différents univers, qui ne sont pourtant que les perspectives d'un seul selon les différents points de vue de chaque monade.[75]

It seems curious that a visual, external figure like the perspective scheme should be applied to metaphysical relations between nonspatial monads. In his early book on Leibniz, Bertrand Russell thought that he had detected a contradiction between the German philosopher's "subjective" view of space and the idea of the point of view, which calls for a degree of objectivity: "Thus Leibniz had two theories of space, the first subjective and Kantian, the second giving an objective counterpart, i.e., the various points of view of the monad." [76] In other words, if spatial connections between monads are not real, how can perspectives, which occupy space, be objective? How is Leibniz able to avail himself of perspectives for a transition from nonextension to space?

Monads are qualitatively different from one another, and one such difference is the fact that each has a special point of view, from which its particular relation to other substances derives. Now, a bare scheme of the perspective figure is a simple cone or pyramid, and its apex can symbolize perfectly not only the nonextensive monad but its point of view, i.e., the actual place where the cone begins. Two points, as it were, coincide: that of the monad and that of its point of view, which results from its internal activity and nature. The comparison holds so far, and it is consistent with Leibniz's argument to affirm in this context that the point of view is metaphysically real, not just a cognitive event. Can we say the same of the rest of the perspective cone?

The monad-composed universe has no extension, no shape, no succession. Space and time enter only the monad's *representation* of the rest of the world. The qualities that are apprehended, such as the physical shapes of bodies, are only appearances, phenomena, like colors and sounds. These appearances are brought together in the process of representation by space and time. Extension is the condition of the monad's perception of multitudes of things.[77]

We do not have a subjective, Kantian space, dependent on a subject's mental structure as it perceives so-called objects. Space in Leibniz, though limited to the activity of representation, depends instead on the response of one substance to other substances, i.e., on the relation between one part and another part of the real. This response is called metaphorically a perspective. It rests on the actual organization of the monads in the nonextensive world which they constitute. "Space and time in Leibniz's system belong to the world of appearance and not to the world of noumenal reality. Yet space and time are not themselves appearances, nor are they objects of perception, they belong to the *order* of perceptions. Space is the order of coexistence, time is the order of succession, in the monad's perceptions." [78]

The point of view, then, is metaphysically real. The perspective is a representational order which ontologically does not exist, but also is neither objective (since it structures appearances) nor subjective (as it rests on real relations between monads). The combination of the two is a mixed metaphor which may be qualified, in conclusion, by the following observations.

Perspectives, firstly, should not be regarded as illusory or erroneous—"as nought but shadows"—in Shakespeare's words—"of what is not." They not only are "shadows" of what *is*, they are also exact, as the quoted passage from the *Théodicée* makes clear ("Rien ne paraît si différent, ni si dissemblable, que ces figures; et cependant il y a un rapport exact de chaque point à chaque point."). There is a mathematically correct and truthful relation between the various parts of a given percept and its point of view. Just as space and time are not appearances, but orders of perceptions, perspectives are *exact orders of perception*. Monads can only know the real on the basis of phenomena, as only these are organized with precision and in agreement with a point of view.

The total figure, secondly, *combines* the ontologically existent point of view with the mirror-like perspective. This articulation is crucial. The total figure at hand is a representational relation between different real entities. Thus Leibniz occupies a middle ground (and I wish to stress this in view of what later thinkers will sustain) between the ontological and the epistemological notions of perspective. Leibniz stresses that monads are subject to change, but that these changes proceed from a *principe interne*, not from external influences (*Monadologie* nos. 10–11). The internal principle, with which the point of view is associated, is ultimately responsible for the development of the monad, for the order imposed on its perceptions. Thus, the point of view controls the perspective and the manner in which each monad experiences the universe.[79] Perspectives are cognitive, but not in any passive sense of the word.

In Leibniz's world view perspectives are, thirdly, legitimate and praiseworthy. I have already shown some reasons for this. Furthermore, the universe, while God knows it as a unity, as far as created substances are concerned, becomes infinitely mirrored and multiplied. There is a harmonious network of relations, which is not illusory but orderly, on the basis of geometrically exact and understandable relations. How splendid that the universe should be both one and multiple, both like a single sphere and like a multitude of perspectives! The simile of the city in the *Monadologie*, which I quoted earlier, was followed by this sentence: "Et c'est le moyen d'obtenir autant de variété qu'il est possible, mais avec le plus grand ordre qui puisse, c'est à dire c'est le moyen d'obtenir autant de perfection qu'il se peut." [80] And in the *Théodicée* the philosopher's rational delight is even clearer: "C'est comme dans les inventions de perspective, où certains beaux dessins ne paraissent que confusion, jusqu'à ce qu'on rapporte à leur vrai point de vue, ou qu'on les regarde par le moyen d'un certain verre ou miroir. C'est en les plaçant et s'en servant comme il faut, qu'on les fait devenir l'ornement d'un cabinet. Ainsi les déformités apparentes de nos petits mondes se réunissent en beautés dans le grand, et n'ont rien qui s'oppose à l'unité d'un principe universellement parfait." [81] Perspectives are a sign of God's preestablished harmony.

I should like to mention, finally, that Leibniz, unlike others, does not utilize the figure of perspective in order to underline distance or a strict subject-object dualism. One is not confronted simply with a thinking mind that contemplates things. Perspectives are relations between equally real and active subjects. In this connection, too, the position of Leibniz is unique in the history of the metaphor.

We do not encounter it again, in a philosophical text, until much later, and it is only during the last eighty years that it has become frequent. The term "perspectivism"—according to José Ferrater Mora in an invaluable article to which the present essay is much indebted [82]—was first used philosophically by Gustav Teichmüller in *Die wirkliche und die scheinbare Welt* (1882). Soon afterwards it reappears in Nietzsche. Before turning to Nietzsche, however, we might well note the date of Teichmüller's book: 1882. The first group exhibition of Impressionist painters had taken place in Paris in 1874. In 1877 Cézanne had painted his *Still Life: Jar, Cup, and Fruit* (Metropolitan Museum, New York); Manet in 1881, his *Bar at the Folies-Bergère* (Courtauld Institute of Art, London), etc. The Impressionist style had reached maturity, and some of its principal exponents were seeking new paths. By the same token, they were expressing a growing dissatisfaction with the conventions of Renaissance perspective; or they were experimenting with alternate procedures. From then on the prosperity of the metaphor of perspective will coincide with the decline of its literal uses in the visual arts (though not in commercial art).

These were the final stages of a convention which had been reduced much earlier, for many artists, to the status of a preliminary technique, a mere support for the painting, or even of a *poncif*. In one of his "Antiquarian Letters" Lessing had described it as a mere device: "Denn die Perspektiv ist keine Sache des Genies: sie beruht auf Regeln und Handgriffen. . . ." [83] For some of Lessing's contemporaries it was like a neoclassical rule, though perhaps a less substantial one than the three unities on the stage. A bad picture, in fact, could be painted with excellent perspective, as Diderot observed more than once.[84]   The value of perspective was often considered pedagogical.   It belonged to an apprentice's schooling in the tradition of his craft, like drawing from natural models.   In his *Gutachten über die Ausbildung eines jungen Malers,* Goethe writes that in his opinion a *young* painter cannot do without the study of anatomy and perspective.[85]   The fact that perspective was often assigned a secondary role may explain partly why Romantic painters did not reject it at the time when medieval art in general was being rediscovered.[86]   The *Beaux Arts* school tradition never considered doing so, of course, and the question of perspective during the 19th century is closely related to the tensions between traditionalism and *avant-garde.*

Pierre Francastel compares to a "grille" the function of the perspective scheme in the works of the main Impressionist period: if placed, as it were, over the canvas, it does not contradict it; but in the picture itself it appears like a mere framework, lightly alluded to.[87] This is especially clear in urban pictures like Monet's *Boulevard des Capucines* (1873) (or later ones by Pissarro, like the *Place du Théâtre Français,* 1898), where the vanishing distances of Parisian streets, or of the Seine River, are an occasion above all for the sensory and luminous effects with which the artist is concerned. During the 1880's, however, certain painters begin to produce pictures which dispense with, or even contradict, the "grille." Degas's interrupted rooms, figures cut off by the picture frame, diagonals plunging into shallow air; Gauguin's voluntary exile from familiar forms, for the sake of fictional spaces and surfaces;[88] Cézanne's unwillingness to "seduce"—Malraux's word—with appearances, to subordinate the surface of the painting to the content of the pictorial illusion [89]—all these constitute important steps in a new inquiry.   I have mentioned earlier Cézanne's *Still Life* in the Metropolitan Museum, which was done in 1877, and about which Sam Hunter writes: "He stresses flatness here by juggling perspective. . . .   Cézanne's great innovations shattered with one blow all painting formulas based on traditional Renaissance perspective." [90]

"Das *Perspektivische,* die Grundbedingung alles Lebens. . . ." [91] These words startle the reader of the Preface to *Jenseits von Gut und Böse* like a road sign barely warning of what follows. Teichmüller's *Perspektivismus* [92] is wielded by Nietzsche in his most mobile and provocative manner and sets off a number of original sparks, particularly in the already mentioned book and *Die fröhliche Wissenschaft.* Yet the sparks all seem to fly off in the same direction.   The starting point is the old notion of perspective as visual illusion, as an infinite series of arbitrary appearances perceived by countless individuals.

"But, why not appearances?" Nietzsche asks characteristically. Are they not the product of man's imagination, of his creative interpretation of mute nature ("die Natur ist immer wertlos" [93])? "Wir, die Denkend-Empfindenden, sind es, die wirklich und immerfort etwas *machen*, das noch nicht da ist: die ganze ewig wachsende Welt von Schätzungen, Farben, Akzenten, Perspektiven, Stufenleitern, Bejahungen und Verneinungen." [94] It is only moral prejudice to believe that truth is superior to appearances and evaluations: "Man gestehe sich doch so viel ein: es bestünde gar kein Leben, wenn nicht auf dem Grunde perspektivischer Schätzungen und Scheinbarkeiten." [95] The new concept of *value* is clearly the relevant one to this context, and for Nietzsche *Perspektiven* belong most often to the area of *Wertungen,* to the formation and creation of values.

The term seems appropriate to Nietzsche's later thinking in at least two ways. First, the notion of perspective as visual appearance supports readily his insistence on error and fallibility as the condition of our lives and of the necessity for the philosopher to comprehend the deep-seated impulses that lead the greatest of men to entertain particular opinions and sustain particular fallacies: "Wir finden Gründe uber Gründe dafür, die uns zu Mutmassungen über ein betrügerisches Prinzip im 'Wesen der Dinge' verlocken möchten." [96] Perspectives, secondly, underline the endless multiplicity of interpretations which any single thing may suggest to an original thinker. All beings are more or less interpretative, all being is in need of meaning, and this very fact can only be grasped through the individual mind's peculiar perspectives:

> Wie weit der perspektivische Charakter des Daseins reicht oder gar ob es irgendeinen andren Charakter noch hat, ob nicht ein Dasein ohne Auslegung, ohne 'Sinn' eben zum 'Unsinn' wird, ob, andrerseits, nicht alles Dasein essentiell ein *auslegendes* Dasein ist—das kann, wie billig, auch durch die fleissigste und peinlich-gewissenhafteste Analysis und Selbstprüfung des Intellekts nicht ausgemacht werden: da der menschliche Intellekt bei dieser Analysis nicht umhin kann, sich selbst unter seinen perspektivischen Formen zu sehn und *nur* in ihnen zu sehn.[97]

Nietzsche is perfectly aware of the visual origin of the metaphor and even refers to it in order to stress the subjective nature of values. The perspective figure is subordinated here—in our terms—to the "point of view," to the apex of the visual angle, and the very act of seeing is considered an essentially personal and inventive effort:

> Hüten wir uns nämlich, meine Herren Philosophen, von nun an besser vor der gefährlichen alten Begriffs-Fabelei, welche ein 'reines,

willenloses, schmerzloses, zeitloses Subjekt der Erkenntnis' an-
gesetzt hat, hüten wir uns vor den Fangarmen solcher kontradiktori-
scher Begriffe wie 'reine Vernunft,' 'absolute Geistigkeit,' 'Erkenntnis
an sich';—hier wird immer ein Auge zu denken verlangt, das gar
nicht gedacht werden kann, ein Auge, das durchaus keine Richtung
haben soll, bei dem die aktiven und interpretierenden Kräfte unter-
bunden sein sollen, fehlen sollen, durch die doch Sehen erst ein
Etwas-Sehen wird, hier wird also immer ein Widersinn und Unbegriff
vom Auge verlangt. Es gibt *nur* ein perspektivisches Sehen, *nur* ein
perspektivisches 'Erkennen'; und *je mehr* Affekte wir über eine Sache
zu Worte kommen lassen, *je mehr* Augen, verschiedne Augen wir uns
für dieselbe Sache einzusetzen wissen, um so vollständiger wird unser
'Begriff' dieser Sache, unsre 'Objektivität' sein.[98]

These perspectives—one might add in modern terms—are not simply
"figurative." Nietzsche raises the concept of perspective (also in
other passages where the stress is more pragmatic and biological),
and that of vision in general, to the level of a process of evaluation
and creation which is closer to the achievement of 20th-century artists
than to the geometrical objectivity of the old Florentine convention.
In this sense he destroys the older idea—reliant as it was on the conception of a *mimesis*-devoted sensibility, and on a subject-object
dualism.[99] Nietzsche's seer is not only an active inventor but a lover
of multiplicity and contradiction. The latter is what "perspectives"
also make clear. The active subject is able to control and exploit
a variety of points of view on a single object, as well as the contrasts
they imply. By having "several eyes," by combining various points
of view—nearly like a Cubist painter—he contributes to the endless
richness of being.[100]

V

In the 20th century "perspectivity" makes numerous and varied appearances, especially after World War I. It responds to an attitude
well attuned—not only in philosophy proper—to a period when no
single truth seemed likely to suffice, and some form of eclecticism, of
cosmopolitan doubt, of intellectual pluralism, or of inexhaustible historical curiosity, tempted numerous minds. Are we confronted here
with a species of relativism? With a blank check to all firmly held
"points of view," all intellectual idiosyncrasies? Normally the notion
of perspective seems most appropriate not to an all-out relativism,
but to the idea that a "point of view" has to yield a "right perspective" on the real, that a diversity of approaches must necessarily be
circumscribed, or supported in each case by an adequate methodology.

Indeed the main stress is often negative, as the perspectivist is conscious above all of his limits as a perceiver of the truth, of his inability to grasp totalities and construct systems. On some occasions perspectivism has been regarded as a sort of historicism—the realization that every activity in the history of culture is relative to the historical-social conditions of the period in which it took place.[101] And it has been attributed to the thinkers whose ancestor, in the broadest sense, one may consider to have been Wilhelm Dilthey. Certain abuses of the German-type *Geistesgeschichte*, such as the failure to evaluate properly individual achievement, or the intoxication with over-all period-by-period generalizations, obviously fall under this category. But perspectivism describes rather more accurately the work of those historians who, like Dilthey himself, regard *Weltanschauungen* as basic existential attitudes.[102] To the perspectivist, historicism does not produce valueless chaos. It suggests that every world view provides us with an ultra-individual aspect of truth, with a partial but loyal perception of man, of his history and of the values he has created. These are the distinctions, I think, that ought to determine the relevance of "perspectivism" to such writers and fields as Spengler's biologically determined relativism, G. Simmel, the *Umweltlehre* of the biologist J. von Uexküll, M. Scheler, K. Jaspers, K. Mannheim's *Soziologie des Wissens*, E. Rothacker, the historicists in literary criticism or art history, and J. Ortega y Gasset.

I shall discuss here a few philosophical instances—from Spain, England, and America. José Ortega y Gasset gave currency to the metaphor among Spanish readers during and after the First World War. That the idea of perspective was central to his thought has been proved abundantly by A. Rodríguez Huéscar in an admirable book, *Perspectiva y verdad: el problema de la verdad en Ortega* (Madrid, 1966). I can only refer my readers to Huéscar's exhaustive account of the numerous meanings—at least thirteen—that the term assumes in Ortega. But I must also direct their attention to a question of method which is pertinent to our subject, and on which I shall venture an opinion. The question is that of the preliminary approach to Ortega's philosophy as a whole. Huéscar, like Julián Marías, tends to regard it as a perfectly coherent body of thought which can be approached systematically. When an idea is not pursued fully in, say, text A, he then proceeds not only to discuss a text B for better comprehension—doubtless a legitimate step—but to suppose that the complete idea was *implicit* in text A. For example, in an early essay by Ortega, "Adán en el paraíso" (1910), the reader is likely to notice that the metaphor of perspective supports a subjective theory of values—a combination that will not reappear in later writings.[103]   While Ortega states already in this essay that as many entities exist as there are points of view, and it is remarkable that the metaphor should have been used by him so soon, what the metaphor actually signifies seems very different from its later meanings.   Yet Huéscar minimizes these differences, and even maintains that Ortega's subsequent idea is potentially present in "Adán en el paraíso." [104]   On the other hand, there are readers of Ortega who regard his achievement primarily as a dynamic inquiry, a constant self-elaboration, an intellectual "narrative" of which no single phase can be said to contain fully what will follow.[105]   This dramatic process, I think, is rather closer to the truth (and to Ortega's truth concerning human life).   Thus, to return to our topic, Huéscar traces the term perspective from "Glosas" (1902) to *El hombre y la gente* (1949–1950).   This covers a wide spectrum, ranging from the strictly philosophical to the notion of an artistic or intellectual "point of view" or even to the normal use of the word in ordinary Spanish speech.   I am not qualified to offer here a full alternative to Huéscar's interpretation.   The following may serve simply as an example of the different method.

Ortega recalls in this context Leibniz rather than Nietzsche [106]— as well as the work, among others, of Jakob von Uexküll (*Umwelt und Innenwelt der Tiere*, 1911), for whom the basic unit of biology is not the isolated organism but the functional whole including each body and its environment.   In the *Meditaciones del Quijote* (1914) the idea is merely sketched, though with an interesting reference to a philosophy of objective values.   There is a hierarchy of perspectives on the real, in agreement with the value attached to each.   The individual, whose point of view is originally limited to his *circunstancia* or environment, should develop a sense of relative position and distance so as to integrate his perceptions with the broad expanses of a larger reality.[107]   While so doing, he must distinguish between what is near or present (for example, the trees he actually *sees* in a wood) and what is distant, latent, or co-present (the wood, which he never sees as a whole).   This *teoría de la profundidad,* as applicable to art or to the structure of things, will remain an important feature of Ortega's thinking.[108]

But Ortega's ideas on the subject do not come to fruition until the first installment of *El espectador*, "Verdad y perspectiva" (1916), and especially *El tema de nuestro tiempo* (1923).   On both occasions he insists that the concept of perspective permits one to avoid the twin poles of relativism (there are only individual opinions, hence truth does not exist) and dogmatism (a single body of truth does exist, hence individual opinions do not matter). Perspectives are like a bridge between the knowledge-seeking person and reality. They are the dimension of man's apprehension of the real. This apprehension is selective and acts like a filter without leading necessarily into error. A "perspective" requires an individual "point of view" in order to be actualized and as such is not a subjective fallacy. An object offers to different persons different perspectives, all of which *can* be authentic, truthful, and, therefore, mutually complementary. One of Ortega's important contributions here is his presentation of the conditions that are needed for a point of view to be authentic and truthful. The opposites to be shunned are not only dogmatism and relativism. Man's knowledge is effective when he succeeds in not isolating "culture" from "life"—cultural aspirations from biological impulses, the imperatives of reason from those of living. The abstract exercise of reason fails to seize the mobility of existence, and a *razón vital* must be developed that is able to do so. A genuinely cognitive point of view must be spontaneous and rooted in experience—be a vehicle of the *razón vital.* A point of view, in order to be illuminating, should be sincere—it cannot be really feigned—while able to recognize its own limits—"La sola perspectiva falsa es ésa que pretende ser la única." [109] Let every man use his own lights as forcefully as he can, instead of attempting to "see" with someone else's eyes, which is sterile, or with everybody's, which is impossible.[110] The relevance, I must add, of this approach to humanistic studies is evident, and Ortega himself has applied skillfully the notion of the point of view to painting, literature, and music.[111]

Ortega's argument, however, is not quite clear or complete as he proceeds from a theory of knowledge and truth to perspectives as qualities of being, as ontology. "La perspectiva"—he writes in *El tema de nuestro tiempo*—"es uno de los componentes de la realidad." [112] Couldn't this be nearly a solipsism? *What* is this reality that perspectives are components of? The objective conception of perspective is dangerously circular, as it implies an independent reality on which the point of view focuses, and then goes on to state that this reality consists in a combination of perspectives. Ortega is quite aware of this and sustains that a perspective is an ontological predicate: "Cuando una realidad entra en choque con ese otro objeto que donominamos 'sujeto consciente,' la realidad responde *apareciéndole.* La apariencia es una cualidad objetiva de lo real, es su respuesta al sujeto." [113] The implication, it seems to me, is unequivocal: Perspectives are appearances, aspects, qualities of the real as perceived by individual subjects. Since Ortega has rejected previously any form of subjectivism or idealism, these appearances presuppose the reality they actualize or offer as a response to the subject. Unlike Nietzsche or Vaihinger, Ortega is not satisfied with perspectives as *mere* appearances, fictions, subjective values. Neither can he insert them into an equivalent of Leibniz's monadology. The reader remains anxious for a broader framework, a support for perspectives as objective appearances.

It can be argued that at this stage of Ortega's philosophy such a support in fact existed: his "circumstantial" theory, as formulated by the *Meditaciones del Quijote*. One can also add that his later insistence on a *filosofía de la vida* is a development of the earlier theory and may also serve as the needed framework. But I have promised to follow an alternate approach to Ortega's thought. It is also possible to indicate a dialectical tension between not only different ideas, but different attitudes—aspects of the Spanish writer's personality as a philosopher. There is perhaps such a tension between the metaphor of perspective and the *idea de la vida*. "Yo soy yo y mi circunstancia" means that the self, instead of being ontologically independent, is inconceivable without its environment—and vice versa. The philosophical concept of life, likewise, signifies that the individual finds himself situated in a broader reality which is his life. "My life," to all intents and purposes, is the radical locus of the real. This radical foundation is not a thing, a substance, but a series of events, constantly renewed and changing, constantly reinvented by man. My life, Ortega insists against the idealists, is submerged in the world. But, on the other hand, perspectives are based on a *sujeto consciente* who apprehends the things that are "out there" and seeks to pursue a dialogue, a kind of coexistence, with them. The metaphor of perspective is anthropocentric, and it normally implies the perception of things—not of the non-thing which is the locus of the self and of its environment. It is true that Ortega was aware of the limits of visual analogies, and even wrote once that "no one has ever seen an orange." [114] While it is impossible to see an orange fully and simultaneously from all sides, it is not impossible to touch it or grasp it three-dimensionally: "Es cosa clara que la forma decisiva de nuestro trato con las cosas es, efectivamente, el tacto. Y si esto es así, por fuerza tacto y contacto son el factor más perentorio en la estructuración de nuestro mundo." [115] Would a tactile analogy be more appropriate to the *idea de la vida?* Ortega, at any rate, held on to a metaphor in which a subject-object distinction was implicit. The notion of perspective is not readily adaptable to a "life" that embraces both the perceiver and the perceived. How do I "see" my life, how do I alter it or reinvent it, without losing touch with its real status? The metaphor at best is partial, or relevant to knowledge and action rather than to reality itself. It corresponds to one attitude only in Ortega—that of the *espectador* whose intelligence is engaged in a form of intellectual vision, of meditation on the spectacle of existence.

In 1914, the year of the *Meditaciones,* Bertrand Russell's *Our Knowledge of the External World* was also published. In this book Russell proposes to deal with the old doubts as to the reality of the world of sense by applying the procedures of the new logic to the examination of ordinary experience. At one point in his argument, he suggests suddenly a hypothesis—each mind sees the world "from a point of view peculiar to itself" and perceives a private world which is a "perspective." [116] A little while later, when he attempts to return from this metaphorical hypothesis to the central discourse of the book, Russell encounters serious difficulties. (Where is the intrapersonal mind that can construct from the various private worlds a public one? How can this logical construction be in itself anything but private? etc.[117]) It should not be necessary, however, to analyze these difficulties in detail, as Russell himself, in an article called "How I Write," seems to have conceded the point: "The book was very imperfect, and I now think that it contains serious errors." [118] In his case as in Ortega's, the student of our subject is likely to observe above all the problems raised by the attempt to turn the metaphor of perspective into a full-fledged ontological concept. Solipsism threatens the effort of relating by means of perspectives a multitude of perceiving entities to a single perceived reality (without regarding, like Leibniz, these entities as substantial). There is also the reduction of the external world to aspects or qualities lacking any real foundation— as W. T. Stace indicates concerning this stage of Russell's philosophy: "The whole object of the theory, we understood at the beginning, was to get rid of hidden substrates, *Ding-an-sich*-like physical objects with unknowable intrinsic qualities. But now all this, which we were to get rid of, is back again on our hands. The only advance made on the theory of *The Problems of Philosophy* is that for the solid *Ding-an-sich*-like thing at the center with its intrinsic qualities, we have substituted *Ding-an-sich*-like *aspects*, with their intrinsic qualities, radiating from the center through space. This change in no way makes the theory more empirical." [119] One is tempted to think that the metaphor of perspective offers a way out of a serious philosophical problem. After Russell, Alfred North Whitehead in his later writings also speaks of perspectives, "perspectival feelings," "perspectival relatives." [120] He uses the term especially in *Modes of Thought* (1938), a series of lectures intended for an audience of nonspecialists.

Students of American philosophy will be familiar with the work of George H. Mead, Samuel Alexander, E. B. McGilvary, the "perspective realists" and "objective relativists" whose work attracted attention before the Second World War. These different philosophers have in common an interest in the concept of perspective. In an article in the *Journal of Philosophy* for 1934 one can read a sentence that is indicative of a moment in the history of American thought: "In recent philosophy, the problem of perspectivity has become of the greatest importance." [121] Another article in the same journal for 1959—a respectful rejection by Arthur E. Murphy of McGilvary's posthumous *Toward a Perspective Realism*—spells out the change in the situation of philosophy over a twenty-five-year period.[122]

I can only recall in passing these philosophers, among whom important differences existed, and mention Arthur O. Lovejoy's powerful critique in *The Revolt Against Dualism* (1930), which is broadly relevant to the notion of perspective. Although he mentions Mead, Whitehead, Donald A. Piatt, Edwin A. Burtt, A. E. Murphy,[123] Lovejoy addresses himself to a general notion of perspectivity, along the following lines. Cognition is a direct relation between mind and object. Only certain aspects of the object enter into a relation of co-presence with the mind. A perspective designates this relation, which makes the content of a given experience unlike the object as it appears in any other relation. The point of view or "standpoint" [124] is the set of conditions responsible for the perception of a certain aspect or appearance. The "face values" of things are seized by the mind as a "continuum of qualities" (S. Alexander's terms [125]). The mind is a focal point for perspectives—it does not create a synthesis. Perspectives are relative to the point of view but are not based on qualities existing independently from the perceiver (hence the "realist" in "perspective realist," and the "objective" in "objective relativist"). These ideas are supported by certain assumptions for which a satisfactory account is not always given. The assumption I have discussed earlier is that of a real foundation for perspectival appearances. But Lovejoy in this context criticizes also the concept of the point of view. Perspectivity, he stresses, does not simply suppose that a percept depends upon a conditioning relation with the percipient; it relies upon the *position* of the percipient. "The notion of a standpoint or point of view apparently implies, in the first place, a situation in which *some* element is initially taken as *not* relative to the percipient. . . . From my point of view the penny may appear elliptical, from yours, circular; but the phraseology implies that the same object, or at least the same region of space or space-time, is in some sense being viewed by both of us." [126]   The point of view would be meaningless if one did not assume the previous existence of a region in space-time common to both the perceived object and the perceiving points of view. Lovejoy, secondly, is of the opinion that perspectivity brings about a subjective dissolution of *knowledge*.   The professedly objective relativist emphasizes that all content is affected by perspectivity.   This means that I can never know "things as they are" and am left with nothing more solid than my own point of view, which can only be the condition, not the goal, of knowledge.   It all leads to "a general deliquescence of the notion of factual truth and falsity." [127]

The last objection turns, of course, on whether knowledge is defined as the apprehension of "things as they are," and in this sense is circular.   But there is an added factor in the equation which should be taken into consideration—what I called earlier the ultra-individual point of view.   Let us not begin by asking that truth should exist independently of any experience of it.   Let us rather question the quality of the experience.   If closely related perspectives *were* only different from one another, objective knowledge would be in peril. Only when an individual receives an impression which others *cannot* receive, is the experience *totally* subjective.[128]   If we notice or assert, furthermore, that the same point of view *can* be shared by several persons, that it can be ultra-individual, Lovejoy's objection loses part of its force.   We have seen that according to Ortega the point of view had to be intensely personal.[129]   On the other hand, some of the American perspectivists have defended the opposite conception— George Herbert Mead, for example.   In the pragmatic philosophy of Mead (1863–1931), thought is a problem-solving activity, instrumental to behavior.   The fundamentals of perception are a distant object and one's selection of that which is related to one's future action.   In this pragmatic sense, then, "the perspective is the world in its relationship to the individual and the individual in its relationship to the world." [130]   But perspectives are combined through action, and in action men function also as members of groups.   The *location* underlying a perspective is a collective one,[131] as "the social individual is already in a perspective which belongs to the community within which his self has arisen. . . .   This involves the assumption of the community attitudes where all speak with one voice in the organization of social conduct.   The whole process of thinking is the inner conversation going on between the generalized other and the individual." [132]   This is Mead's view of the locus of the standpoint.   As

for the question of the real basis for perspectival aspects, Mead thinks
there is no absolute reality analogous to Newtonian absolute space
and time, of which the perspectives would be but partial representa-
tions. The universe itself consists of perspectives, which exist not
"on" an absolute behind the scenes, but "on" one another within a
time-space continuum as revealed by Einstein's relativity.[133]

VI

The notion of the ultra-individual point of view, then, is useful to the
perspectivist insofar as it compensates for a certain degree of subjectivism in his position. As an illustration of this, let us turn for a moment to literary theory. Let us suppose that a perspectivistic aesthetics exists in literary criticism and attempt to formulate briefly
(and very imperfectly, I am afraid) what some of its principles
might be. The work of art is a structure—one would begin—of potentialities, which criticism tries to actualize. There can be no actualization without the individual critic. A total, supra-individual realization is an abstraction inimical to the nature of the aesthetic experience, based as the latter is on perception. The literary work of art
is a finite structure that is able to release infinite effects. As a structure, it presents objective forms to the critic, and as a work of art it
multiplies itself endlessly through the aesthetic experience. Criticism
consists of a temporal series of critical acts. No single critical act
can encompass the wealth of the aesthetic experience, though it must
proceed from it. This channeling or funneling of the experience into
the act is the perspective. It is not an abstract method or a general
approach, but an empirical relation between the one and the many.
The work of art coincides solely with itself. Only certain aspects
of its actualization by the aesthetic experience enter at any single
moment into a relation of co-presence with the critic's mind. This
relation, or perspective, is the condition for the critic's reflective and
verbal effort. It leads to his active apprehension of the work, to his
own "creative" achievement. This achievement, if at all successful,
brings us back to the work itself, in a kind of constant voyage between the finite structure and the endless critical perspectives. In
this sense the existence of the work of art is not static or immutable,
and the articulate discovery by the critic of real perspectives is irre-
versible. The perspective is relative, of course, to the critic's point
of view, but this does not mean that either of the two are "his"
alone. The point of view must be nourished by an individual sensibility, or no aesthetic experience would occur. At the same time, the

point of view cannot be just private, or criticism would be either illusory or sterile. The point of view assumes the existence of a public region where the critic's gifts and the objective structure of the work of art *can* meet. Although two critics are not likely ever to write identical essays, they are able to work with or from the same perspective—in the hope, besides, that their readers will follow suit. The genuine critical perspective combines precisely an individual creative effort with the actualization of a public truth through an ultra-individual point of view, so that it may be transferable to future readers or critics who are capable of occupying a similar position.

But it is not my purpose here to develop new perspectives. Broad though my topic has been, I have tried to confine myself in this survey to the conscious use of the term by painters, writers, and philosophers of past periods. It would be another matter, and a subject for another essay, to envisage the possible uses of the term as *our* own critical instrument—to study in, say, music or literature, perspectives as "symbolical forms." The idea of "seeing things in perspective," for example, has been applied particularly to history and to the individual's experience of it. This experience is relevant to those historical novels whose characters proceed with some difficulty from the hard truths of private life to the wider and more questionable ones of history. Nikolai Rostov at Austerlitz was no more aware of the larger patterns in which he found himself than Fabrice del Dongo had been at Waterloo; and the hedgehog—to borrow Isaiah Berlin's terms concerning Tolstoy [134]—could be regarded as a fox who is able to see things in perspective (or the fox as an animal too involved in action to benefit from distant vision). In this connection, the notion of perspective has been applied to Manzoni's archetypal *Promessi sposi*, as far as I know, only in the most perfunctory fashion.[135] I should like to suggest, also briefly, the usefulness of such an approach.

In *I Promessi sposi*, perspectives are introduced first of all by the illustrious description of Lake Como and the mountain called *Resegone*. This mountain towers over the novel, shifts and changes before the eyes of the various characters as significantly as the steeples of Martinville will many years later for Proust. (Only when seen from the region of Milan does the *Resegone* appear like a saw—hence its original name.) The entire landscape description stresses mutability, especially in terms of the human eye and the innumerable standpoints it can occupy:

> E da qui la vista spazia per prospetti più o meno estesi, ma ricchi
> sempre e sempre qualcosa novi, secondo che i diversi punti piglian

più o meno della vasta scena circostante, e secondo che questa o quella parte campeggia o si scorcia, spunta o sparisce a vicenda. Dove un pezzo, dove un altro, dove una lunga distesa di quel vasto e variato specchio dell' acqua; di qua lago, chiuso all' estremità o piuttosto smarrito in un gruppo, in un andirivieni di montagne, e di mano in mano più allargato tra altri monti che si spiegano, a uno a uno, allo sguardo, e che l'acqua riflette capovolti, co' paesetti posti sulle rive; di là braccio di fiume, poi lago, poi fiume ancora, che va a perdersi in lucido serpeggiamento pur tra'monti che l'accompagnano, degradando via, e perdendosi quasi anch'essi nell'orizzonte.

(Ch. 1)

Gina Alani has pointed out, concerning Manzoni's descriptions, the writer's fondness for the observation of linear contour, his fascination with distance and wide spaces: "Il suo sguardo è attratto dall'orizzonte." [136] Yet his concern for detail, for the insoluble riddles of the human heart—"questo guazzabuglio del cuore umano" (Ch. 10)—is just as evident. The private truth is the most enigmatic of all. How does the narrator reconcile this puzzled presentation of detail with his faith in God's over-all design, with the long *prospettive* of Providence? The possibility, at any rate, of such a reconciliation—or its impossibility for those persons whose viewpoint is all too human—is what Manzoni seeks to integrate into the form of the novel. The dimensions of time rejoin those of space. The constant movement from narrative incident to the large expanses of history underlines the necessity of a temporal perspective. In the conventional novel, time before and after the action—whatever its span, even beyond the plot—simply ceases to exist. Fictional time has a beginning and an end. But Manzoni needs endless time as the dimension of permanence or the revelation of design, or as a foil for transformation and mutability. In this manner the blending of novelistic action with real history becomes not just a means for the revival of the past, or for pretending that the events in the story actually did happen, but the only method by which the reader can be supplied with temporal vistas that have truly an existence beyond the limits of the fictional plot. The historical novel becomes with Manzoni an instrument for placing the complexities of life on earth "in perspective"— in the temporal perspective of a philosophy of history.

Perspectivity in the novel was discovered and studied many years ago, particularly by Hispanic critics. In 1925 Américo Castro singled it out as one of the achievements of Cervantes in *Don Quixote:* "El mundo en Cervantes se resuelve en puntos de vista." [137] This was one of the ideas to which Castro's influential *El pensamiento de Cer-*

vantes gave currency: The external world in *Don Quixote* is a many-faceted "prism" that only subjectivity can interpret and endow with meaning; human situations, basically problematic, cannot be judged "from above," but rather from the points of view of individual lives, etc. The concept of perspectivity in Cervantes was adopted by a number of critics, such as Jean Cassou and Manuel Durán,[138] and has found a traditional illustration in the famous discussion of Mambrino's helmet (I, Ch. 44), which to Don Quixote was a helmet, to Sancho Panza a barber's basin, and—Don Quixote added *at a certain point*—to other men could appear as other things as well. The fact that in such scenes Cervantes' actors take a stand on the basis of their *visual* interpretations of single objects lends special support to the use of the perspectival metaphor. Cervantes was subtly able to combine the narrative presentation of the problematic experience of truth with his contemporaries' fascination with visual trickery and optical fallacy—*el engaño a los ojos*—which I have discussed earlier with reference to Shakespeare's anamorphic simile in *Richard II*.[139]

Leo Spitzer, furthermore, associated in a well-known article this feature of Cervantes' art with what he called his "linguistic perspectivism," i.e., the instability of proper names, certain common words, popular etymologies and styles, through a functional connection in each instance with the individuality of the speaker. The novelist is interested not in a monolithic world, not in a static language-in-itself, but in the co-presence of both with singular minds on singular occasions. Dialect or slang words, for example, which to a Dante would have been inferior manifestations of an ideal or superior language, in Cervantes are modes of expression that respond to individual realities and as such are justified.[140]

Spitzer, unfortunately, believed that this aspect of *Don Quixote* was a form of "relativism," as well as an inherent characteristic of Christian thought.[141] A number of important Hispanic critics, on the contrary, regard it as an anticipation of the modern novel (in relation with an entire current of Spanish and Latin American literature, from *La Celestina* to a recent work like Carlos Fuentes' *La región más transparente* [142]). Whether an idea is right or wrong—such a critic might say—is not really the point in a novel, but how men confront, test, defy, neglect, are able to live with or from, ideas. To state that *Don Quixote* gives us a "relativistic" approach to ideas or beliefs is likewise beside the point, because it assumes that these exist, like fixed stars, primarily outside the orbit of the novelistic action. The novelist does not ask what truth *is;* and if a character in the novel does, the center of gravity lies in his questioning, in his thought as an existential "occurrence." His procedure is radically different from the medieval debate (between the cleric and the layman, between water and wine, etc.) on a certain issue, around which the discussion revolves. The question is not the diversity of human opinions ("quot homines, tot sententias," in the words of Terence), but the diversity of human lives under the banner of identical opinions. A perspective, then, is a changing relation between the level of judgment and the level of existence. A novelistic perspective discloses a choice of values rooted not in the fixed character or status of the hero, but in his entire life, so that the process unfolded in the narrative is a constant manifestation and testing of a developing point of view.

This, I should add, is normally distinct from the varied use that Anglo-Saxon critics make of Percy Lubbock's "point of view." Lubbock (whose terms were often visual and well adapted to Flaubert and Henry James, to a period when artistic *correspondences* were fashionable) applied in *The Craft of Fiction* the notion of the point of view not so much to the character in the novel as to the relationship between the narrator and his material, or to the reader's participation in this relationship.[143]

VII

Although only the expert or the very adventurous should speak on the subject of modern painting, I will risk some observations with a principal purpose in mind: that of discussing the different results which a single concept may give rise to in different cultural areas. Many years ago René Wellek warned us against the perils of parallel-hunting between the various arts, or between the arts and intellectual history. His caveat has not lost its pertinence. As far as literary history is concerned, we need only recall the continuing tendency to totalitarian periodization, or the simple-minded uses of sociology by Marxist critics. "Just as fallacious"—Wellek wrote—"as the assumption of a common social background of the arts at a given time and place is the usual assumption that the intellectual background is necessarily identical and effective in all the arts." [144] This is singularly relevant to the 20th century and the "modern" scene. One welcomes, naturally, the examination of concrete relations between poetry, painting, and ideas during the "banquet years" in Paris: Herman Meyer's authoritative study, for example, of Rilke's early enthusiasm for Cézanne and later rejection of what Klee and Picasso stood for.[145] But the adoption by scholars of such comparisons as those proposed by Apollinaire in *Les peintres cubistes* (1913), or the charting in more than negative terms of a similar course for cubism and atonal music,[146] has been far from persuasive. Generalizations of this sort usually become valid as soon as they cease being illuminating. Careful analysis reveals "an intricate pattern of coincidences and divergences" [147] at any given point in time, as each form of creative activity tends to find its own direction or its own rhythm within the larger pattern of a period. That is to say, in a synchronic sense most cultural moments contain dialectical tensions, stresses and strains, balances and counterbalances. Diachronically, "the various arts . . . have each their individual evolution, with a different tempo and a different internal structure of elements." [148] Thus the question is not simply one of—if I may say so—perspective, of distance or of proximity to the subject under study. A culture as a mobile combination of "stresses" is not easily explained by any *reductio ad unum,* or indeed by any reduction, by any single point of view.

I am referring not to the inertia of the metaphor of perspective in everyday speech, but to philosophy. We saw that in 1914 Ortega y Gasset and Lord Russell sought support for their ideas in the figure of perspective, which Leibniz (on whom both wrote books) had first applied to metaphysics, and that numerous thinkers followed suit during the nineteen twenties and thirties. The year 1914 was one of the *anni mirabiles*—those of the decade before the First World War—that witnessed the emergence of radically new styles in painting. These would tend to dislodge or replace the convention of Florentine perspective, as well as the traditional conception of pictorial space. Furthermore, the "perspective realists" indicated their satisfaction with appearances, with a common-sense approach to ordinary experience, at a time when the plastic arts tended to do the opposite. I do not think that these contrasts reflect merely a distinction between traditionalism and *avant-garde*. Russell and Ortega were forward-looking thinkers, highly sensitive to the discoveries of their age. Only a student of modern philosophy, of its "internal structure" and itinerary and rhythm, is qualified to elucidate the situation I am describing. And whatever the appropriate comments may be, we should not be tempted—to recall our own caveat—by any single "reduction." Our contrast involves but a limited group of thinkers, and we are confronted with only one stress, one tension, within a cluster of stresses. The origin of the tension resides perhaps—this is my hypothesis—in changing attitudes toward vision as the possible instrument of knowledge and understanding.

Renaissance perspective had applied to painting the laws of medieval optics. These laws were simplified into an orderly, practical presentation of the facts of vision. Modern painting as a whole seeks alternatives not only to this simplification but to the absolute dependence of the work of art on everyday optics—on the purely visual process against which Diderot had protested, in his own way, when he wrote: "En un mot, la peinture est-elle l'art de parler aux yeux seulement? Ou celui de s'adresser au coeur et à l'esprit . . . , par l'entremise des yeux?" [149] I must add, however, that any general consideration must be empirically adapted to the sinuous course of the visual arts in our day. I have in mind two obvious features of the modern scene. The *avant-garde* attacks on a number of fronts at once and occupies extraordinarily varied, and even opposite, positions. The stresses and tensions of which I have spoken affect not only the particular arts but individual styles as well. This does not mean, secondly, that every style, every group, every "ism," is truly a fresh start or an independent affair that ought to be sealed off from the others. There are not as many significant styles in 20th-century art as one might gather from the proliferation of movements and labels in which museum directors, art critics, and dealers have a more than sentimental interest. I find myself in sympathy with those historians who sustain that the entire career of painting since Cézanne constitutes a single process and an unbroken quest.[150] It appears to me that this is the most fitting approach, at any rate, to the problem of perspective in modern art.

The seemingly boldest movements rely sometimes on conservative techniques like perspective. Recent "optical art" or "op art" (Vasarely, etc.) almost revives the assumptions of *Quattrocento* perspective. It proposes a return to the merely visual, and to an *esprit de géométrie* as illusion-producing and as painstaking as that of the most Euclidian of Renaissance theorists. It requires the spectator to be the extension of an eye, to *see* exclusively and intensely — from singular angles and points of view. Like commercial art, of course, or at least an important sector of it, so-called "pop art" cannot do without perspective, an element of its identification with the trivial and the photographic. Then there is the interesting case of Salvador Dalí. The liberation of pictorial content by surrealism led to either an analogous formal freedom (Ernst, Masson) or an exacerbated traditionalism (Dalí, Tanguy). The Catalan painter's remote horizons and vanishing vistas (in his surrealist phase, as in the work called *Perspectives*, c. 1932 [151]) have a Renaissance flavor in common with the "silent and infinite" perspectives of Giorgio de Chirico. But the chilling coherence of his pictorial dreams makes Dalí's academic hand curiously effective and functional.

Many of the outstanding achievements of 20th-century art can be regarded as a development, a metamorphosis, or a destruction of the perspective scheme—rather than as a full emancipation from it. An extreme instance is the naive painter, whose rejection of conventional spatial relations implies—at least as far as the sophisticated spectator is concerned—a reference to the "museum" in order to be fully significant. A similar observation could be made, to a certain degree, about a series of antiperspective canvases by Matisse, such as his *La liseuse distraite* (1919), where the lovely Florentine ground plan or checkerboard is made to *look* rectangular (instead of converging on a vanishing point). A decorative effect is of course involved. The ironic allusion to the old convention emphasizes, besides, the lack of unified space: the forlorn, daydreaming figure of the woman does not seem to belong to the surrounding room. One could argue further that the cubists were still preoccupied with perspective when they combined shifting points of view toward a simultaneity of vision (as the authors of dynamic montages and cinematic sequences obviously did—like Marcel Duchamp in the *Nude Descending a Staircase* (1912), and the Italian futurists). But the formal arrangements of cubism were also "real" in their own terms—autonomous and self-seeking. The possibility of an "abstract" space was one of its important contributions. This contribution would pose ultimately as many problems as it would solve. Is a fictional space to find some other principle of organization than perspective? How is it to be seen, to be approached by the beholder? I can only indicate here the pertinence of these questions— to Chagall and Kandinsky, for example. Chagall's spaces, to be sure, are mythical and unreal. Roosters and violins, clocks and bridal couples float in a never-never atmosphere that does not answer to the law of gravity. Yet this fabulous world is to be surveyed and seen *as if* it were real. One is allowed a bird's-eye view of it, by a kind of miraculous dispensation. As for Kandinsky, his abstractions move in a not-so-abstract space about which Clement Greenberg has written: "The atmospheric space in which his images threaten to dissolve remains a reproduction of atmospheric space in nature, and the integrity of the picture depends on the integrity of an illusion." [152]

Though there have been other relevant departures (like the divided, afocal picture), the various styles of abstract painting appear to have faced most boldly the consequences of the rejection of perspective. Let us consider them briefly with one question in mind: the relation between pictorial surface and pictorial depth. Art critics have discussed how Cézanne and the late impressionists sought to coordinate the decorative surface of the canvas with the illusion in depth of the "inside"; and Clement Greenberg interprets in the same terms the discovery of collage by Braque and Picasso, who found that *"trompe l'oeil* could be used to undeceive as well as to deceive the eye. It could be used, that is, to declare as well as to deny the actual surface. If the actuality of the surface—its real, physical flatness—could be indicated explicitly enough in certain places, it would be distinguished and separated from everything else the surface contained." [153] The various "abstract" painters—*sensu lato*—have tended, similarly, to "declare" the surface of the picture at the expense of the illusion of coordinated three-dimensional space, or to subordinate the calligraphy of the surface to the suggestion of fictional depth, or to pursue intermediate directions. These are of course mere polarities. Generally speaking, there has been a tradition of the surface (from Mondrian and Klee to Tobey, Still, de Stäel, Tàpies, etc.), as well as a tradition of space (from Kandinsky, Tamayo and Masson to Pollock, Riopelle, etc.). I do not mean to imply that the surface painters, who, like Tàpies, convert the surface into significant matter (or also tear and break it apart, like Burri and Millares), are not capable of producing fictional "worlds." They obviously are. But in their case the problem of perspective is simply solved by dispensing with the illusion of organized space. The pictorial surface has ceased to function as a window—Alberti's *finestra aperta*. The spectator's response, likewise, ceases to be merely visual. These works undeceive the eye so thoroughly that they seem above all to *exist,* to exist like objects—fragments or symbols of a larger reality.

This trend manifests itself most forcefully in the work of the space painters, whose fictional structures transcend the perspective scheme. The entangled patterns of a Jackson Pollock, for example, provide us with uniform, unified spaces. But these are not unified by the act of seeing—either within the interior of the picture or with respect to the beholder. The surface, though open to inner space, is no mere open window, calling for the single glance or the appropriate point of view. The observer is asked not only to see but to *confront* the artist's created spaces. The act of seeing presupposes and maintains a fundamental gap between the order of reality which is the locus of the spectator and the order of the painting. Vision is an "introduction" to the painting. A fuller "confrontation" is now prompted by the fact that the picture begins to occupy the place of everyday reality, to dislodge it or to supplement it. The spectator is now invited to enter, to "find himself" in, the order of the work of art. This order (like Ortega's "idea of life," which I discussed earlier) becomes the radical, enveloping condition of the observer's consciousness. The coordinates of perspective are superseded by the search for an illusion of life which uses and transcends the visual.

Contemporary painters, by the same token, strain against the limits of the single canvas. The abstract artist is again a central example (though there have been earlier ones, like Monet, in his late *Water Lilies*). The dense tracery of the "all-over" picture, where every inch is charged with line and color (Tobey, Pollock, Riopelle), or the total metamorphosis of the surface into texture and matter (Tàpies) produces a work with no absolute beginning and end. The painter needs no longer the aesthetic function of the frame—or the reduced angle of vision of the spectator.[154]

This emergence of the picture from the frame requires a full collaborative effort on the part of the spectator. Here contemporary painting—painting as confrontation and illusion of being—joins hands with the other arts. The enveloping effects of an art-in-the-round, in which the spectator is asked to exist, to participate without reservations, are not only the province of "happenings," pop-art "environments," or the theater of the absurd. They are also sought by the plastic arts. D.–H. Kahnweiler has told that in 1929 Picasso "was thinking of huge monuments which could be both houses for living in and enormous sculptures of women's heads, and which could be set up along the Mediterranean coast." [155] Similar monuments are being constructed today.[156] And, to give a recent example from painting, Matta exhibited in Paris in the spring of 1966 a series of canvases assembled like the faces of a cube: "Enfermant le spectateur dans le cube"—a reviewer writes—"Roberto Matta veut, symboliquement, le plonger au centre d'un espace en extension: le spectateur occupe la place du peintre." [157]

VIII

Although little can be said in conclusion without simplifying the subject we have just surveyed, there remain some questions that need to be asked. We have seen that the metaphor of perspective has fulfilled a number of functions in different cultural areas. Is it valid to speak of *a* metaphor at all, in the singular? Does it "exist"? Or are we confronted with a row of particulars, beyond which only fruitless abstractions are possible? To a certain extent, it is true that every metaphor is a concrete particular that cannot be dissociated from its context. This applies not only to poetry, but to rational thought. Modern critics such as Northrop Frye have observed the crucial role of single terms in the writings of important philosophers: "One often feels that a full understanding of such a word would be a key to the understanding of the whole system. If so, it would be a metaphorical key, as it would be a set of identifications made by the thinker with the word." [158]   I think I have begun to show some of these identifications, with regard, for example, to Leibniz and Ortega.

On the other hand, every particular occurrence of a metaphor implies an origin, a *fundamentum analogiae,* which lies outside the single work and has a previous existence. If every metaphor is based on a "let A be B," [159] and both B and the connection between A and B are uniquely related to the context, there are at least two elements which the writer inherits and employs: A; and the "let A be . . . X"—the very possibility and momentum of the metaphor, in those cases where A has already been used figuratively. One would otherwise deny that there is any expressive contact between the product and the initial figuration on which it rests, that is, one would deny the existence of the metaphor not only in general but in singular instances. A metaphor "fades" both in everyday speech and in cultured writing when the force of its origin is no longer felt. Thus, although its use may be contextually unique, its nature implies an extrinsic relation. A metaphor is the transformation of an extrinsic relation into an intrinsic one. Furthermore, if we consider for an instant the former, we may be able to recognize the elements in the *fundamentum analogiae* which condition the final result. These elements compose a structure of possibilities. It should be feasible to point out, for example, that certain analogies are *not* likely to arise, or at least to occupy a central position in the over-all area of the metaphor. For, as every good perspectivist knows, if the barber's headpiece looked like Mambrino's helmet to Don Quixote, and like a basin to Sancho, there are many things it could not have looked like to anyone.

These remarks are especially relevant to the figure of perspective, which is a "cultural" one. The metaphor was not latent in ordinary language, nor in a Christian symbol, nor in an ancient myth, nor in an archetypal image (though its cognitive uses were supported by the archetypal identification of vision with knowledge). It derived from a European, historically conditioned discovery in the visual arts, which was amenable to theory and as such could be called a cultural concept. It is probable that the metaphor will fade in the future, if not disappear altogether, as the framework of the concept and the *funda-*

mentum analogiae—namely, the close kinship of painting with optics and mathematics—loses its validity, just as it may reappear with the renewed vigor of the framework.

To analyze our metaphor as a structure of possibilities would extend unduly this essay. Suffice it to suggest that its controlling elements could be found in the six assumptions which I indicated in my presentation of artistic perspective. I do not think that any of these assumptions were unequivocal or did not prove capable of producing contradictory results. Point 2 (the point of view) gave rise to a personal metaphor (Ortega) and an ultra-personal one (Mead), both of which enter ordinary speech. Yet these polar uses retain a core in common—the connection between location and sight, percipient and knowledge. Similarly, the metaphor could lead to a stress on truthful appreciation (La Rochefoucauld, Ortega) or on problematic, subjective interpretation (Shakespeare, Baroque styles, Nietzsche). The concern with illusion or subjective value could be regarded as an emphasis on points 1 (painting as mimetic fiction) and 2 (the point of view, and its exaggeration by anamorphic pictures) at the expense of point 5 (structures are geometrically correct). Distance (point 6) is stressed frequently both in everyday speech (perspective as mental outlook; seeing things in perspective) and by moral or philosophical writing (La Rochefoucauld, Ortega). Point 4 (perspectives are relational) is basic in Leibniz's use of the metaphor, together with points 2 and 5; and also in that of later thinkers (Mead). We have admired in Leibniz, however, a particularly coherent utilization of the full structure of the metaphor.

Our glance at the idea of perspectivity in the 20th century has shown, I think, that the second assumption, the point of view, has been most fruitful and adaptable to the intellectual circumstances of the modern age. This assumption meant that the structure and unity of the picture were dependent on the beholder; it also meant that several beholders, several points of view, could equally support the final result. The relevance of this notion to a certain intellectual attitude has been expressed most forcefully by Ortega, who called it a rejection of both dogmatism and relativism. The intermediate position is a methodological beginning rather than an end, though also in an undogmatic way, the only method that is certain to be wrong being (to paraphrase Ortega) the one that pretends to be unique. I need not emphasize the kinship of this position with the procedures of modern science: the loyalty to the test of experience, the idea that knowledge is a continuing inquiry working within certain limits. As far as the humanities are concerned, I should like to quote some of the opening words from E. B. McGilvary's *Toward a Perspective Realism:*

> The perspective realist makes no claim that he can speak for the universe as it is for *itself*. He does not consider himself as an outsider looking on, a stranger, as it were, from some supernatural realm, passively contemplating a world of nature with whose goings-on he has no active business. On the contrary, he is a natural organism responding to natural stimulations and acquiring thereby such knowledge as nature thereupon puts at his disposal. This knowledge, as far as he can integrate it into a system, is his philosophy. As this knowledge and the integration of it develops, his philosophy develops. . . . A mature philosophy for him is an ideal never realized. He sees in part, he knows in part, he prophesies in part; and that which is perfect never comes, except as a goal that lies afar off before him.[160]

The immensity of the thinker's goal, which McGilvary stresses, goes hand in hand with a growing refusal to begin with the hypothesis of a systematic support, in the universe as it is "for itself," for our efforts to apprehend it. Modern science, to recall a classic example, no longer assumes that Newtonian laws, which are suited for the description of mechanical systems, are of use to the description of the atom. The philosophy of history also tends to eschew the unitarian hypothesis, as "the problem of history"—in Karl Löwith's words—"is unanswerable within its own perspective. Historical processes as such do not bear the least evidence of a comprehensive and ultimate meaning."[161] Thus, the modern scholar is filled with the awareness both of his own necessary limits as an observer and of the huge complexity of his task. The cry for "perspective" often expresses, in fact, a desperate longing for order in a cluttered, helter-skelter world. It seems to me that, in this context, the metaphor of perspective has provided us with a modern version of Nicholas of Cusa's *docta ignorantia.* There is no plausible proportion between the individual mind and our "cultural world." Yet, in the words of the same theologian, "homo non potest iudicare nisi humaniter."[162] Our metaphor serves to underline the necessity of avoiding the individualistic chaos of knowledge while keeping in mind the endlessness of experience, the basic incongruity between man's limited capacity for understanding and the immense, expanding universe of which he is a part.

I have already discussed the limits of the perspectivistic figure—like the difficulties that were met when turning from epistemology to ontology, from a metaphor for knowledge to a metaphor for being (Ortega, Russell). The passage of time, besides, has reduced the cognitive force of the analogy. Generally speaking, Renaissance perspective was founded on a common-sense approach to the facts of vision, which under the scrutiny of modern psychologists—or of a philosopher like Wittgenstein [163]—appear increasingly complex and problematical. The environment of the post-Renaissance painter receded from him in all directions and underwent distortions which, as he looked at them, were compatible with a simple set of mathematical coordinates.[164] He lived in a geometrically organized world from which the human spirit considered itself distinct. Distance (our sixth assumption) was the premise of this basic distinction between nature and mind. It has become for the same reasons a stumbling-block for modern artists. I have just said that the metaphor of perspective underlined the individual's limits vis-à-vis the expanding universe of which he is a part. The inertia of the metaphor also works against the feeling that he *is* a part, not simply a beholder. It seems sometimes necessary, in order to live and understand, to see things "out of perspective," to correct the foreshortenings and the vanishing convergences which impose their order of urgency on us. Curiously enough, it was a physicist, Niels Bohr, who stressed the truism that "we are both actors and spectators in the great drama of existence." [165] The reader who may be familiar with Bohr's "complementarity" and Werner Heisenberg's "principle of uncertainty" will also recall the arguments among physicists concerning the extent to which the situation of the scientific observer affects the contents of his study: "Natural science"—Heisenberg writes—"does not simply explain and describe nature; it is a part of the interplay between nature and ourselves; it describes nature as exposed to our method of questioning. This was a possibility of which Descartes could not have thought, but it makes the sharp separation between the world and the I impossible." [166] Similarly, contemporary art is no longer devoted to a description of nature based on a sharp separation between the world and the I. It may be that all sensory metaphors—including tactile ones—are insufficient to render the total experience of man's intimate involvement in his life and time.

NOTES

1. (New York, 1949), p. 35.
2. Cf. "Six Types of Literary History," *English Institute Essays* (New York, 1946), p. 121.
3. As quoted by A. Parronchi, *Studi sulla dolce prospettiva* (Milan, 1964), p. 10.

4. *The 'Opus Majus' of Roger Bacon*, ed. J. H. Bridges (Frankfurt/Main, 1964), *II*, 3.

5. Cf. Parronchi, *op. cit.* On the contribution of Alhazen, see H. Bauer, *Die Psychologie Alhazens* (Münster, 1911).

6. On this topic, see J. A. Mazzeo, "Light Metaphysics, Dante's 'Convivio' and the Letter to Can Grande della Scala," *Traditio*, 14 (1958), 191–229; and J. Ferrater Mora, "Luz," *Diccionario de Filosofía*, 5th ed. (Buenos Aires, 1965), *II*, 99ff.

7. Cf. *De Genesi ad Litteram, IV*, XXVIII, 45, and *XII*, IV, 15, 18; and *Soliloquiorum Libri Duo, I*, 3; also Mazzeo, *op. cit.*, p. 199.

8. *In Aristotelis Librum de Anima Comentarium*, ed. A. M. Pirotta (Turin, 1959), *II*, XIV, 420, p. 105.

9. Cf. F. Sardemann, *Ursprung und Entwicklung der Lehre von lumen rationis aeternae, lumen divinum, lumen naturale, rationes seminales, veritates aeternae bis Descartes* (Kassel, 1902), p. 20.

10. Mazzeo, *op. cit.*, p. 212.

11. Cf. Lorenzo de' Medici, *Opere*, ed. A. Simioni (Bari, 1939), pp. 45, 96–97, etc.

12. Cf. Descartes, *Principes Philosophiques, I*, 30; and Leibniz, *Die philosophischen Schriften* . . . , ed. Gerhardt (Berlin, 1960–1961), *VI*, 494, 496.

13. Cf. M. H. Nicolson, *Newton Demands the Muse* (Hamden, Conn., 1963), Ch. 2.

14. Cf. R. Longhi, "Giotto spazioso," *Paragone* (Arte), 3 (1952), 18–24.

15. Cf. E. Panofsky, *The Life and Art of Albrecht Dürer*, 4th ed. (Princeton, 1955), p. 247ff.; R. Krautheimer, *Lorenzo Ghiberti* (Princeton, 1956), Ch. 16; and Parronchi, *op. cit.*, p. 226ff.

16. L. B. Alberti, *Della Pittura*, in *Kleinere Kunsttheoretische Schriften*, ed. H. Janitschek (Vienna, 1877), pp. 69, 79.

17. *Ibid.*, p. 99.

18. *Ibid.*, p. 93.

19. Though with a particular degree of beauty and truth. The notion that reflected images—images in a mirror or in a fountain—are more truthful or "ideal" than the objects they represent is Neoplatonic.

20. Panofsky, *op. cit.*, p. 247.

21. Cf. E. Panofsky, "Die Perspektive als 'symbolische Form'," *Vorträge der Bibliothek Warburg* (1924–1925), pp. 258–330.

22. *The Diary of John Evelyn*, ed. W. Bray (Washington & London, 1901), *I*, 53.

23. Ruskin, in his Introduction to the *Elements of Perspective* (1859), *The Works of John Ruskin*, ed. E. T. Cook and A. Wedderburn (London, 1901), *XV*, 241, asks the student to sit near a window and consider every pane as a "glass picture," and he adds: "But, to do this, you must hold your head very still. You must not only not move it sideways, nor up and down, but it must not even move backwards or forwards; for if you move your head forwards, you will see more. . . ."

24. K. Müller-Vollmer, *Towards a Phenomenological Theory of Literature. A Study of Wilhelm Dilthey's Poetik* (The Hague, 1963), p. 60.

25. Cf. P. Francastel, *Peinture et société* (Lyon, 1951), p. 87.

26. Historians have drawn parallels between the rise of perspective, during the Renaissance and the 17th century, and certain cultural assumptions of the period, like the opening of empirical reality to the notion of infinity and the growing primacy of the theory of knowledge, from Nicholas of Cusa to Kant. Cf. Panofsky's suggestion in "Die Perspektive als 'symbolische Form'," p. 287: "man könnte die Funktion der Renaissanceperspektive geradezu mit der Kritizismus, die der hellenistisch-römischen Perspektive mit der des Skeptizismus vergleichen." In his later *Dürer* (4th ed., p. 261ff.) Panofsky mentions these parallels: the Renaissance inserted "historical distance" between itself and the past, as the picture does between the image and the point of vision (is this historical distance not a later idea, in our sense of the term?); the mind of man was placed in the center of the universe (i.e., the earlier reference to "Kritizismus"); and Renaissance aesthetic canons were based on correct mathematical relationships (a point mentioned in my fifth assumption). I shall discuss in a later section of this essay the problems raised by such comparisons.

27. Uccello, besides, stresses perspective only in certain portions of the *Battle of San Romano;* cf. J. Pope-Hennessy, *The Complete Work of Paolo Uccello* (London, 1950), p. 21: "The background has no spatial reference to the episode in front, and the compositions resemble scenes played before a drop curtain, in which we are perpetually aware of a disparity between the false space represented on the backcloth and the real space of the stage."

28. Mazzeo, *op. cit.*, pp. 205–206, 207.

29. On these and other facts concerning the history of perspective theory, see A. Flocon and R. Taton, *La Perspective* (Paris, 1963), p. 49ff.

30. *Comedias* (Madrid, 1762), *VIII*, 414.

31. Cf. Flocon and Taton, *op. cit.*, p. 61.

32. Cf. R. Alewyn, "Feste des Barock," *Aus der Welt des Barock*, ed. R. Alewyn, et al. (Stuttgart, 1957), pp. 101–111.

33. Burton speaks of "perspective pieces" or paintings and of "perspectives," meaning magnifying glasses, with the same sense of wonder; cf. *The Anatomy of Melancholy* (London, 1827), *I*, 420: ". . . to do strange miracles by glasses, of which Proclus and Bacon writ of old, burning glasses, multiplying glasses, perspectives, *ut unus homo appareat exercitus*, to see afar off, to represent bodies, by cylinders and concaves, to walk in the air. . . ."

34. Cf. Flocon and Taton, *op. cit.*, p. 59. There were also the simplifiers, of course; in 1661 P. Bourgoing published in Paris a *Perspective affranchie de l'embarras du point de vue.*

35. Cf. Il Donzello, I, in *Comedie di M. Gianmaria Cecchi Fiorentino* (Venice, 1585), p. 7: "Il caso loro è prospettiua vera."

36. *Nuovi canti carnacialeschi del Rinascimento*, ed. C. S. Singleton (Modena,

1940), p. 18. The poem is attributed to Guglielmo, "detto il Giuggiola." Cf. also *Tutti i trionfi, carri, mascherate, o canti carnacialeschi* (Lucca, 1750), *II*, 321.

37. "Inapprehensiveness," *The Complete Poetic and Dramatic Works of Robert Browning* (Boston & New York, 1895), p. 991. Cf. also G. Keller, "Der Schmied seines Glückes," *Die Leute von Seldwyla*, 4th ed. (Stuttgart, 1883), *II*, 64; and Letter of February 3, 1818, *Goethes Briefe* (Weimar, 1904), *XXIX*, 38. The German *Perspektive* appears to have been borrowed from the French *perspective;* cf. J. C. Adelung, *Grammatisch-Kritisches Wörterbuch der Hochdeutschen Mundart . . .* (Vienna, 1808), *III*, 694: "Gryphius suchte dieses Wort durch Schaukunst zu ersetzen, welches aber keinen Beifall erhalten hat."

38. *Gargantua, I*, Ch. 10: "Car, comme le blan exteriorement disgrege et espart la veue, dissolvent manifestement les esprits visifz, selon l'opinion d'Aristoteles en ses *Problemes* et des perspectifz (et le voyez par expérience, quand vous passez les monts couverts de neige, en sorte que vous plaignez de ne pouvoir bien regarder). . . ."

39. *The Text of the Canterbury Tales*, ed. J. M. Manly and E. Rickert (Chicago, 1940), p. 235. The *Roman de la Rose*, ed. Langlois (Paris, 1914–1924), lines 18234–18387, also refers to these writers on optics.

40. *The Poetical Works of William Drummond of Hawthornden* (Edinburgh, 1913), *II*, 80.

41. Particularly in certain poems by the English metaphysicals. Cf. "Obsequies to the Lord Harrington," *The Poems of John Donne*, ed. H. J. C. Grierson (Oxford, 1912), *I*, 272 (where "by perspective" is the equivalent of "diminished in proportion"—which could apply to either an optical instrument or a picture, probably the former); and "Sinne II," *The Complete Works of George Herbert*, ed. A. B. Grosart (London, 1874), p. 48: "so devils are our sinnes in perspective" (i.e., devils are our sins represented, symbolized—an earlier line is "as in sleep we see foul death"; this *could* allude to painting, as the second line of the poem refers to it: "We paint the devil foul," etc.).

42. *The Works of Ben Jonson*, ed. W. Gifford (New York, 1879), p. 359; cf. also *Every Man out of His Humour, ibid.*, p. 151.

43. "Of Seeming Wise," *The Complete Essays of Francis Bacon*, ed. H. L. Finch (New York, 1963), p. 68. The term "prospective" is probably an Italianism, as well as a plausible encounter of the forms deriving from *perspicere* (like "perspicacity," "perspicuous," and "perspective") with those deriving from the classical Latin *prospectus*, "a view," and *prospicere*, and the late Latin *prospectivus* (said of windows which permit a view, a prospect) (Italian *prospettiva*, English "prospect"). The English "prospect" was an old medieval word, and the cultured derivative from *perspectiva* could have been blocked in some cases by the living "prospect." Spanish *prospectiva* appears, as we shall see, in a 15th-century work by Alfonso de la Torre. John Ruskin (*op. cit., XXIV*, 478) thought it was a flaw of the English language that "prospect" and "prospection" should exist, but not "perspect" or "perspection."

44. Cf., for example, *Henry V*, V, ii; *Twelfth Night*, V, 1; *Sonnets*, 24, 4.

45. Cf. L. Spitzer, "Le vers 830 du Roland," *Romania*, 68 (1944–1945), 471–477.

46. Cf. L. J. Friedman, "Occulta cordis," *Romance Philology*, 2 (1957–1958), 103–119.

47. Cf. E. Engelberg, "Tragic Blindness in *The Changeling* and *Women Beware Women*," *Modern Language Quarterly*, 23 (1962), 23. The original meaning of "insight" seems to have been "internal sight," "with the eyes of the mind"; cf. *The Oxford English Dictionary* (Oxford, 1961), *V*, 337.

48. For example, cf. R. Burton, *The Anatomy of Melancholy, II*, 2, 4: "many pretty landskips and perspective pieces. . . ."

49. *The Poetical Works of John Dryden*, ed. R. Hooper (London, 1891), *II*, 279.

50. *The Poetical Works of Wordsworth*, ed. H. Reed (Philadelphia, 1851), p. 32; see also "The Excursion," *ibid.*, p. 629.

51. *Le Génie du Christianisme, II*, III, 1.

52. Before *perspectiva*, the word *prospectiva* appears—Prof. Stephen Gilman kindly tells me—in the *Visión delectable* (c. 1440) by Alfonso de la Torre. Cf. *Biblioteca de autores españoles* (Madrid, 1855), *XXXVI*, 348. It has there the medieval meaning of "optics."

53. Letter of August 26, 1676, to Madame de Grignan.

54. Letter of January 15, 1690, to Madame de Grignan. The term is often used optimistically; cf. *The Works of Oliver Goldsmith*, ed. P. Cunningham (New York, 1900), *III*, 197: "I saw a long perspective of felicity before me." The adverbial expression "to have in perspective," *avoir en perspective*, etc., has first a spatial application; cf. *Oeuvres de Voltaire*, ed. Beuchot (Paris, 1834), *LXX*, 168: "Je suis, comme j'ai toujours été, entre le lac de Genève et le mont Jura, ayant en perspective les neiges éternelles des grands Alpes. . . ." But it soon refers to the future—to having a plan, a prospect, etc. Cf. Mme. de Sévigné, Letter of November 1, 1688: "J'ai en perspective de vous allez voir, et cette pensée me fait subsister."

55. See Bertrand Russell's definition of "Perspective, historical" in the *Dictionary of Mind, Matter, and Morals* (New York, 1952), p. 178: "The military superiority of Europe to Asia is not an eternal law of nature, as we are tempted to think; and our own superiority in civilization is a mere delusion. Our histories, which treat the Mediterranean as the center of the universe, give quite a wrong perspective." Also in this historical sense "perspective," which often means "view of the future," as we saw in the last note, refers to the ability to have a vision of the future. The University of California, which prides itself in having one, in its Academic Plan for 1965–1975, *Unity and Diversity* (Office of the President, 1965), stresses five overriding imperatives: "Growth," "Diversity," "Balance," "Freedom," "Responsibility," plus—in this sense—"Perspective."

56. Cf. *Letters of Queen Elizabeth and King James VI of Scotland* (London, 1849), XCIII, 173: "for I have not so small a perspective in my neighbors' actions. . . ."

57. "Pensée 381," *Oeuvres de Blaise Pascal,* ed. L. Brunschvieg (Paris, 1921), *XIII,* 291. Cf. also "Pensée 383," *ibid.,* p. 292.

58. "Réflexions Morales," No. 104, *Oeuvres complètes,* ed. L. Martin-Chauffier (Paris, 1950), p. 258.

59. Cf. "Maximes Supprimées," No. 563, *ibid.,* p. 335.

60. "Réflexions Diverses," No. 2, *ibid.,* p. 361.

61. *Morales du grand siècle* (Paris, 1948), p. 98.

62. "Réflexions Morales," No. 97, *Oeuvres complètes,* p. 257.

63. "Réflexions Diverses," No. 19 ("De la retraite"), *ibid.,* p. 400.

64. "Réflexions Diverses," No. 16, *ibid.,* p. 384.

65. "Réflexions Morales," No. 26, *ibid.,* p. 247.

66. Littré's *Dictionnaire de la langue française* (Paris, 1962) gives examples from Mme. de Sévigné, Bourdaloue, Fontenelle, etc.; the *OED, VII,* 1051, quotes Coleridge and 19th-century writers; the *Diccionario de la lengua castellana . . . ,* called "de Autoridades" (Madrid, 1726–1739), *V,* 435, gives Tomas Vicente Tosca's *Compendio matemático* (1670). The term obviously was due to a growing familiarity with perspective theory. *Viewpoint* seems to be a later abbreviation (*OED, XII,* 196: first example from the year 1856). *Standpoint,* as I shall mention later, is a loan from the German *Standpunkt* (*OED, X,* 821: examples from the 19th century).

67. "Lettre 116," *Lettres Persanes.*

68. It also enters everyday speech. The individual may regard as indispensable *his* "point of view," which is alone capable of revealing his particular experience of a thing. But there are moments in the workings of social or political institutions when the individual is expected to represent a group. If a Prime Minister, for example, appoints a commission to investigate a certain issue, and assigns to it a banker, a general, and an ambassador, we may surmise that he does not wish them to submit merely their personal opinions, but the "points of view" of the economist, the military man, and the diplomat, respectively.

69. Cf. Y. Belaval, *Leibniz: Initiation à sa philosophie* (Paris, 1962), p. 60.

70. Cf. H. W. Carr, *Leibniz,* 2nd ed. (New York, 1960), p. 96.

71. *Ibid.,* pp. 81–82.

72. Cf. Belaval, *op. cit.,* pp. 60–61.

73. Carr, *op. cit.,* p. 69.

74. *Essais de Théodicée,* No. 357, *Die philosophischen Schriften . . . ,* ed. Gerhardt (Hildeshelm, 1960–1961), *VI,* 327.

75. *Monadologie,* No. 57, *Oeuvres philosophiques de Leibniz,* ed. P. Janet (Paris, 1900), *I,* 716. The comparison of the city appears already in the *Letter to Thomasius* of 20–30 April, 1669, ed. Gerhardt, *I,* 19.

76. *A Critical Exposition of the Philosophy of Leibniz* (Cambridge, 1900), p. 122.

77. Cf. Carr, *op. cit.,* p. 91.

78. *Ibid.*, p. 154.

79. The lines of the perspective figure, spreading from the apex outward, may also be regarded as forces, rays, tendencies, or efforts (*Letter to Sophia of Hanover*, ed. Gerhardt, VII, 566).

80. *Monadologie*, No. 58, *Oeuvres philosophiques, I*, 716.

81. *Essais de Théodicée*, No. 147, *Die philosophischen Schriften, VI*, 197.

82. "Perspectivismo," *Diccionario de Filosofía, II*, 405–408.

83. *Briefe antiquarischen Inhalts*, IX, *Gesammelte Werke* (Berlin, 1955),*V*, 411. A characteristic example of the neoclassical view may be found in Dryden, who thought perspective was a Greek discovery that the barbaric Middle Ages had forgotten and the time of Raphael had revived; cf. the Epistle "To Sir Godfrey Kneller," *The Poetical Works of John Dryden, II*, 274. On the other hand, Perrault, in order to praise the *Modernes*, had reproached the *Anciens* with not having had perspective. For a recent opinion on this—still today—unresolved issue, cf. J. White, *Perspective in Ancient Drawing and Painting* (London, 1956).

84. For example, he describes in this fashion a painting by Hallé; cf. "Salon de 1767," *Oeuvres Complètes de Denis Diderot* (Paris, 1821), *IX*, 42.

85. Cf. *Gedankenausgabe . . . ,* ed. E. Beutler (Zürich, 1949), *XIII*, 130. See also the conversations with Eckermann for December 13, 1826, and December 21, 1831, *ibid., XXIV*, 186, 506.

86. Cf. Ruskin, *op. cit., XV*, 17: "Turner, though he was a professor of perspective at the Royal Academy, did not know what he professed, and never, as far as I remember, drew a single building in true perspective in his life."

87. Cf. *Peinture et société*, p. 153.

88. Cf. *ibid.*, pp. 166, 193, etc.

89. Cf. C. Greenberg, *Art and Culture* (Boston, 1961), pp. 52–54.

90. *Modern French Painting, 1855–1956* (New York, 1956), p. 118.

91. F. Nietzsche, *Werke*, ed. K. Schlechta (München, 1955), *II*, 56.

92. I have not been able to see Teichmüller's book, but it appears from the text that Nietzsche had it in mind on more than one occasion: cf. *Werke, II*, 221, 599.

93. *Ibid.*, p. 177.

94. *Ibid.*, p. 177.

95. *Ibid.*, p. 599.

96. *Ibid.*, p. 598; cf. also *ibid.*, p. 860.

97. *Ibid.*, pp. 249–250.

98. *Ibid.*, pp. 860–861.

99. On this point, cf. K. Löwith, *Nietzsches Philosophie der ewigen Wiederkehr des Gleichen* (Stuttgart, 1956), Ch. 6.

100. I have discussed only one direction of Nietzsche's perspectivism. In another direction it tends toward pragmatism, the idea that intelligence is an instrument that life creates toward action, and life an interplay of

forces constantly striving to surpass one another and themselves. Perspectives are vehicles of *Triebe*, biological and vital impulses: cf. *Werke, III*, 903. These forces work within the limits, and according to the needs, of each being; they act on others through limited channels: "Der Perspektivismus ist nur eine Komplexe Form der Spezifität. Meine Vorstellung ist, dass, jeder specifische Körper danach strebt, über den ganzen Raum Herr zu werden und seine Kraft auszudehnen (sein Wille zur Macht)" (*Ibid., III*, 705). On this level perspectives are not necessarily personal or conscious, but rejoin collective needs (and what I call elsewhere the ultra-personal point of view). On this aspect of Nietzsche's perspectivism, cf. R. Berthelot, *Un Romantisme utilitaire. Etude sur le mouvement pragmatiste* (Paris, 1911–1913), *I*, Ch. 1.

101. Cf. the article "Prospettivismo," *Enciclopedia filosofica* (Venice, Rome, 1957), *III*, 1671.

102. Cf. Müller-Vollmer, *op. cit.*, p. 40 and elsewhere.

103. Cf. "Adán en el paraíso," *Obras completas* (Madrid, 1946), *I*, 495.

104. Cf. *Perspectiva y verdad* (Madrid, 1966), p. 51.

105. To a certain degree, and with important qualifications, this is the view of J. Ferrater Mora's brief but excellent *Ortega y Gasset: etapas de una filosofía* (Barcelona, 1958).

106. Cf. "Verdad y perspectiva," *Obras completas, II*, 18, n. 1. After quoting the *Monadologie*, Ortega affirms that he follows neither Nietzsche nor Vaihinger. The latter had adapted the former's perspectivism to his own "fictionalism": cf. H. Vaihinger, *Die Philosophie des Als Ob* (Berlin, 1911), p. 780ff. On Ortega's originality with respect to these philosophers, cf. J. Marías, *Ortega* (Madrid, 1960), *I*, 392ff.

107. Cf. *Meditaciones del Quijote, Obras completas, I*, 321–322.

108. Cf. Rodríguez Huéscar, *op. cit.*, pp. 74–85.

109. *El tema de nuestro tiempo, Obras completas, III*, 201.

110. Cf. *ibid.*, p. 202.

111. Especially in "Musicalia" (1921), *La deshumanización del arte* ("Una gota de fenomenología") (1925), "Don Juan y el resentimiento" (1921), "Sobre el punto de vista en las artes" (1924). For other texts, cf. Rodríguez Huéscar, *op. cit.*, pp. 262–408.

112. *Obras completas, III*, 199.

113. *Ibid.*, p. 236.

114. "Nadie ha visto jamás una naranja" (*Meditaciones del Quijote*), quoted by Rodríguez Huéscar, *op. cit.*, p. 76.

115. *El hombre y la gente*, quoted by Rodríguez Huéscar, *op. cit.*, p. 389.

116. (London, 1952), p. 95. (A revised edition had been published in 1926.)

117. Certain sense data are primitive—Russell had begun—because they are not inferred from anything else, and others are derivative. The question is: Can the existence of anything other than our own hard or primitive data be inferred from them alone? As I walk around an object—

say, a table—I find that my sensations are changing in a continuous way, not by sudden replacement but by the experience of a progressive correlation of muscular and other sensations with changes in visual data. After proposing the hypothesis that each mind thus sees a private world which is a perspective, Russell goes on to state that these private worlds do exist. By relating them, moreover, one *infers* a space that is not *in* any perspective, but is a system of relations between perspectives. The aspects of a thing seen from various perspectives are real, but the "thing itself" is a logical construction—which does not contradict our experience. My comments are: 1. The metaphor of perspective is not mobile or three-dimensional enough to deal with the progressive correlation of tactile or auditory data; 2. the notion of the single angle of vision is not a hard datum of experience: I may have to walk around a table to know that *it* exists, but I perceive immediately that the moving forms of a dancer correlate; the metaphor "freezes" both the subject and the object; 3. from a particular position what I see coincides with what another can see from the same place; in this sense the perspective is not "private"; 4. and 5.: the two questions asked in my text above.

118. *The Basic Writings of Bertrand Russell*, ed. R. E. Egner and L. E. Denonn (New York, 1961), p. 64.

119. "Russell's Neutral Monism," *The Philosophy of Bertrand Russell*, ed. P. A. Schilpp, 3rd ed. (New York, 1951), p. 370.

120. Cf. V. Lowe, *Understanding Whitehead* (Baltimore, 1966), pp. 54, 259, 279.

121. P. L. DeLargy, "Perspectivity and Objectivity," *The Journal of Philosophy*, 31 (1934), 29–38.

122. "McGilvary's Perspective Realism," *ibid.*, 56 (1959), 148–165.

123. Lovejoy associates the "perspective realists" and "objective relativists" with the scientific positivism of Mach and Petzoldt. Cf. *The Revolt Against Dualism* (Boston, 1930), p. 81.

124. These writers often use "standpoint"—probably a German influence. Cf. J. Petzoldt, *Das Weltproblem von positivischem Standpunkte aus*, 2nd ed. (Leipzig, 1912), p. 142: "Wir können die Welt immer nur von dem Standpunkt aus denken, auf dem wir wirklich stehen, nicht von einem Standpunkt aus, auf dem wir überhaupt uns gar nicht stehend denken können, oder von gar keinem Standpunkt aus. Es gibt keinen absoluten Standpunkt und es gibt keine Standpunktlosigkeit, es gibt allein relative Standpunkte, diese aber auch stets. . . ."

125. Cf. B. D. Brettschneider, *The Philosophy of Samuel Alexander* (New York, 1964), pp. 82–83.

126. Lovejoy, *op. cit.*, p. 120.

127. *Ibid.*, p. 123.

128. Cf. DeLargy, *op. cit.*, p. 32.

129. Cf. Rodríguez Huéscar, *op. cit.*, p. 101: "Dos individuos situados sucesivamente . . . en el mismo lugar y mirando en la misma dirección . . . representan, sin embargo, *dos puntos de vista diferentes* y, por consiguiente, *no ven lo mismo*."

130. G. H. Mead, *The Philosophy of the Act* (Chicago, 1938), p. 115.

131. Cf. *ibid.*, p. 64.

132. *Ibid.*, p. 157. Cf. also E. B. McGilvary, *Toward a Perspective Realism*, ed. A. G. Ramsperger (La Salle, Ill., 1956). On other uses by philosophers of the metaphor of perspective (Merleau-Ponty, Sartre, A. P. Ushenko, C. F. Graumann, R. A. Tsanoff, etc.), cf. Ferrater Mora, "Perspectivismo."

133. Cf. Mead, *op. cit.*, pp. 118–119.

134. Cf. I. Berlin, *The Hedgehog and the Fox* (London, 1954).

135. Cf. G. Zibondi, *Divulgazioni manzoniane*, 2nd ed. (Milan, 1934), p. 274.

136. *La Struttura dei Promessi Sposi* (Zürich, 1948), p. 19.

137. *El pensamiento de Cervantes* (Madrid, 1925), p. 88.

138. Cf. M. Durán, *La ambigüedad del Quijote* (Xalapa, 1960), p. 184ff.

139. The interpretation of visual enigmas in *Don Quixote* is not unrelated to those modern novels where a quest for truth culminates in vision: from Stendhal and Flaubert to, in the 20th century, Kafka and Malraux; Proust's scrutiny of the hawthorne bush near Combray; Dos Passos' camera eye; the perspectives of Robbe-Grillet's heroes failing to penetrate opaque surfaces, to find knowledge in what is seen, etc.

140. Cf. "Perspectivismo lingüístico en el Quijote," *Lingüística e historia literaria* (Madrid, 1955), p. 161ff.; or (in English), *Linguistics and Literary History* (Princeton, 1948).

141. Cf. *Linguistics and Literary History*, pp. 61, 73, 85 (n. 37).

142. Cf. *La región más transparente* (Mexico, 1958), p. 226: "porque las verdades están metidas en nuestros días y se quiebran en mil aristas a la luz de cada mirada, de cada golpe de corazón, de cada línea del azar. . . ."

143. Cf. *The Craft of Fiction* (New York, 1947).

144. "The Parallelism between Literature and the Arts," *English Institute Annual 1941* (New York, 1942), p. 54. The substance of this essay was incorporated into the *Theory of Literature*, III, Ch. 11.

145. Cf. *Zarte Empire* (Stuttgart, 1963), pp. 244–336.

146. A. Neumeyer in *The Search for Meaning in Modern Art* (Englewood Cliffs, N.J., 1964), p. 121, indicates that Kandinsky's first nonrepresentational pictures were created at the same time (1911–1912) that Schönberg was writing his first atonal compositions. But C. Greenberg, *op. cit.*, p. 156, finds a correlation between Schönberg and the "all-over" picture (Pollock).

147. Wellek, "The Parallelism between Literature and the Arts," p. 62.

148. *Ibid.*, p. 61.

149. "Salon de 1767," *Oeuvres choisies de Diderot*, ed. F. Génin (Paris, 1886), p. 168.

150. Cf. Francastel, *op. cit.*, p. 173ff.

151. Reproduced in A. Neumeyer, *op. cit.*, Plate XXVI.

152. *Art and Culture*, p. 112.

153. *Ibid.*, p. 72.

154. Cf. *ibid.*, p. 125.

155. As quoted by Greenberg, *op. cit.*, p. 68.

156. Like the huge, open figure of a lying woman built recently in the Stockholm Museum by Jean Tinguely, Niki de Saint-Phalle, and Per Olof Ultvedt.

157. O. Hahn in *L'Express*, Paris, June 13–19, 1966, p. 90. What, and how many, spectators? I can only mention here the evident but complex tensions between this search for existential three-dimensionality and the popular forms of our "image culture." The contradictions between the tradition of perspective and its modern replacements reflect only partially the relations in our time between mass-art and the *avant-garde*. The most sophisticated spectator is himself submitted to these tensions. His visual habits are also conditioned, not only by a film like Resnais's *L'année dernière à Marienbad* (its search for alternate solutions to the limits of cinematic montage, which can offer no more than one perspective at a time, as panoramic shots cannot be abused), but by photography, advertising, that largest of *finestre aperte*, the cinemascope screen, and even that most faithful replica of Alberti's glass-pane, the television set.

158. N. Frye, *Anatomy of Criticism* (Princeton, 1957), p. 335.

159. Cf. *ibid.*, p. 123.

160. McGilvary, *op. cit.*, p. 1.

161. As quoted by H. Meyerhoff, *The Philosophy of History in Our Time* (Garden City, N.Y., 1959), p. 24.

162. *De Visione Dei*, 6. Cf. E. Zellinger, *Cusanus-Konkordanz* (Munich, 1960), p. 57.

163. Cf. *Philosophical Investigations* (Oxford, 1953), pp. 202, 213.

164. Cf. J. White, *op. cit.*, p. 86.

165. As quoted by P. J. Doty, "Complementarity and Its Analogies," *The Journal of Philosophy*, 55 (1958), 1100.

166. *Physics and Philosophy* (New York, 1962), p. 81.

Joseph Szili

Recent Trends of Marxist Criticism
in the Countries of Eastern Europe

The appreciation of Marxist criticism by non-Marxist authors is often based on the assumption that it is a closely limited sociological approach to literature. Although far from being a branch of sociology, Marxist criticism is, by definition, "sociological." It is deeply conscious of the fact that literature is a social phenomenon and has to be dealt with as such. Marxism is "sociology" in the sense that it aspires to present knowledge about the basic laws of society and social development. It also implies profound awareness both of the great possibilities and of the practical and historical limitations of the scientific approach.

The scope of Marxist criticism is not confined to the task of detecting the socio-economic determinants of literary development, or the ideological and social implications of literature. Formal analysis of individual works and of various literary kinds, exploration of relevant symbolic reference, psychological study and speculative examination of the sources of the aesthetic effect are as important components of Marxist criticism as direct socio-historical studies. In the course of its development Marxist criticism emphasized many aspects of literary analysis. Like most kinds of criticism, it frequently yielded to the demands of social and literary evolution, and from time to time it suffered from the vice (or virtue) of having overstated a good case.

Owing to the common grounds they have in social and literary history, and to the fact that they have common objects of interest, there are obvious parallels between Marxist and non-Marxist criticism. The various trends of positivism and of the *Geistesgeschichte* school of criticism exerted notable influence on some Marxist critics. There were attempts to apply the findings of anthropology and Freudianism to literary criticism within the framework of Marxism. Persuasive aesthetic systems have been drawn up as a result of the determination of Marxist critics to offer an alternative to the teachings of Benedetto

Croce and other representatives of idealistic aesthetics in the 20th century. Sometimes their preoccupation with the establishment of universal aesthetic standards based on a single aspect (style or species) of literature created an artificial distance between life and literature, while a failure to see the difference between them culminated in efforts to base criticism solely on the immediate didactic and political impact of literary works, the direct appeal of artistic representation, or the close resemblance of the literary creation to its model. The intellectual claims of the ever-growing reading public also influenced the development of Marxist criticism in the Socialist countries, where it had to initiate millions of working people in the enjoyment of literature.

At the present time, the "new" trends of Marxist criticism turn with great love and interest toward Socialist literature. These trends indicate dissatisfaction with standards that impede its development and impatience with aesthetic systems which fail to meet their demand for a thoroughly Marxist system and methodology of aesthetics.

The Socialist countries are often referred to as the countries of Eastern Europe. The terms "East" and "West" and the phrase "Eastern Europe" have no exact geographical meaning in this context. After all, as Professor Eugen Kogon, editor of *Frankfurter Hefte*, told the *Europa-Gespräch* conference in Vienna in June, 1965, where the theme "Bridges between the East and the West" was discussed, "Every schoolboy is supposed to know that Prague is 140 kilometers *west* of Vienna." Nevertheless, the Socialist countries of Eastern and Central Europe do form a kind of regional unity not only geographically but also socially and economically, in terms of their cultural structure and their historical development.

The Eastern European countries, or more precisely the peoples that formed them, belonged for centuries to an "underdeveloped" area of Europe. Czarist Russia was no exception. The Eastern European peoples were involved in long, dramatic struggles for national independence and social progress. They had to defend themselves against the Ottoman Empire, or Czarist Russia, or the Austro–Hungarian Monarchy. The Hungarians fought back the Turkish invasion, and then their Austrian rulers. The Slovaks, the Rumanians, and the Serbians fought for independence from their Hungarian rulers. The age-old principle of empire-building, *divide et impera* was fruitfully applied by the rulers of the Monarchy; it yielded the bitter fruits of national hatred and extreme chauvinism. Progressive political and intellectual leaders, among them the Hungarian poets Endre Ady and Attila József, spoke out against the blind chauvinism of the ruling classes in prose and poetry, and called for the fraternity of Hungarians, Rumanians, Slovaks, Czechs, Serbians, and Croatians. National and social oppression, technical and cultural backwardness characterized the situation in this area. In Hungary serfdom was abolished as late as the middle of the 19th century. The law was passed under the government of Lajos Kossuth, who led Hungary's war of national liberation against Austria in 1848 and 1849. Social progress was impeded by the vested interests of the ruling classes. In 1919 the struggle of the oppressed culminated in the establishment of the first Socialist state in Hungary. In less than a year the Hungarian Republic of Councils was overcome by foreign anticommunist intervention, and the fruits of that victory were handed to Nicolaus Horthy, under whose reign the rule of the landowning classes and of the aristocracy of wealth was restored. White terror, the massacre of progressive people, and extreme chauvinism paved the way to Fascism.

Though in different forms, their age-old desperate struggle against social and national oppression is a common feature of the histories of the peoples of Eastern Europe. Writers, poets, artists, and critics were involved in that struggle not only as individuals but also as writers, poets, artists, and critics. Literature as such was also involved in it. National consciousness began with the cultivation of national languages and with the rise of national literatures. Social and national aspirations inspired the main trends of Hungarian literature in the 19th century. The realistic and messianistic tendencies of 19th century Russian literature arose from the writers' preoccupation with the social conditions of Czarist Russia.

Western stylistic trends also influenced the literatures of these nations. Romanticism and realism underwent a "sea change" entering the climate of thought and feeling that characterized the cultural life of these areas. Conditioned by the writers' national and social consciousness, the artistic tenor of these trends was restrained in some aspects and amplified in some others. In his book *Romantika és realizmus* (*Romanticism and Realism*, 1955) István Sötér analyzes this type of evolution in the Hungarian literature of the 19th century and refers to parallel developments in some of the neighboring countries.

In this part of Europe the social and political engagement of literature arose as a result of hard necessity. Social and national strivings could hardly find more effective means of expression than what was offered by literature. Did "commitment" reduce the chances of genuine literary achievement? Hardly so. Pushkin and Petöfi, Mayakovsky and Attila József are key figures in a poetic tradition which is entirely alien from *l'art pour l'art* poetics.

The "sea change" that characterized the reception of Western stylistic influence in the 19th century can also be observed in the 20th century. Endre Ady, a Hungarian follower of the French symbolists, created a language of symbols revealing the profound contradictions of Hungarian society before and during the First World War. His deeply moving poems have also expressed the human crisis of standing helpless against the powers of destruction. He is a symbolist, but his poetic practice modified the meaning of the term considerably. In his symbolism, the expression of social consciousness plays a far more integral part than in the poetry of the French symbolists or their followers in the West. The "symbolism" of Bulgarian symbolists (Botev, Milev, Smirnensky) presents similar problems. According to István Sipos and Péter Juhász, authors of a new history of Bulgarian literature (Budapest, 1965), a new term should be invented to indicate the difference between symbolism as it appears in Western poetry and its counterpart in Eastern Europe.

Despite its generally negative role the Austro–Hungarian Monarchy did serve to create a common basis of reference for the literature of this region. Discussions on the interpretation of the works of Franz Kafka have raised this problem repeatedly. Lecturers at the *Liblice Kafka* conference in 1963 referred to it, and in 1965 a Hungarian historian, Ervin Pamlényi, argued that Kafka's dream-world, nightmarish as it is, is an accurate artistic reflection of the absurd world of the Monarchy. György Szabó, an editor of *Uj Irás*, a Hungarian literary magazine, thinks that the existence of the Monarchy had an all-embracing influence on creative writing in the early part of the 20th century. The omnipresent state bureaucracy and the way of life it promoted finally succeeded in creating its own "anti-matter" in the realm of the arts.

New trends emerged which bore on them the image and likeness of their originator, the Monarchy. Writers, poets, artists, and musicians felt to the bone the impact of that strange, fiendish, overwhelming, though somewhat clumsy, power. Negating the innermost essence of all that the Monarchy stood for and rejecting it in a more or less abstract and irrationalistic way, these artistic trends got rid of the provincialism and selfish nationalism of the ordinary loyal citizen of the Monarchy and reflected the revolutionary situation in its true light. What was absurd had to be shown as absurd, and social contradictions had reached an absurd and incomprehensible stage in that society, even though the surface appeared to be calm and normal. The exuberance of grotesque and abstract elements, the atmosphere of nightmare, the vision of absurdity, and the logic of madness prevail in the *art nouveau* as it appeared in Eastern Europe. Such features are detectable in the works of the Hungarian novelist Gyula Krudy, the poet Endre Ady, the Trieste writer Italo Svevo, the Czech Miroslav Krleza, or in the writings of Franz Kafka and Robert Musil, or in the early compositions of Béla Bartók and the messianistic paintings of Tivadar Csontváry. Most of these common elements may be termed "grotesque." Among the Eastern European critics there has been increasing interest in this mood or form of literature in recent years. Professor Oleg Sus, of Brno, and György Szabó have proved to be competent exponents of the issue.

In Eastern Europe most of the modernist trends which arose in the 1920's and the 1930's were inspired by profound social responsibility. Humanistic and socialist attitudes characterized the aspirations of the German Activists (the left wing of German expressionism), the movement of Czech poetists, and the poetry of Blok and Mayakovsky. In Hungary Lajos Kassák, a pacifist, a communist, and an anarchist in succession, followed closely the new experiments and introduced the tones of futurism, expressionism, constructivism, and Dadaism in Hungarian poetry. Attila József is a classic of modernism as well as a classic of Socialist realism. The poetry of Aladár Kómjat, another important modernist representative of Socialist poetry, exemplifies the affinity between the aspirations of revolutionary humanism and the attempts to revolutionize the language of poetry. Such facts provide sufficient evidence against the view of Stephen Spender, who in *The Struggle of the Modern* (London, 1963) says something to the effect that the truly modern idiom is necessarily combined with the rejection of social progress. His view is based on the achievement of Yeats, Eliot, Wyndham Lewis, and Ezra Pound, and it is a reaffirmation of the views presented by T. E. Hulme and the militant conservative exponents of the "new criticism." In deprecating the modernity of Picasso's art, Mr. Spender takes sides with Wyndham Lewis, in whose opinion Picasso indulged in "sentimental humanism." (Can humanism be anything but sentimental from the viewpoint of antihumanism?) In a review in *Kritika*, I took the liberty of quoting Mr. Spender's own words against his poetics.[1] In *World Within World* (London, 1951), a book written long after his renunciation of what he thought to be Communism, he recalls how deeply he was moved and inspired by some early Soviet films he had seen in the Weimar Republic. He praises their modernism, poetic sensibility, satire, and visual beauty, i.e., all the qualities he found exciting in other forms of modern art, and adds that all this conveyed a message of hope, as if an answer to *The Waste Land.*

There is an answer to *The Waste Land,* and there is no reason to believe that it cannot be given in the same grand manner as used by its great poet. On the other hand, while the "objective," stationary, and pseudo-rationalistic trends in art were irrationalistic to the core, the modernism of left wing poets was inspired by a new type of rationalism: not the soulless, restricted, mechanical rationalism whose main value is a negative trait—lack of sentimentalism—but the rational humanism of Socialist action.

This fresh development of progressive literary achievement demanded fresh insight from the critics. Not all of them had this insight. It was easy to label the new formal achievements as formalism and to stand aside at a time when conservative and reactionary critics did their best to expropriate theoretically the qualities of the new stylistic trends. The fact that the idiom of 19th-century realism could be applied to themes and forms arising from the new socio-historical and psychical conditions of the 20th century and had the advantage of immediate appeal to large sections of readers also influenced progressive criticism. The fruitful revival of the realistic tradition in the works of Gorky, Sholokhov, and numerous other Socialist writers underlined the claim that this was the only usable tradition of Socialist literature. Even some very erudite Marxist critics could not rid themselves of the influence of the typological approach to the problems of stylistic and aesthetic qualities. They conceived the confrontation of literary styles in the literary process as a form of the struggle between conflicting social ideas. All-embracing aesthetic systems were based on a selective approach to literary values and on oversimplified notions concerning the interdependence of artistic and political attitudes. The fact that all great art functions as a specific case of epistemological "realism" was presented as a proof that one specific case, the realistic idiom of literary portrayal of events, scenes, and characters, was the only possible form of great art, or of "realism" in the epistemological sense. Much had been done to throw light on the socio-economic determinants of the development of literary genres and styles, but some of this work was seriously hampered by the weaknesses of the aesthetic theory. In the hands of epigoni and academic critics the ideas borrowed from the more sophisticated aesthetic structures underwent further distortion and became ready-made clichés of superficial and naive views on literature.

Still Marxist criticism has made great progress in establishing a systematic approach to aesthetic phenomena and the problems of criticism. Its emphasis on the basic aesthetic fact that art is a reflection of reality has helped us to get closer to the understanding of the true nature of the relationship between art and reality and has provided practical criticism with a set of critical concepts which, with minor modifications, are valid and applicable to new literary phenomena.

Socialist realism, a new phase or trend in the development of Socialist literature, found its appreciation in the works of Marxist critics and aestheticians who could detect some of its essential features and estimate, sometimes in an abstract way only, its great possibilities. Mikhail Lifshitz, Georg Lukács, Alfred Kurella, or the Bulgarian aesthetician Todor Pavlov accomplished pioneer work and created a climate of Marxist opinion in the field of literary criticism. Their accomplishment serves as a point of departure for any further research. Critics who, unlike these pioneers of systematic Marxist aesthetics, did not put the blame on the *avant-garde* (Anatoli Lunacharsky, Attila József, Bertolt Brecht, or Béla Balázs, an early theoretician of the film art) have greater influence among the young critics today. What appear to be the deficiencies of Lukács's theory are refuted by Hungarian critics in terms of József's position. József emphasizes the active character of the artistic reflection of reality and gives prominent place in it to the artist's subjective consciousness. Lukács, although he admits that artistic reflection may not be conceived as passive representation of external reality, wraps in mystery those ingredients of artistic creation which would make artistic reflection psychically and intellectually wholesome and effective.

There is a characteristic difference in the way Lukács and József criticize the subjectivist aesthetics of Croce. Lukács creates an almost symmetrical counterpole of the Crocean system, laying emphasis on the socio-economic determinants of literary development, on objective imitation rather than subjective expression, explaining artistic value as a result of the inherent laws of literary species, and basing his norms on the virtues of the novel. József appears to have raised himself above the somewhat overdone objectivism of Lukács and the downright subjectivism of the Crocean theory, and outlines, roughly, an open system of Marxist aesthetics. The issue has been taken up by young Hungarian critics. Attila Tamás and Ervin Gyertyán have devoted studies to the problem, and László Forgách wrote a book entitled *József Attila esztétikája* (*The Aesthetics of Attila József*, Budapest, 1965).

There is great interest in the critical views of Bertolt Brecht too. In a study in *Kritika*, László Illés drew attention to the 1938 controversy between Lukács and Brecht and expressed the view that

Lukács's conservative theoretical position set him in contrast with an important trend of Socialist literature.[2]   The issue has also been dealt with by Paolo Chiarini in *L'Europa letteraria* [3] and in his book *L'avanguardia e la poetica del realismo* (1961), and by Viktor Žmegag in "Brecht o realizmu" ("Brecht on Realism").[4]   Brecht's apology of experimental writing was called forth by an attack Lukács launched on German expressionism and on Brecht's artistic innovations.   In Lukács's opinion any type of "modernism" or of *avant-garde* literature represents bourgeois decadence and paves the way to Fascism.   Based on his theory of the "objective form" (implying that artistic forms express social tendencies and ideological positions independently from the intentions of the artist), he declared that the forms of expressionism and the montage technique were "antirealistic."   Brecht, in return, defined realism as the attitude of the artist who does not necessarily depict reality in conventional terms when he attempts to draw attention to or increase awareness of so-far unexplored tendencies of reality.   Like József, Brecht stood for an active, creative attitude to reality, for a nonconformist art that urges its recipients to reestimate and reformulate their attitudes.   Through Illés's well-documented study and the debates which followed its publication, the Lukács-Brecht controversy has become an asset of the current literary and aesthetic polemics in Hungary.

Dealing with these polemics in "The Hungarian Shores of Realism," Mrs. Ann Demaitre quotes the present writer and his colleagues, only to draw the conclusion that Hungarian criticism is drifting away from the shores of Socialist realism.[5]   Mrs. Demaitre appears to have lost her way among the questions of terminology that accompany the polemics and overlooks the fact that none of us, not even those who propose that the term "Socialist realism" should be replaced by the term "Socialist literature," ignore the existence of the literary facts which are commonly referred to by means of the term "Socialist realism."   All the facts point to the emergence in the 20th century of a new and broad literary trend in the Socialist movement, which has weathered long spells of hardship and continues to grow, whether I and my colleagues choose to drift toward, or to drift away from, its shores.

The classical stature of Lukác's *œuvre* explains why polemics in Hungary are centered around his views on aesthetics.   Criticism of his standards of value arose in 1955 when a congress of Hungarian literary historians was called to discuss a consistent way of applying his concept of realism to the history of Hungarian literature.   Instead, the congress "threw light on the contradictions of Lukác's *œuvre* and brought discredit on it, due to fruitful inspiration from the contributions of foreign guests, primarily those of the Soviet guests, which reflected a new attitude." [6]   Lukács has never made a clear distinction between *realism* as a general principle of artistic value and *realism* as a historical or typological term of style.   In his usage the terms "realist" and "classic" appear to be interchangeable.   His term "great realism" would comprise all great classics of world literature, giving prominence to Homer, Sophocles, Shakespeare, Cervantes, Goethe, Balzac, and Thomas Mann.   According to this theory, the historical trend of realism was constantly exposed to attacks by antirealistic tendencies exemplified by romanticism, symbolism, naturalism, and the trends of the *avant-garde*.   Lukács declared that the true method of Socialist realism was the method used by Balzac to portray his age.

Theories of "realism versus antirealism" were in vogue in the years of the "personal cult."   They represented an Arian conception of literary development with less erudition and refinement than Lukács's theory.   This type of theorizing suffered a serious blow in 1957 when a conference of the Institute of World Literature of the Soviet Academy of Science saw the failure of Professor Nedoshivin's theory to withstand the pressures of rational argument.   His conception of artistic development was based on the idea of constant struggle between realistic and antirealistic tendencies.   In his ОСНОВЫ ТЕОРИИ ЛИТЕРАТУРЫ (*The Bases of Literary Theory*, Moscow, 1963), L. I. Timofeev explains that realism and nonrealism (e.g., romanticism) express correlative artistic dispositions based on correlative aspects of human activity, on experience and creation, or on reproductive and productive attitudes to reality.   Consequently, typological classifications are only of limited value, and critical theories which give prominence to one of the two components of artistic creation have no universal validity.   In "The Specific Object of the Artistic Reflection of Reality," Jaroslav Volek, a Czechoslovak aesthetician, points out that the dual character of art is rooted in the fact that art differs from science not only in the way it reflects its object but also in the fact that its object is different from that of the scientific reflection of reality. [7]   As Péter Rákos comments in "The Questions of Realism in Czechoslovak Literary Criticism," Volek's view represents an "explicit break with the prevailing opinions of some exponents of Marxist literary criticism." [8]   The "prevailing opinion" is that of Lukács, i.e., that the arts and the sciences reflect the same object.   But even theoreticians who agree with Lukács on this point do not follow the course he takes when he charges the *avant-garde* with the distortion of the picture of objective reality. Květoslav Chvatík is one of these theoreticians. In *Bedřich Václavek a vývoj marxistické estetiky* (*Bedřich Václavek and the Development of Marxist Aesthetics*), he points out that Václavek (the greatest pioneer of Marxist theory in Czechoslovakia) did not accept Lukács's views on the *avant-garde:*

> Václavek's views on the fundamental issues of Socialist art and aesthetics were diametrically opposed to the position taken by Lukács. The sign of equation Lukács placed between the problem of the *avant-garde* and that of decadent bourgeois literature was always alien to the thinking of Václavek and the other Czech theoreticians and is attributable to Lukács's one-sided interest in reactionary German romanticism and the pre-Hitlerite and Hitlerite irrationalistic and mythological trends which followed in its wake. Václavek and the other Czech theoreticians were well aware of the significance of the left wing of the artistic *avant-garde* in the 1920's, which, especially in the advanced capitalist countries, was an important landmark of the artists' break with bourgeois society on their way to a new system of values undistorted by capitalism. In Czechoslovakia the ties between the artistic and the political *avant-garde* were particularly close and durable due to the powerful democratic traditions of Czech culture and the maturity of the revolutionary movement. Artistically this circumstance was revealed in the pronounced anti-decadent and to some extent antiromanticist attitude of the Czech *avant-garde;* in its optimism this trend clearly mirrored some traits of the life-style of the new class.[9]

Volek's view on the object of artistic reflection comes very close to the propositions of A. I. Burov, a Soviet aesthetician whose book, entitled ЭСТЕТИЧЕСКАЯ СУЩНОСТЬ ИСКУССТВА (*The Aesthetic Substance of Art,* Moscow, 1956), is based on the idea that art has its specific object, viz., the aesthetic qualities of objective reality. This line of thought is carried to its logical conclusions by V. V. Vanslov and V. I. Stolovich, who claim that art cannot be sufficiently well defined in terms of epistemology. Based on the Marxist concept of "the socio-historical practice (activity) of humanity," their definition states that art, in the ontological terms of a philosophy of history, is a special type and medium of social act which has basic functions in the development of human sensibility and man's capacity to *humanize* those strata of man's nature which evade direct rational control. They turn with special interest toward the problem of the work of art as a relatively autonomous artifact and provide a philosophical clue to the understanding of the social nature of artistic creation. They emphasize the active character of the work of art, which is being realized through the fact that its mode of existence is a type of social existence. A work of art is, under proper conditions, able to create an audience for itself. Such and similar views, including the views of Roger Garaudy, a French Marxist, and Ernst Fischer, an Austrian Marxist critic, have exerted considerable influence on the recent development of literary criticism in Eastern Europe.

The polemics around the question of "realism" also draw attention to problems of terminology. Statements to the effect that "realism" denotes all great art are in direct conflict with the view that it should be used only for "that stylistic period of European literature which comprises roughly the period between 1830 and 1870." [10]   There is, however, a school of critics, especially those who follow Lukács's teachings or the concept of "realism versus antirealism," which strives to ignore the difference between the various meanings of the term "realism." Another school of critics, associated with the Budapest Institute of Literary History, is striving to discipline the language of criticism. These critics propose that the term "realism" should be used in one sense only, preferably in the sense denoting the 19th-century movement of realism and its stylistic characteristics. Such and similar proposals to clear up terminological and theoretical issues, especially those pertinent to the issue of Socialist realism, were raised by Lajos Nyirö in a study in *Kortárs*.[11]   Mr. Nyirö is head of the Department of Literary Theory at the Institute of Literary History.

The main organ of this new school of criticism is *Kritika*, a critical and theoretical monthly. Studies and articles by its principal contributors (András Diószegi, Miklós Béládi, László Illés, Tibor Klaniczay, Lajos Nyirö, Pál Miklós, the late Béla Osváth, István Sötér, György Szabó, Miklós Szabolcsi, and György Mihály Vajda) are focused on the facts, conditions, and prospects of the development of Socialist art and literature. These writers base their opinion on the conviction that Socialist realism is a great new trend in the historical development of literature and that its idiom (or idioms) should not be restricted to that of 19th-century realism. As Mr. Klaniczay argues, the specific style of Socialist art and literature is still in the making, and its form, when fully developed, will not be a uniform idiom of artistic expression, but *style* in the broad historical sense of the word, the sense we use when we speak about the "style" of the Renaissance. In Mr. Klaniczay's opinion there is ample evidence that this new style will be indebted more directly to some trends of the *avant-garde* (especially to the *oeuvre* of those writers who achieved a synthesis between tradition and innovation) than to the poetics of the Balzac school of realism. This view does not involve the rejection of the term Socialist realism. As Mr. Nyirö pointed out in several studies, this term should be conceived as the name of a given phenomenon, and the task of the critic is to study the phenomenon itself.

Critics of this new school start out from the assumption that literature is a social institution and a species of art. They are convinced that though the specifically formal elements of art play a great role in defining art as art, in reality art cannot exist as merely a kind of formal achievement or as the materialization of an abstraction—of its "artistic substance." Art tends to incorporate ever-new fields of experience. Mr. Miklós and Mr. Nyirö argue that the social function of the arts and of literature may undergo substantial changes in the course of history; new forms and species of art may arise, and nonartistic qualities may be recognized as artistic attributes. They add that definitions of art are valid only if they reflect this vitality and mobility. Norms of artistic value are useless unless they are based on laws of development, instead of the outstanding qualities of past achievement. Mr. Klaniczay, Mr. Nyirö, and Mr. Diószegi lay special emphasis on the social consciousness of the artist. They disapprove of the view that any straightforward expression of the artist's conviction creates greater risk to his artistic achievement than the risks he has to face anyway entering this particular realm of human potentiality.

These critics' preoccupation with structural and rhetorical studies is combined with the use of what István Sötér describes as "the complex method of literary scholarship" (the combination of sociological, psychological, historical, and critical approaches with the methods of comparative studies, including the comparative study of the relationship between literature and the other species of art). This school of criticism is one of the trends mentioned in connection with the discussion of the concept of realism in "Of Socialist Realism: A Basis for Further Discussion" issued by the Panel on Cultural Theory attached to the Central Committee of the Hungarian Socialist Workers' Party.[12]

In Hungary as well as in other Socialist countries, there is a new interest in structural and formal analysis, although Hungary has no live traditions of structuralism such as exist in the Soviet Union, in Czechoslovakia, and in Poland. In those countries attempts to combine the structuralist approach with a socio-historical approach are especially successful. There are similar strivings in Rumania and in Yugoslavia (e.g., the circle of aestheticians around the Zagreb periodical, *Umjetnost riječi*). In Hungary, László Antal, Imre Bata,

András Martinkó, Ferenc Papp, and Gyula Tellér came forth with interesting ideas, and Professor Elöd Halász (Szeged University) presented a paper on his findings concerning the role of the time factor in the structure of 20th-century novels to the 9th Congress of the International Federation for Modern Languages and Literature.

Paralleling the structuralists' fresh or renewed efforts to develop logical methods of analysis, theoreticians also strive to apply the theory of information and of cybernetics to the questions of art and literature. This relatively new approach is widely cultivated among scholars in the Soviet Union. Yury Filipev, in ТВОРЧЕСТВО И КИБЕРНЕТИКА (*Art and Cybernetics*, Moscow, 1964), bases a theory of the creative process on the functioning of the "negative feedback." In "ОБРАЗ КАК ИНФОРМАЦИЯ" ("The Image as Information"), I. Zaretsky conceives a work of art as a complete image, or an organized series of images functioning as units of information.[13] A Polish critic based an analysis of Tolstoy's *War and Peace* on the principle of "redundancy." In "Teorie informace a literární proces" ("The Information Theory and the Literary Process"), Jeřy Levy deals with the use of the theory of information in the exploration of the laws of the literary process.[14] Mrs. Nora Krausová, a Slovak critic, has applied conceptual means provided by the theory of information to the definition of literary species in "K Teórii Informácie v Literárney Vede" ("The Theory of Information on the Literary Genres").[15] Another Slovak critic, Jiří Zeman, is engaged in research on the use of cybernetics for the solution of aesthetic problems. As articles and studies in *Útunk* and *Korunk* (Hungarian literary periodicals in the Rumanian People's Republic) indicate, there is similarly great interest in the theory of information and in cybernetics among Rumanian students of literature.

In Hungary Mr. Tellér, Mr. Papp, and Mr. Nyirö have devoted studies to the use of these new theoretical approaches in literary criticism. Mr. Papp deals with the general aspects of aesthetics, while Mr. Tellér combines the findings of the information theory with those of structuralism in defining the structural qualities of some trends of 20th-century poetry. In his study, "Müvészet és kibernetika" ("Art and Cybernetics"), Lajos Nyirö criticizes a view presented by the French aesthetician Abraham Moles in *Théorie de l'information et perception esthétique* (Paris, 1958) that art is but a medium of information.[16] He rejects similar views he detects in the works of Ukraintsev, Kovalgin, Medvedev, Tukhtin, and some other Soviet scholars. Moles states that all information available through a work of art consists of semantic and aesthetic information. According to

Mr. Nyirö, the French aesthetician fails to take account of the nature of what he describes as aesthetic information. The Hungarian critic points out that the difficulty arises from the fact that a work of art is not merely a neutral channel of information; in this case the channel itself functions as information, as it is capable of modifying aesthetically neutral semantic information. Dealing with the functional changes of literature, Mr. Nyirö offers the view that the model of the "negative feedback" or that of the "homeostatic state," which characterize the functioning of autoguided dynamic organizations, may be of major help in determining the basic laws of the literary process. Describing the epistemological and ontological status of the individual work of art, he points out that it is not a duplicate copy of reality; though modeled on the laws of reality, a work of art also assumes the characteristics of a new construction, and, in the sense that it is a real challenge to its recipients, it is *a new reality*. Thus a work of art is both a self-sufficient entity and an "open world," i.e., a structure that becomes live in the context of larger structures.

In conclusion, here are a few facts about the recent development of Hungarian criticism and literary scholarship.

Prolonged debates about new novels by Endre Fejes, Ferenc Sánta, and József Darvas, new poems by Mihály Váczi and Ferenc Juhász, or new dramas by Gyula Illyés and László Németh reflect diverse attitudes toward the new qualities that arise in the development of Socialist literature. In an interesting study entitled "A mai regény világképe" ("The World Image of the Novel Today"), Mr. András Diószegi, editor of *Kritika*, draws attention to formal innovations that represent a new phase in the evolution of the novel and a widespread trend in the recent development of Socialist fiction.[17] Mr. Diószegi confronts the technical and aesthetic achievements of Socialist writers with those of non-Socialist writers and arrives at the conclusion that in recent years Socialist novelists developed a concise, highly dramatic, and tense novel structure based on the montage and similar techniques. Unlike the conventional forms of the novel, this new form is powerful enough to sustain an intensive philosophical and moral consciousness. This form characterizes recent novels and stories by Soviet novelists Sholokhov, Simonov, Kazakevich, Tendryakov, Aytmatov; Czech writers Otčenašek and Fried; Slovak novelists Karvaš and Mnacko; Polish writers Brandys and Andrzejewski; Dimov, a Bulgarian writer; Davico, a Yugoslav novelist; and Hungarian writers Endre Fejes, József Darvas, Ferenc Sánta, Lajos Mesterházi, Gyula Fekete, Sándor Tóth, and Lajos Galambos.

Much of the work done by Hungarian literary scholarship is centered in the universities and in the Institute of Literary History of the Hungarian Academy of Science. In 1965 the Institute published a comprehensive *History of Hungarian Literature* in 6 volumes. The editors are István Sötér, Tibor Klaniczay, Pál Pándi, and Miklós Szabolcsi. Painstaking textual research and the application of modern critical standards and methods characterize this work, the end result of a well-coordinated, collective effort of scholars working at the Institute or at various other places. The Institute plans to publish a history of Hungarian criticism, a textbook of literary theory, and a history of world literature based on the methods of comparative literature.

Tibor Klaniczay's essays collected in *Marxizmus és irodalomtudomány* (*Marxism and Literary Scholarship*, 1964) provide information about the preparation, the methods, and the principles of the *History of Hungarian Literature*. István Sötér's monograph of 19th-century Hungarian literature, *Nemzet és haladás* (*Nation and Progress*, 1963), threw new light on the main spiritual trends of the period. *A szimbolizmus és a magyar líra* (*Symbolism and Hungarian Lyrical Poetry*, 1965) by Aladár Komlós; a collection of essays entitled *Tanulmányok a magyar szocialista irodalom történetéből* (*Studies on the History of Hungarian Socialist Literature*, 1962) edited by Miklós Szabolcsi and László Illés; Antal Pirnát's study, *Die Ideologie der Siebenbürger Antitrinitarier in den 1570er Jahren* (1961), on the Anti-Trinitarian movement in Transylvania; studies by Miklós Szabolcsi (on Attila József), by Pál Pándi (on Petőfi), by István Király (on Kálmán Kikszáth), by János Barta (on 19th-century realism and on aesthetic issues), by József Szauder (on Hungarian romanticism and contacts between Hungarian and Italian literature), and numerous other scholarly works prepared a synthetic approach to the general and specific questions of Hungarian literary history, decided questions of its periodization and questions pertinent to the appreciation of individual authors and literary trends.

The Department of Comparative Literature of the Institute devotes special attention to contacts between the literatures of the Central and Eastern European countries. Comparative studies on Polish and Hungarian, Russian and Hungarian literatures (the latter in 3 volumes) have been published in Budapest, Warsaw, and Moscow. Hungarian comparatists attended the Moscow conference on comparative literature in 1960 and the Utrecht and Fribourg conferences. In October, 1962, comparatists of the East and the West met in Budapest. The proceedings of the conference were printed in *Acta Litteraria*,[18] including a brief outline of the history of comparative literature studies in Hungary by György Mihály Vajda.[19] Hungarian Slavists attend Slavistic congresses held every five years. *Acta Litteraria* (polyglot), *Helikon,* and *Filológiai Közlemények* (*Philological Review*) are the main forums for Hungarian comparatists.

As to the standard of the work of Marxist comparatists, here is a quote from a review of the *Proceedings of the 3rd Congress of the International Comparative Literature Association* (The Hague, 1962):

> The congress was enormously enriched by the participation of so many scholars from Eastern Europe and the Far East. Their papers illuminate areas beyond the familiar confines of Western literature, and, through their use of the best comparative methods, throw back new light on the Western tradition. Furthermore, the explicit attention in several Eastern papers to basic theory of comparatism in assessing the method and purpose of studying East-West or major-minor literary relationships provides a significance too often lacking in the more routine influence and fortune studies among the Western papers. The most penetrating of these theoretical considerations appear in I. Sötér's impressive survey of the effect of the West upon the growth of modern Eastern European literature, in "Phénomènes parallèles de la littérature hongroise et de la littérature russe du XIXe siècle," and in B. Munteano's paper on Rumanian literature, "La Vocation européenne et humaniste de la littérature roumaine." [20]

The achievement of Hungarian Anglicists and Americanists, among them Miklós Szenczi, László Kéry, László Országh, and the late Dr. Tibor Lutter, also deserves notice. A survey by Béla Köpeczi, entitled "Vingt années de philologie moderne en Hongrie," [21] gives a factual account of the work done by Hungarian students of foreign literatures in the past twenty years. A history of Hungarian literary scholarship and criticism since 1945 is outlined by Tibor Klaniczay in "Les sciences littéraires hongroises après la libération." [22] These works provide the broad view necessary to the student who would seek to understand the development of criticism in Middle Europe since the Second World War.

NOTES

1. Cf. *Kritika,* No. 5 (1964).
2. Cf. *Kritika,* No. 2 (1963).
3. *L'Europa letteraria,* No. 1 (1960).
4. *Umjetnost riječi,* No. 1 (1963).

5. *Comparative Literature Studies*, No. 4 (1964).

6. Tibor Klaniczay, *Marxizmus és irodalomtudomány* (*Marxism and Literary Scholarship*) (Budapest, 1964), p. 257.

7. *Otázky teorie poznáni* (1957), pp. 263–359.

8. *Világirodalmi Figyelö*, No. 4 (1963), 377.

9. (Prague, 1962), p. 126.

10. Fran Petrè and Zdenko Škreb, *Uvod u književnost* (*Introduction to Literature*) (Zagreb, 1961), p. 544.

11. Cf. *Kortars*, No. 1 (1962).

12. *Társadalmi Szemle*, No. 2 (1965); in English, *The New Hungarian Quarterly*, No. 19 (1965).

13. Вопросы Литературы, No. 2 (1964).

14. *Česká Literatúra*, No. 4 (1963).

15. *Slovenská Literatúra*, No. 1 (1964).

16. *Kritika*, No. 9 (1965).

17. *Kritika*, No. 1 (1963).

18. *Acta Litteraria*, *5* (1962).

19. *Ibid.*, pp. 306–313.

20. *Comparative Literature*, *15* (1964), 77.

21. *Acta Litteraria*, *7* (1965), 415–430.

22. *Ibid.*, pp. 395–411.

II | PRACTICAL CRITICISM I: THEORY OF THE NOVEL

Neal Oxenhandler

Character and Emotion in Balzac's Novels

I

"Monsieur, votre chapeau, s'il vous plaît?" [1] Raphaël Valentin, desperate and distracted, shows his ignorance of the gambling house by forgetting to check his hat. A moment later, the fact of his desperation is confirmed by this authorial comment: "Oui, je conçois qu'un homme aille au Jeu; mais c'est lorsque entre lui et la mort il ne voit plus que son dernier écu." [2] The young man's desperate innocence is further emphasized through contrast with the suroundings—the worn and dirty floor, the drawn faces of the other players who "tous en voyant l'inconnu éprouvèrent je ne sais quel sentiment épouvantable. Ne faut-il pas être malheureux pour obtenir de la pitié, bien faible pour exciter une sympathie, ou d'un bien sinistre aspect pour faire frissonner les âmes dans cette salle où les douleurs doivent être muettes, où la misère est gaie, et le désespoir décent?" [3] This is not mere description of the character, mere rendering of the gambling house; rather, locale and character illuminate each other. The character is revealed less through description than through the sense of an emotion, a pitiable urgency, an urge to leap into the void. We will find, indeed, that character is always revealed to us in Balzac's novels through emotion.

As we follow Monsieur Crevel, "le capitaine bourgeois" with the "ventre piriforme," through the streets of Paris, toward the house of the Baron Hulot, where he will make his shameless proposition to the Baron's wife, we are moving toward the outrage and indignation of this virtuous, indeed saintly, lady:

> Après avoir sonné, le capitaine bourgeois fit de grands efforts pour remettre en place son habit, qui s'était autant retroussé par derrière que par devant, poussé par l'action d'un ventre piriforme. Admis aussitôt qu'un domestique en livrée l'eut aperçu, cet homme important

et imposant suivit le domestique, qui dit en ouvrant la porte du salon:

—Monsieur Crevel!

En entendant ce nom, admirablement approprié à la tournure de celui qui le portait, une grande femme blonde, très bien conservée, parut avoir reçu comme une commotion électrique et se leva.

—Hortense, mon ange, va dans le jardin avec ta cousine Bette, dit-elle vivement à sa fille qui brodait à quelques pas d'elle.[4]

We know instantly that the "commotion électrique" is one of distaste and revulsion. Dismissing her daughter with the words "mon ange," she reveals something of her own purity of character, that purity which all the demonic male sexuality of the book is going to attack and finally demolish. The Baronne Hulot stands quivering at the book's overture like a magnificent yet somehow weakened (obvious negative implication of "très bien conservée") angel.

While emotion in Balzac's novels is to some degree an essence or quality, expressed by substantives such as "hate," "love," or "passion," and reinforced by metaphors and analogies, it is also situational, for Balzac seems to have anticipated the view of Maurice Merleau-Ponty that emotion is given to the individual as a function of his being-for-others:

Si j'essaye d'étudier l'amour ou la haine par la pure observation intérieure, je ne trouve que peu de choses à décrire: quelques angoisses, quelques palpitations de cœur, en somme ces troubles banaux qui ne me révèlent pas l'essence de l'amour ni de la haine. Chaque fois que j'arrive à des remarques intéressantes, c'est que je ne me suis pas contenté de coincider avec mon sentiment, c'est que j'ai réussi à l'étudier comme un comportement, comme une modification de mes rapports avec autrui et avec le monde, c'est que je suis parvenu à le penser comme je pense le comportement d'une autre personne dont je me trouve être témoin.[5]

In spite of the use of an "essentialistic" language, Balzac does not rely on introspection, interior monologue, or even "narration indirecte libre" as means of revealing inner states; the inner states serve only as reflectors of the action. Raphaël Valentin is rendered desperate by a hopeless love; his love-sickness causes him to barter his life for the magic skin. His desperation is a force constantly thrusting outward, modifying all the other characters of the book in turn. The Baronne Hulot listens to Crevel's proposal only out of the desperation into which her husband has plunged her; she pleads with the dastardly "capitaine bourgeois" only out of a mother's desire to save her family. Once again, we know the character through her "comportement, comme une modification de (ses) rapports avec autrui et avec le monde" rather than directly, through the communication of her emotional states. We might indeed be tempted to say that in fiction emotion always appears as *action in situation,* response to others, attempted modification of circumstances. We might then make the equation: character equals situation.

Yet in one of the most important of contemporary works on the novel, Nathalie Sarraute's *L'Ere du soupçon,* we learn that "character is dead," killed in fact by Balzac:

> La vie, à laquelle, en fin de compte, tout en art se ramène (cette "intensité de vie" qui, "décidément, disait Gide, fait la valeur d'une chose"), a abandonné ces formes autrefois si pleines de promesses, et s'est transportée ailleurs. Dans son mouvement incessant qui la fait se déplacer toujours vers cette ligne mobile où parvient à un moment donné la recherche et où porte tout le poids de l'effort, elle a brisé les cadres du vieux roman et rejeté, les uns après les autres les vieux accessoires inutiles. Les loupes et les gilets rayés, les caractères et les intrigues pourraient continuer à varier à l'infini sans révéler aujourd'hui autre chose qu'une réalité dont chacun connaît, pour l'avoir parcourue en tous sens, la moindre parcelle. Au lieu, comme au temps de Balzac, d'inciter le lecteur à accéder à une vérité qui se conquiert de haute lutte, ils sont une concession dangereuse à son penchant à la paresse—et aussi à celui de l'auteur—à sa crainte du dépaysement.[6]

If character and situation are no longer "interesting," as Madame Sarraute claims, if readers have grown "suspicious" of the author's insistence that the people and events of his book merit more attention than "real" life with its "petits faits vrais" and its beings of flesh and blood whom he may observe by merely opening his eyes, then it must be that character and situation are not after all the ultimate categories of fiction, that there is something else, something further that must be uncovered if we are to continue to read and write novels. Nathalie Sarraute does in fact take us further, does reveal to us the ultimate category of fiction—consciousness of itself. Yet consciousness is charged with affectivity, as Madame Sarraute suggests in this description of Dostoevsky:

> Quoi de plus propre, en effet, que ces interrogations passionnées et ces réponses, que ces approches, ces reculs feints, ces fuites et ces poursuites, ces agaceries et ces frottements, ces chocs, ces caresses, ces morsures, ces étreintes, quoi de plus propre à chauffer, agiter, faire affleurer et se répandre au dehors l'immense masse tremblotante dont le flux et le reflux incessants, la vibration à peine perceptible est la pulsation même de la vie?[7]

To summarize this passage and others: Madame Sarraute sees characters as "props" or "vehicles" through which the affectively charged consciousness of the writer is communicated. This consciousness, especially in the great moderns such as Dostoevsky, Kafka, and Proust, manifests a tentative movement outward, a probing search or grasping for others, a "need for contact." For contact with whom or what? With me, with you, "hypocrite lecteur, mon semblable, mon frère." To carry the argument one step further: the emotions of characters are simply analogies or metaphors for the emotional thrust of the novelist's "need for contact" with the reader. As Sartre points out "l'objet littéraire n'a d'autre substance que la subjectivité du lecteur." [8] He goes on to say that characters exist only in the reader's subjectivity. Our point is somewhat different: The characters are both the locus of and the medium through which an emotional communication or exchange between novelist and reader takes place. In the light of this view, I turn to several novels of Balzac. Our question will be: What is the nature of Balzac's reaching-out to the reader? Is it hostile or imperialistic? Or is it dominated by generosity?

II

Jean-Paul Sartre's theory of the novel, as developed in "Qu'est-ce que la littérature?" is based on the rejection of a type of 19th-century novel which is attributed to Balzac. The basis for this rejection is socio-political: Balzac, the greatest of bourgeois writers, solidifies in his works and implicitly justifies the myriad inequities of his time. But it is not merely the portrayal of an unjust world that Sartre criticizes, it is the attempt to make us accomplices of this world through the manipulation of our emotions. This led to an attack on Balzacian narration, an attack echoed in greater or less degree by novelists of the following generation, such as Alain Robbe-Grillet and Michel Butor.[9]

Balzacian narration was attacked not so much for inherent defects, as for the manner in which it manipulated reader emotion. Balzac was seen as a sorcerer who changed his readers into slaves, a hypnotist or seducer. He was accused of bad faith and of emotional imperialism. There was indeed a tendency to megalomania in Balzac, an impulse to political as well as erotic domination. The two are combined in this passage from a letter written to Zulma Carraud in June, 1832:

> Si je suis pour quelque chose dans le gouvernement du pays, plus tard, je serai jugé. . . . Il y a des vocations auxquelles il faut obéir,

et quelque chose d'irrésistible m'entraine vers la gloire et le pouvoir. Ce n'est pas une existence heureuse. Il y a chez moi le culte de la femme et un besoin d'amour qui n'a jamais été complètement satisfait; désespérant d'être jamais bien aimé et compris de la femme que j'ai rêvée, ne l'ayant rencontrée que sous une forme, celle du coeur, je me rejette dans la sphère tempétueuse des passions politiques, et dans l'atmosphère orageuse et desséchante de la gloire littéraire.[10]

The theme of "power" returns in a remark quoted by Jules de Petigny, a friend of his youth: "Je contraindrai les hommes a m'obéir, toutes les femmes à m'aimer. . . ."[11] Or, since all clues serve in the establishment of a motive, we can quote Raphaël, the character whom we observed enter the gambling house at the start of *La Peau de chagrin:* "Je voulus me venger de la societé, je voulus posséder l'âme de toutes les femmes en me soumettant toutes les intelligences. . . ."[12] It is also worth mentioning Gautier's observation in 1835 that Balzac had pasted to the sword-hilt of a statue of Napoleon, which he kept in his study, the inscription: "Ce qu'il n'a pas achevé par l'épée, je l'accomplirai par la plume."[13]

We must contrast these feverish statements with the attitude toward the reader offered by Sartre: "Je le considère comme liberté pure, pur pouvoir créateur, activité inconditionnée; je ne saurais donc . . . m'adresser à sa passivité, c'est-à-dire, tenter de lui communiquer d'emblée des émotions de peur ou de colère." In brief and total contrast to Balzac: "L'écrivain ne doit pas chercher à bouleverser."[14]

But what are the specific emotional effects produced by a Balzacian novel? We must make an effort to identify and describe these effects before we pronounce a verdict on Balzac the seducer. For the very nature of the verbal medium contradicts this all too human dream of seduction. And surely the writer's megalomaniac daydream is purified by the terrible discipline of continuous and unrelenting creation. "Savez-vous ce que je fais? Je travaille vingt-quatre heures de suite, je dors cinq heures, ce qui me donne vingt-et-un heures et demie de travail par jour."[15] Or this: "Je suis si cloué par mes épreuves, mes travaux qui renaissent d'eux-mêmes que vous seriez en vérité charitable de venir me voir aujourd'hui même lundi, et ne pas trop regarder si j'abuse de votre amitié, car il me faut prendre comme un prisonnier, prisonnier d'une idée et d'une œuvre elle est aussi féroce que les créanciers."[16] The Balzac of the novels is not only seducer but sufferer, not only master but victim, and our relationship with him as readers is complex, despite the fact that it is structured by specific aesthetic principles which we shall now try to lay bare.

Antoine Roquentin, the hero of Sartre's novel *La Nausée,* finds an open copy of *Eugénie Grandet* on a table in the Bouville public library and begins to read at page twenty-seven. He reads several pages for distraction, then goes to work. The novel has had its effect, however; a moment later Roquentin gives a brief description of the Autodidacte which is suspiciously Balzacian: "Il porte des vêtements rapés, mais son linge est d'une blancheur éblouissante." [17] But the real influence of Balzac in the novel is not in the descriptions, of which we find other and lengthier ones later; rather it is in the use of the Balzacian novel as a vision of life which Roquentin is to reject:

> Je n'ai pas eu d'aventures. Il m'est arrivé des histoires, des événements, des incidents, tout ce qu'on voudra. Mais pas des aventures. Ce n'est pas une question de mots; je commence à comprendre. Il y a quelque chose à quoi je tenais plus qu'à tout le reste— sans m'en rendre bien compte. Ce n'était pas l'amour, Dieu non, ni la gloire, ni la richesse. C'était. . . . Enfin je m'étais imaginé qu'à de certains moments ma vie pouvait prendre une qualité rare et précieuse . . . autrefois, à Londres, à Meknès, à Tokio j'ai connu des moments admirables, j'ai eu des aventures. C'est ça qu'on m'enlève à present. Je viens d'apprendre, brusquement, sans raison apparente, que je me suis menti pendant dix ans. Les aventures sont dans les livres et naturellement, tout ce qu'on raconte dans les livres peut arriver pour de vrai, mais pas de la même manière. C'est à cette manière d'arriver que je tenais si fort.[18]

Roquentin returns to *Eugénie Grandet* again ("il faut bien faire quelque chose") and reads at random a section which reveals by typical Balzacian devices Eugénie's love for her handsome cousin. He has only read a few lines when he begins to listen to a real-life conversation at a nearby table of the *brasserie.* By contrast to the constructed scene of the novel, "real-life" conversation is disjointed, incoherent. It does not carry the listener forward upon the paths of "aventure" but conveys only a sense of psychic density and obscurity. The book cannot move Roquentin. He rejects adventures in fiction as he has already done in life. He reacts adversely to what is, for many readers, the most powerful and delightful of Balzacian effects— expectation.

The novel posits a temporal order in which events are foreshadowed and then indeed come to pass as we have expected and feared. The very first line of the book tells us to expect a tale of unhappiness: "Il se trouve dans certaines villes de province des maisons dont la vue inspire une mélancolie égale à celle que provoquent les cloîtres les plus sombres, les landes les plus ternes ou les ruines les plus tristes." [19] Numerous other devices establish the antithesis between youth and age, love and avarice, Paris and province which controls the reader's expectation of the tragic stifling of Eugénie's pure love. If, as Georges Poulet has suggested, the Balzacian imagination is always soaring into the future—"Voler, nager, voyager, se projeter, s'élancer, tels sont les termes égaux par lesquels s'exprime cette expérience première et mille fois recommencée de la pensée créatrice" [20]—the reader too is always carried forward in time and space. In its most general form, expectation is the temporal dimension of the novelist's world. It is the response he must shape in the reader's subjectivity, the emotion which he must bring into existence if his book is to have a future. Yet expectation is not certainty. The reader may guess that Eugénie will never marry her cousin Charles, but he does not guess that Eugénie will one day become the mirror image of her miser father. There is a fine line between what we might call a narrative determinism, which would be objectionable, and the sense of indeterminacy that may coexist with expectation. Expectation is the emotional weight of the question: What will happen next? It is the sign of the novelist's power to intervene in the reader's subjective world with a continuous gesture that structures the surge of the reader's emotive and perceptual life. It constitutes, in short, the "pleins pouvoirs" of the novelist without which the meaning of his art is lost. There could be no novel without it.

Roquentin's scorn of the *a priori* form which Balzac has built into *Eugénie Grandet* is nothing more than the reappearance of the dream of the realistic novel. Roquentin says, in effect, No, *that* is not the way "real life" is. *This* is the way it is. For the Balzacian structure of expectation, he substitutes a structure of indeterminacy. But indeterminacy, or contingency, is just as metaphorical as Balzac's determinacy. Neither can be validated in an absolute sense, neither can be proved to be "the way it is" once and for all. If Roquentin had been as consistent as his creator was later to become, he would have followed his insight to its logical conclusion and seen that there can be no realistic novel. Instead, he resists the temporal and causal ordering of Balzac's world because that world does not correspond to his own internal sensing of these categories; but why indeed should it? Surely the psychic reality of Balzac is as valid as that of Roquentin—or of Sartre. As a final point, we should be aware that there is expectation, foreshadowing, and even a touch of determinacy in *La Nausée*, just as there is a large measure of freedom and contingency in *Eugénie Grandet*.

Expectation is doubled by another effect—intensification. From the first powerful duet of *La Cousine Bette,* the great dramatic confrontation in which the evil Crevel attempts to seduce that incarnate virtue, the Baroness Hulot, we are led onward through a series of coincidences and convergent plots which transform expectancy into a desire for crisis and release.

Early in the novel two simultaneous meetings occur. They are almost random. Baron Hulot takes his daughter, Hortense, to visit an art dealer, and while she enters the store, he stands outside, looking thoughtfully up at the apartment of one of his employees, Marneffe. Just at that moment the seductive Madame Marneffe appears —and Hulot is started on the most destructive liaison of his career; a few moments later, his daughter meets the sculptor, Wenceslas, with whom she is, we realize, already half in love; she too has met her destiny.

What tempted Balzac onto this dangerous path of coincidence? Why did he so frequently use a device which threatened to destroy the authenticity of his stories? Do these meetings indicate some fatal tropism in Balzac's characters which leads them to seek out those very persons who will destroy them? Or shall we assign some realistic valence to coincidence? Is Balzac showing us the mobility of a society where money can replace human relations and class distinctions? Surely this is the case for such "vertical" coincidences as those we have described early in *La Cousine Bette.* The coincidence indicates that in the 1830's people could meet and mingle much more readily, could form improbable if passing combinations more easily than under the *ancien régime.*

Certain formal patterns and repetitions seem to have appealed to Balzac for aesthetic reasons: The scene of mutual commiseration between Crevel and Hulot is echoed by one between Hortense and the Baroness; or these internal *rimes* may appear in inverted form: the Baroness refuses Crevel, then summons him back, Hulot courts Marneffe and then is refused by her.

But any attempt to explain coincidence through purely social or aesthetic values would overlook the dominant motive behind all of Balzac's writing—the intensification of the emotional experience. Balzac is above all an emotional writer; he makes his novelistic decisions always in terms of the emotional effect.[21] Balzac never loses sight of the fact that the novel exists for the reader; the novel is above all the way in which Balzac chooses to exist for us, his readers; it is his being-for-us. It is through the intensification of that emotional effect which begins with expectation that the polarity of the novel, the equilibrium between writer and reader, begins to assume definitive form.

Those first coincidences, early in the novel, intensify expectation to that critical point at which events, new and pregnant events, begin to happen. Only when this point is reached has the novelist assumed command of his universe, only then can he exercise his "pleins pouvoirs," only then too does the reader exist as a responding subjectivity.

We cannot therefore fault Balzac on his "unrealistic" use of coincidence except at those points, later in the book, where coincidence works against emotional intensification. We are amused when Marneffe's lovers whiz in and out of her bedroom, hiding in cupboards in the belief that they are duping others, only to be duped themselves; yet the "comic relief" does not help the novel. The "vaudeville" stringencies of plot reveal Balzac, the failed dramatist, too directly; the patterns of action reach us without sufficient diffusion; yet the great comic scene in which Crevel and Hulot compare notes on Valérie Marneffe redeems this lapse into vaudeville. Coincidence momentarily threatens the autonomy of the fictional world; yet, in the end, it is part of the foundation of that world.

One of the richest of Balzac's effects, an effect that may indeed produce expectation but is distinct from it, is clouded insight. Balzac's narrators are by no means totally omniscient and Godlike, as Alain Robbe-Grillet has described them:

> Qui décrit le monde dans les romans de Balzac? Quel est ce narrateur omniscient, omniprésent, qui se place partout en même temps, qui voit en même temps l'endroit et l'envers des choses, qui suit en même temps les mouvements du visage et ceux de la conscience, qui connaît à la fois le présent, le passé et l'avenir de toute aventure? Ça ne peut être qu'un Dieu.[22]

Robbe Grillet claims that his novels are more "subjective" than those of Balzac because they present a narrower vision of reality; but he has simply failed to recognize the quality of Balzac's subjectivity and the principle in terms of which he selects which aspect of reality he will reveal to us. It is possible to show, for example, that Balzac's narrators are often limited. Their knowledge of events is often intermittent, incomplete, and inadequate. Here are several small but significant examples.

In his description of Mademoiselle Michonneau, who appears early in *Le Père Goriot* as an inhabitant of La Pension Vauquer, the narrator indicates doubt as to her past history:

> Quel acide avait dépouillé cette créature de ses formes féminines?
> elle devait avoir été jolie et bien faite: était-ce le vice, le chagrin, la
> cupidité? avait-elle trop aimé, avait-elle été machande à la toilette,
> ou seulement courtisane? Expiait-elle les triomphes d'une jeunesse
> insolente au-devant de laquelle s'étaient rués les plaisirs par une
> vieillese que fuyaient les passants?

The same doubt is indicated a few lines later in the description of
Monsieur Poiret:

> "Ce qu'il avait été? mais peut-être avait-il été employé au Mini-
> stère de la Justice . . . Peut-être avait-il été receveur à la porte
> d'un abattoir, ou sous-inspecteur de salubrité." [23]

Several explanations offer themselves for the narrator's attitude of
doubt expressed by the interrogations and the use of "peut-être." It
may be simply that Michonneau and Poiret are types. They might
have done any of the things suggested; the end result would still be
the same. But it is idle to discuss these characters as if they were
entities in themselves, when they are instruments of a total purpose;
that total purpose is the achievement of a powerful emotional effect.
We are given a clouded insight into Michonneau and Poiret to develop
their potentiality for a sinister function later in the book; and, equally
important, the clouded insight keeps the emotional focus somewhere
else. We do not learn enough about them to become involved with
them; our focus stays on Rastignac.

A bit later, the narrator suggests that he knows a mystery about
Vautrin that he will not tell us. At this point Vautrin has already
been introduced to us in a character sketch charged with significant,
revelatory detail, including the fact that he knows how to dismantle
locks. The clouded insight into Vautrin now functions not as a
buffering device but as a means of intensifying interest.

All this is maddening to those readers who demand sincerity from
their narrators, but it is perfectly acceptable to those of us who hold
that the novel is not supposed to give us "true" facts about a fictive
world but rather to be itself a world whose truth we have no right
to legislate.

A novel cannot both *be* real and *seem* real at the same time; it
cannot reproduce or transcribe real phenomena and at the same time
create, in a reader, the *effect* of witnessing real phenomena. Balzac
has chosen seeming over being. Although he seems to have fallen
into the trap of realism, it is only to ignore the problem of realism
and to proceed as if the real point at issue were the "making contact," the achievement of that being-for-others in an act of generous
communication which calls forth a free yet imperious response from

the reader who freely chooses to structure his own psychic experience along the lines of force the novelist proposes to him. By accepting, indeed even posing, the conventions of a realism, Balzac once and for all transcends them and becomes free to write a totally subjective novel.

The famous Balzacian descriptions, descriptions of places or of a character's clothes or appearance, which are often cited as examples of Balzacian realism, often function in reality as vehicles of this same clouded insight of which we are speaking. Clothes or bodily features both reveal and conceal. They hide the inner man while symbolically revealing him; they are both a key and a disguise. Thus Colonel Chabert is hailed first by the clerks of Derville's law office as a scarecrow in a tattered overcoat: "Allons! encore notre vieux carrick!" [24] We wish to pierce the mystery of this overcoat under which the man is hidden. The clerks themselves express our curiosity: "Je parie qu'il a été portier, repliqua Godeschal. Les portiers sont seuls doués par la nature de carricks usés, huileux et déchiquetés par le bas comme l'est celui de ce vieux bonhomme! Vous n'avez donc vu ni ses bottes éculées qui prennent l'eau, ni sa cravate qui lui sert de chemise? Il a couché sous les ponts." [25] Our desire to know "the character" is whetted yet held in restraint. The narrator's partial view at this point gives us a clouded insight which is itself emotionally charged, which is the very substance of our response to Balzac who is, at this moment, in contact with us in the intimacy not merely of language but of life itself.

Again in *Le Père Goriot* the first description of Rastignac subtly awakens our expectation of conflict by a carefully controlled insight: "Sa tournure, ses manières, sa pose habituelle dénotaient le fils d'une famille noble. . . ." But the description continues: "Ordinairement il portait une vieille redingote, un mauvais gilet, la méchante cravate noire, flétrie, mal nouée de l'étudiant, un pantalon à l'avenant et des bottes ressemelées." [26] Rastignac's feelings of bitter deprivation are conveyed by the antithesis between "fils d'une famille noble" and the enumeration of his *garde-robe,* in which each miserable article of clothing has its pejorative modifier ("vieille," "mauvais," "méchante," "noire," "flétrie," etc.). Again the device whets and controls our appetite to know more about the character. Our pity for him is compounded with puzzlement about him, and these emotions are controlled by a careful dosage of information. At issue is not how much the reader knows but *how* he knows; his knowledge must be charged with the right degree of affectivity. It is this concern that governs Balzac's use of narration, not a desire to play God.

We are viewing effects as characteristics of the work's structure, but it should be clear that nothing can really *determine* the response of a reader; contemporary readers often express disaffection from Balzac.

The last effect we shall discuss is the most "cathartic," the most total and demanding of effects, though in the last analysis the reader cannot experience "éblouissement" apart from a structure in which there is expectation and intensification. *Eblouissement* is akin to frenzy, to ecstasy, to revelation; it is the very *bouleversement* that Sartre rejects; it gives rise to the mythical awareness which is the ultimate dimension of Balzac's work. Albert Béguin in his *Balzac visionnaire* shows that there is an effect of ascension, of breaking-through in the novels, and that this may be signaled by a number of devices. The device used most often, indeed with almost compulsive regularity, is the comparison with the work of an. artist: "If a Rembrandt, if a Raphaël, if a Turner could have witnessed this scene. . . ." An example among hundreds occurs in the description of the antique dealer of *La Peau de chagrin:*

> Un peintre aurait, avec deux expressions différentes et en deux coups de pinceau, fait de cette figure une belle image du Père Eternel ou le masque ricaneur du Méphistophélès. . . .[27]

Balzac describes by refusing to describe; the truth lies beyond words, in vision itself. The following example strives for an even more specifically visual effect:

> Ce *Patiras* était l'ancien vermicellier, le pére Goriot, sur la tête duquel un peintre aurait, comme l'historien, fait tomber toute la lumière du tableau.[28]

as does this famous sentence:

> Pour bien peindre la physionomie de ce Christ de la Paternité, il faudrait aller chercher des comparaisons dans les images que les princes de la palette ont inventées pour peindre la passion soufferte au bénéfice des mondes par le Sauveur des hommes.[29]

Balzac says, in effect: Words fail me, I cannot describe what I *see*. He is, in truth, a visionary, so ecstatic that he can only express his vision by poetic approximations:

> Il arrive qu'un charbon ardent touche ce crâne, ces mains, cette langue; tout à coup, un mot réveille les idées; elles naissent, grandissent, fermentent. Une tragédie, un tableau, une statue, une comédie, montrent leurs poignards, leurs couleurs, leurs lazzis. C'est une vision, aussi passagère, aussi brève que la mort; c'est profond comme

un précipice, sublime comme un bruissement de la mer; c'est une richesse de couleur qui éblouit; c'est un group digne de Pygmalion, une femme dont la possession tuerait même le cœur de Satan; c'est une situation à faire un pulmonique expirant; le travail est là, tenant tous ses fourneaux allumés; le silence, la solitude ouvrent leurs trésors, rien n'est impossible.[30]

When Balzac is writing under the stress of such emotion, we often find incoherencies or lyrical flights, or passages of surreal intensity. At these moments, Balzac wishes to provoke in the reader an emotional submission, ecstatic in nature, to the otherness of the work. But these moments in which he threatens to overwhelm us ("bouleverser," in Sartre's phrase) are brief. Balzac tempers and controls our response to such passages by many modulatory devices. For example: Long prolix passages can provide a bridge between peaks of intensity. Or moments of "dead time" (e.g., long contemplative or descriptive passages) may create a temporal zone whose spaciousness allows us once again to breathe and to relate in a more leisurely way to characters who themselves are once again released into freedom by their author after the ecstatic seizure.

In reading Balzac, I am struck less by his imperialism or his seduction than by his generosity. At the start of his career, in a letter written to Madame de Berny in 1822, the twenty-year-old Balzac recognized that the role of the writer, the role to which he momentarily hesitated to aspire, was to possess "ce pouvoir de distribuer les grandes émotions." [31] His concern was to share the richness of his own imagination. True enough, the impulse that brought him to his writing desk was economic or erotic need; but, by the terrible discipline of his craft, the impulse was spiritualized. The seducer then became the giver of a marvelous gift, the gift of the phenomenal world of a human mind, demanding from the receiver of the gift not passivity or surrender but heightened emotion, a sense of risk, and a willingness to share. If a Rembrandt could have painted Balzac, might he not have painted him as consciousness crucified?

NOTES

1. *La Peau de chagrin, La Comédie humaine* (Paris, 1961), *IX*, 11.
2. *Ibid.*, p. 13.
3. *Ibid.*, p. 15.
4. *La Cousine Bette, La Comédie humaine, VI*, 136.
5. Maurice Merleau-Ponty, *Sens et non-sens* (Paris, 1948), pp. 106–107.

6. Nathalie Sarraute, *L'Ere du soupçon, essais sur le roman* (Paris, 1956), pp. 62–63.

7. *Ibid.*, p. 39.

8. "Qu'est-ce que la littérature?" *Situations, II* (Paris, 1948), p. 95.

9. Butor recognized the distortions of these criticisms when he himself, in a considerable change of position, wrote: "Il m'est d'autant plus agréable de parler de Balzac que la plupart du temps on se sert de lui comme d'une sorte d'épouvantail pour essayer d'intimider toute tentative de rénovation, d'invention dans le roman contemporain. On oppose d'une façon simplette le roman dit 'balzacian' au roman moderne, c'est-à-dire à toutes les œuvres importantes du xxᵉ siècle, or c'est un jeu d'enfant de montrer que ce roman 'balzacian' actuel ne s'inspire en réalité que d'une infime partie de l'œuvre de Balzac et que les seuls héritiers véritables de ce grand homme dans les cinquante dernières années sont Proust, Faulkner, etc." "Les Deux univers de Balzac: Le réel," *Balzac*, ed. Jules Bertaut (Paris, 1959), p. 248.

10. *Correspondance avec Zulma Carraud* (Paris, 1951), pp. 52–53.

11. Bertaut, ed., *op. cit.*, p. 10.

12. *La Comédie humaine, IX*, 85.

13. As quoted by Marcel Bouteron, "Une Année de la vie de Balzac," *Etudes Balzaciennes* (Paris, 1954), p. 138.

14. Sartre, *op. cit.*, pp. 98–99.

15. Letter to Madame Hanska, as quoted in Bouteron, *op. cit.* At this moment of the year 1835 Balzac was working on *Séraphita* and *Le Contrat de mariage*.

16. Letter to Théodore Dablin, 1835. As quoted in *L'Œuvre de Balzac*, ed. Albert Béguin (Paris, 1953), *XVI*, 164.

17. Jean-Paul Sartre, *La Nausée* (Paris, 1938), p. 48. An almost explicit parody of Balzac's description of Saumur in *Eugénie Grandet* is introduced on p. 63 by the words "Ça ne pouvait pas se décrire. . . ." Phrases such as "Il y a soixante ans nul n'aurait osé prévoir le miraculeux destin de la rue Tourneridge . . ." represent a typically Balzacin way of situating description in the mind of a hypothetical viewer.

18. *Ibid.*, p. 58

19. *La Comédie humaine, III*, 480.

20. Georges Poulet, *La Distance intérieure* (Paris, 1952), p. 126.

21. Two books published in 1964 have once again attempted to find a unitary explanation of Balzac's work. André Wurmser, *La Comédie inhumaine* (Paris, 1964), gives a Marxist explanation which is disputed by Maurice Bardèche, *Une Lecture de Balzac* (Paris, 1964), whose explanation is esthetic and ideological. But these dimensions are merely functions of the emotional effect which is Balzac's overriding concern.

22. *Pour un nouveau roman* (Paris, 1963), p. 149.

23. *La Comédie humaine, II*, 855–856.

24. *Ibid.*, p. 1086.

25. *Ibid.*, p. 1091.
26. *Ibid.*, p. 858.
27. *Ibid., IX*, 32.
28. *Ibid.*, II, 860.
29. *Ibid.*, p. 1026.
30. As quoted in *Balzac par lui-même*, ed. Gaëtan Picon (Paris, 1956), pp. 21–22.
31. *Correspondance* (Paris, 1960), *I*, 194.

George Gibian

The Forms of Discontent in
Dostoevsky and Tolstoy

In a short story published a year or so ago in *The New Yorker,* John Updike describes the visit to an East European country of an American writer on a cultural exchange mission. He meets poets and critics, who, it seems to me, are thinly disguised portraits or caricatures of Soviet writers whom John Updike met when he was in Russia. Before veering off into an account of a deeply-felt understanding with a woman poet, the story makes fun of one trait common to several East European nationalities: the impression people give that while they admit unashamedly that in many respects their nation does not amount to very much, they insist with pride that in suffering they are supreme.

A similar situation prevails in Russian literature in regard to discontent. Whatever else may have been absent or weakly represented in Russian 19th-century literary characters, this quality comes through strongly. Two well-known illustrations will introduce the subject. First, the exchange in Turgenev's *Fathers and Sons* between Arkady, Bazarov, and Arkady's uncle. The uncle says:

> "I do not understand how you can avoid recognizing principles, rules. What is the motive of your actions?"
> "I have already told you, uncle, that we don't recognize any authorities," Arkady intervened.
> "We act by the force of what we recognize as beneficial," Bazarov declared. "At the present time rejection is the most beneficial of all things, and so we reject."
> "Everything?"
> "Everything."
> "How? Not only art, poetry—but also—it is a terrible thing to say . . ."
> "Everything," Bazarov repeated with complete imperturbability.[1]

The second example is longer, but it shows several aspects of rejection in Russian prose classics—both in its theme and manner. Lebezyatnikov is speaking in *Crime and Punishment*, first about Sonya's being a prostitute:

> "Well, what about it? In my opinion, I mean, according to my personal conviction, this is a woman's most normal condition. Why not? . . . I regard her present actions as a forceful and personal protest against our present organization of society, and I respect her greatly for it. Why I even rejoice when I look at her." [2]

When he is accused of having turned her out of her room, he says:

> "That's another libel. . . . I was simply enlarging her mind, completely disinterestedly, trying to arouse a feeling of protest in her. All I was after was her protest. . . ." [3]

He continues a little later:

> "Environment is everything, and man by himself is nothing. . . . We have advanced in our convictions. We deny more. And if Dobrolyubov rose from his grave, I should have a real argument with him. And as for Belinsky—I'd make mincemeat out of him." [4]

We have advanced more, we have progressed more—"We deny more." "Rejection is the most beneficial of all things, and so we reject." Lebezyatnikov is a character very different from Bazarov; each serves a very different function in the novel in which he lives; the authors' attitudes toward them differ, and we must observe these distinctions. But the two passages do suggest the topic with which we are concerned: how Tolstoy and Dostoevsky express dissatisfaction and use strongly discontented characters, how the narrators in their works show rejection or strong disapproval, and what various forms such expressions of discontent assume in these literary works.

It may be fruitful to place the topic in another setting—both a contemporary and a long-range, historical one. My own interest in it has been aroused through irritation at the fad, observable these past five or ten years, of talking about "Alienation in the Modern World." There are discussions and anthologies of alienation, and the sometimes fuzzy introductions often either state or tacitly assume that "alienation" is, first of all, just any kind of very strong dissatisfaction and pessimism and, secondly, a phenomenon of the modern world—perhaps of the post-World War II period only, shown in Genet, Beckett, Burroughs, and so forth—or something at most characteristic of the 20th century and the very end of the 19th, exemplified by Albert Camus' *The Stranger* and by Franz Kafka, with his beautifully alienated quintessential quip: "What do I have in common with the Jews? I have nothing in common with myself."

When I tried to define just what about all this was bothering me, I decided that it was the assumption that there had been no previous comparable expressions of discontent in other ages. I had a similar feeling about some of the analyses of the "student movements" of the past few years. Again one senses the presupposition that somehow the present times are worse to live in than any previous one, that our problems are unique, and discontent and *anomie* widespread and acute as never before, because of unprecedented conditions. It is as though people may have been unhappy before, but nobody has ever been as unhappy as we are.[5]

Yet the literary history of previous ages, in widely separated countries, could supply analogous expressions of discontent. I do not mean to deny that the disaffections of our age are in some respects unique; what I do wish to dispute is that they are totally unprecedented. It is the responsibility of literary historians and critics, if literary antecedents exist, to define and characterize them; if there are parallels and analogies, to draw them; and if there is anything to be learned from juxtapositions, to formulate the conclusions from them.

Who are some of the authors whom I should like to see comparatively studied from this point of view? Among the ancient Greeks and Romans, Euripides, the satirists, and Propertius; in England, certain Jacobeans, Shakespeare's "dark plays" (perhaps the tragedies also), Jacobean drama in general, and some of the Romantics; and in Russia, the entire 19th century. Expressions of rejection are particularly strong and revealing among the Russians, and I believe an examination of them may throw some light on that very fertile period. It is, of course, a large topic, a very general theme; but I do not think we should allow the pitfalls and vastness to deter us from attempting it. Now may be the time to generalize and to attempt a synthesis; perhaps it may be done without altogether losing sight of the actual text of literary works, of the details and minutiae which give them life in the first place.

Particularly tempting would be to hear what Orientalists think about this topic. I have tried out the idea on a few of them and have been told that, at least in Chinese literature, no parallel exists to Western expressions of rejection, that only in certain limited periods of rapid social change and political as well as social dissolution was there any literature closely comparable to such Western authors or periods as I have mentioned. If this is so, it is a very interesting difference.

In other words, I should like to encourage an inquiry into the history of human discontent as embodied in literature: a study of world literature in this perspective—almost as if it were a literary genre.

Before we turn to Tolstoy and Dostoevsky, it may be well to raise certain walls or compartments. It may be useful to remind ourselves that we must do a great deal of distinguishing, of discriminating, and not merely comparing. Thus, we must always distinguish between the negation *in a person* (character or author) and *circumstances* which may produce or justify such negation; in other words, between subjective dissatisfaction and an environment which seems likely to produce dissatisfaction.

Further categories may be those of Marx—the distinctions between alienation from things and others, and alienation from oneself, or, as he puts it, alienation from the means of production, from the product produced, from society or community, and from oneself. Hegel's quite different use of the two kinds of alienation, *Entfremdung* and *Entäusserung*, may be useful also.

The discontent expressed may be with various objects or based on various reasons, and here I hope I shall be pardoned for merely listing such possible causes of discontent:

1. Social organization—society of the time: the state, the political system, or the economic system; the middle class; the dominant values. This may be called the Czarist autocracy, or the Puritan middle class, the Establishment, the rat race, or the Soviet totalitarianism, etc.

2. Eternal conditions of human life—the fact of death; *la condition humaine;* the smallness of man, the vastness and silence of the universe; the meaninglessness of life, the injustice of suffering.

3. God's injustice, or remoteness, or incommensurability with human concepts of justice; God's ways with man.

4. Poverty, exploitation; irrationality of social structure; tyranny; national oppression by an enemy nation.

The deductions or conclusions drawn from intense discontent with these circumstances can be various. One may be impelled to words, political revolution, social reform; resignation, quietism; toward advocacy of science, rationalism (Bazarov), rejection of traditional society and adoption of new social forms, ways of thinking, and acting; or one may hope for a cataclysm—or give up hope altogether. Again, the reaction may be either gloom or—paradoxically—joy, exultation, as it sometimes comes close to being in Dostoevsky.

The author, or his narrator, we must remember, may condemn along with his character—he may, so to speak, join him in his dissatisfaction and protest; or he may condemn him for his protest. There is yet a third possibility: The narrator may present a character who is perfectly at home in his environment, unalienated, adjusted, and in harmony—as, for example, Oblomov in at least parts of the novel or

Monsieur Homais and Charles Bovary, happily accepting and assenting to their society—and may condemn the character for this very lack of dissatisfaction.

But let us turn from this scheme, or catalogue, of possible variants of literary attitudes and expressions of discontent to something more particular—Dostoevsky's manner of dealing with the topic. His works are a panorama of great deniers, from the Underground Man to Ivan Karamazov, with many great and small characters between them.

In the young Dostoevsky, we find a curiously tentative approach to the theme. Makar Devushkin, in *Poor Folk* (1846), is a man extremely in harmony with society; in fact, he impresses by his willed acceptance, his shrilly proclaimed (if Devushkin may be said to be shrill in anything) adherence to society, his faith in its justice, stability, and unquestionability. But the humble copying clerk writes letters to Varenka, who is beset by the dishonorable pursuit of Bykov, the rich landlord bent on seduction. Makar himself is made fun of by colleagues at the office; he reads Gogol and is horrified by the fate of Akaky Akakevich in *The Overcoat*. He refuses to believe that the world in which he lives is unjust and brutal, and that he and other clerks may be doomed to lives never relieved of humiliation and poverty. He is particularly scandalized by scenes in which Akaky's colleagues throw pieces of paper on his head and protest, not against his own life, but against Gogol. Gogol should have had Akaky transferred by his superior, promoted, given a raise, Makar argues, "so that, you see, evil would be punished, virtue triumph, and his fellow clerks would remain empty-handed. That's how I'd do it." [6]

Makar's problem, a cardinal difference between him and some of Dostoevsky's later heroes, is that while his life is wretched, his aspirations frustrated, and his beloved Varenka oppressed, he refuses to push his criticism beyond very narrow limits. He is reluctant to draw the conclusions which the facts warrant—that good people cannot secure justice and are defeated by life, highly placed personages are callous and cruel, injustice triumphs not as an exception but as the norm, innocence perishes.

Makar refuses the thought that there may be no recourse to any higher court of appeal. He has a permanent psychological set toward expectation of human kindness. He calls attention to his troubles, but he is a Pangloss who only occasionally comes close to the breaking point. He boasts of his loyalty—of never having broken regulations or been impertinent. Public order is sacred to him. Only in his last letter, after Varenka has consented to marry Bykov and is leaving Petersburg for his steppe estate, is Makar distraught, semi-incoherent, in despair. Makar is an unreform-minded unprotester. He is shaken by injustice and shocked mainly by becoming aware himself that he is shocked. He is the humiliated man in the process of becoming socially conscious despite himself. The book is the story of the discovery of one's own resentments and of the effort to combat them. Makar's motivations and presuppositions about society and life are all traditional and Christian, not theoretical or revolutionary.

The House of the Dead (1861), describing with only small changes Dostoevsky's experience in a Siberian prison, brings to light his fascination with two subjects: the psychology of "naked" man in an extreme situation, and the sense of class distinction between peasants and educated prisoners. The book is permeated by Dostoevsky's concern with solidarity (the sense of kinship, of belonging, or being on the same footing as others—understood by everyone and known to everyone), with the sense of community based on belonging to a common, peasant humanity, and with its opposites—isolation, aloofness, and humiliation.

The peasants' sense of belonging to a community, Dostoevsky observes, gives them a sense of security. His discovery of this was one of his central experiences in his stay in Siberia and had a lasting effect on his later outlook, as expressed in his fiction and journalistic writings.

A shattering experience was the brutality and physical torture of prison life, well known to every reader of *The House of the Dead;* but an element insufficiently noticed is Dostoevsky's awareness of class separations. Dostoevsky quotes in a letter describing his Siberian experiences the abuse heaped on "gentlemen" like himself by one of his peasant companions in misery, who reproached them: "You gentlemen, you iron beaks used to peck us to death. Formerly you were the masters—you tormented the people; now our brethren have become lower than last." [7]

"This was the theme which they played upon for four years," Dostoevsky wrote in the same letter. He also analyzed the pleasurableness—to the gentleman—"of administering floggings": "a thrill at once sweet and painful." "There are people who are like tigers thirsting for blood." He speaks of "this power, this unlimited mastery of the body, blood, and soul of a fellow man" and says, "tyranny is a habit. It may develop, and it does develop at last, into a disease." [8]

Dostoevsky links his psychological insight with his sociological criticism:

> The possibility of such depotism has a perverting influence on the whole of society: such power is a temptation. Society which looks indifferently on such a phenomenon is already contaminated to its

very foundations. In short, the right of corporal punishment given to one man over another is one of the sores of social life, one of the strongest forces destructive of every germ, of every effort in society towards civil feeling, and a sufficient cause for its inevitable dissolution. . . . Every manufacturer, every capitalist, must feel an agreeable thrill in the thought that his workman with all his family is sometimes entirely dependent on him. . . . The characteristics of the torturer exist in embryo in almost every man of today.[9]

Dostoevsky did not again speak out so unequivocally, and in such general, diagnostic terms. But his works became more powerful for their subsequent decrease of explicitness and one-sidedness and for their change of direction toward ambivalence and inner struggle. The two early works we have noticed, *Poor Folk* and *The House of the Dead*, mark two unilinear overt expressions of discontent. Makar, who is far from identical with Dostoevsky, is a yea sayer, to whom the thinking of Positive Thoughts about the universe and his hierarchical society is a necessity. Dissatisfaction arises in him as a result of several experiences which are difficult, perhaps impossible, for him to deny.

In *The House of the Dead*, on the other hand, the narrator is very close, perhaps identical with, the author's voice. Despite the violent experiences which emotionally tear him apart, he is nevertheless of one mind: he analyzes rationally, and he speaks his conclusions clearly, unequivocally; he does not change his views. He is the clear-headed, intellectual, unified consciousness—praising, rejecting, warning. In Makar's epistolary novel the dissonant, secondary voice (of disturbance) comes to be heard only seldom, sporadically. It ruffles the surface and leaves us, in his last letter, as pure lament, a wailing.

A far more complex picture exists in Dostoevsky's later writings. Expressions of dissatisfaction become numerous, varied, and powerful.

Let us first distinguish from all other spokesmen of discontent those characters, like Lebezyatnikov, whom we have already quoted, and Rakitin, who turn against traditional social values and forms, but from whom Dostoevsky disassociates himself—whom he even satirizes. They are nihilists, or rationalists, self-proclaimed Westernizing liberals and radicals. In the terms of Daniel Lerner and other contemporary American historians and sociologists, they are "modernizers," dissidents from a traditional society—or, more accurately, parodies on "modernizers." Dostoevsky makes Lebezyatnikov expose himself:

"What is there so shameful and contemptible in, let us say, cesspools?" he says; "I'd be the first to be ready to clean out any cesspool you like. . . . It's simply work, honorable work, work useful to society, which is as good as any other work, and indeed it is of a much higher level than say the work of a Raphael or a Pushkin, because it is more useful . . ."

"And more honorable?"

"What do you mean more honorable? I don't understand such expressions in the sense of a definition of human activities. 'More honorable,' 'more high-minded,' all that is sheer nonsense, absurdities, obsolete clichés, which I flatly reject. Everything that is useful to mankind is honorable. I only understand one word—useful. You can titter as much as you like, but that's true." [10]

Mitya Karamazov says about Rakitin: "Rakitin means to go to Petersburg. There he'll go in for criticism of a progressive tendency. . . ." Rakitin is a parody on Ivan's and Dmitri's "All things are lawful." As he puts it:

"Didn't you know? A clever man can do what he likes. A clever man knows his way about, but you've put your foot in it, committing a murder, and now you are rotting in prison." [11]

The two brothers, Mitya and Alyosha, say like a refrain that Rakitin would not understand, and Rakitin does not understand.

However, the point about Lebezyatnikov, Luzhin, and Rakitin and their like is not that they are wrong because they are radicals and rebels. They are laughable because they are hypocritical and shallow. Their discontent is paltry and weak as well as misguided and misdirected. The chief deniers and questioners in Dostoevsky surpass the petty, parodied ones. Just as Lebezyatnikov thought he outdid Dobrolyubov and Chernyshevsky in denying more, so in fact Mitya and Ivan—and Raskolnikov—far surpass, in Dostoevsky's opinion, Rakitin and Lebezyatnikov, for their dissatisfaction is a far more deeply felt one. The intensity of their discontent is one of its main features. Dostoevsky wrote about Ivan's atheism:

Ivan Fedorovich is profound, not one of your modern atheists, demonstrating in his disbelief merely the narrowness of his conception of the world and the obtuseness of his own stupid abilities. . . . The villains teased me for my ignorance and reactionary belief in God. These thickheads did not dream of such a powerful negation of God as that put in the Inquisitor and the preceding chapter, to which the whole novel serves as answer. . . . Their stupid natures did not dream of such a powerful negation as I have lived through. [12]

The second important feature of Dostoevsky's champion malcontents, so to speak, is their inner division. They are torn. Unlike the narrator of *The House of the Dead*, who knows his own mind, Ivan

Karamazov and Raskolnikov are split. They vacillate; they change their minds often; they see the force of arguments on both, or even on several, sides. It is this which I consider the cardinal feature of Dostoevsky's mature, later works and the chief factor in setting their characteristic form, from the *Notes from the Underground* (1864) to *The Brothers Karamazov*. It permeates every cell of them; it constitutes the structure of the whole, and of the constituent parts. The narrator in *The House of the Dead* is devoid of inner conflict. Compare the well-known beginning of the *Notes from the Underground:*

> "I am a sick man; I am a spiteful man. I am an unattractive man. I believe there is something wrong with my liver. But I do not understand my sickness and do not really know whether there is anything really wrong with me." [13]

And so forth: one turn after another, a constant dialectic *within himself:* disagreement with what he has just said, backtracking—and the same is true of his relationship with the reader.

The Underground Man puts his hooks into the reader, and a drama develops in the changing relationships between the two, full of twists and surprises. Rejection in the Underground Man combines with spite, injured pride, craving for freedom, self-assertion. He rebels against "the stone wall"—"the laws of nature, the conclusions of natural science, mathematics." He is as full of contradictions as his relationship with the reader is full of turns, leaps, and jumps. He is dissatisfied with his age, with eternal conditions of human life, and above all, perhaps, with himself. Far from being in a condition of stability, equilibrium, in which we found the narrator of *The House of the Dead*, the Man from the Underground is in constant motion, leaping from one extreme intellectual or psychological position to another. He attacks reason, propounds volition and suffering. "Suffering is doubt, it is negation"—"man will never renounce real suffering, that is to say, destruction and chaos." We have here an opponent of the rationalism and progressiveness of his age who overtly preaches negation—a denier who practices denial; the form of his sermon is backtracking, clawing, at his audience, his age, himself.

The Underground Man—self-designated as anti-hero—has two direct descendants: the "Ridiculous Man" and the pawnbroker in the story *Gentle Spirit* (1876). The pawnbroker denies several things: first, the code of honor which demands that he fight a duel because someone has insulted a fellow officer in his regiment. He resigns and becomes a pawnbroker—defying the contempt felt for money-lending and pawnbroking. He goes beyond this point in his "plan": he deliberately shows himself in a bad light toward his young wife, since he wants her to grasp his intentions, to admire his greatness and goodness despite appearances to the contrary and without his stooping to praise or even explain himself. He deliberately refrains, then, from normal communication and self-revelation with his wife. He repudiates the social expectations of an honorable occupation and the personal demands for outgoingness, meeting someone else halfway. His motive is pride and injured self-esteem—on the familiar Dostoevskian principle: If I am humiliated, very well, I shall humiliate myself deliberately, of my own will, still further; "if it has to be shame, then let it be shame."

His wife asks him: "Are you revenging yourself on society?" He answers "half-jokingly, half-mysteriously" with Goethe's Mephistopheles' words: "I am part of that power which still doeth good, though scheming ill." [14] What he is really doing is assuming the guise of doing ill, wishing to be recognized as intending ultimate good. His "system," as he calls it, together with what we should call the "treatment" he puts his wife through, leads to her complete withdrawal from him, and after his reversal, to her suicide.

The final effect of it all is to make him feel how alone people are, living in silence, apart from each other.

The narrative form of this story is similar to the *Notes from the Underground:* a confused, bewildered succession of thoughts in the first person—a turbulent confession. Such is also the opening part of *The Dream of the Ridiculous Man* (1877)—the confession of the completely alienated person, who has already decided to kill himself, with the only remaining question being to decide when to do it. He, too, felt ridiculous, not liked, laughed at, absurd.

The Ridiculous Man is utterly indifferent to all. But then, an apparently trivial incident occurs which sets in motion a change in him. When a little girl in the street asks for his help, he fails to respond and then *feels sorry* for her. If he is indifferent to everything anyway and is about to kill himself, shouldn't he be still more indifferent now? Why did he feel sorry for her? He falls asleep, and the tiny kernel of attachment to life, the sole remaining bond—a thread of pity for a little girl whom he did not help—is the seed out of which comes his tremendous dream. "I feel sorry, therefore I am." He is transported to another planet where "children of the sun," beautiful and innocent, on ground unstained by the Fall, show him an existence without desire, at peace with themselves, unstriving, loving nature, communing even with the stars, without any cruelty.

In his dream, he gradually corrupts them by teaching them isolation, the concept of honor, separation, personality, mine and thine—a catalogue of Dostoevskian bugaboos—until they come to know sorrow, thirst for suffering, crimes; and the Ridiculous Man wakes up, back on earth, now completely, passionately reattached to it, dedicated to preaching that "people can be happy and beautiful without losing their ability to live on earth," persuading people to "establish a heaven on earth."

The significant thing about the second part of the story is that it is a vision similar to the medieval convention—like the *House of Fame.*

Dissatisfaction, then, which is serious, unlike Lebezyatnikov's which was only laughable, in this story calls for the literary form of a confession, a gurgling, stumbling first-person narration, full of stops, contradictions, with inner struggle in every component part of it. The answer to it—absent in both the *Notes from the Underground* and the *Gentle Spirit*—calls for the form of a vision, complete with a prelapsarian Utopian population. Only a leap to the ecstatic visionary joy of another planet is powerful enough to outweigh, cancel, and convert the powerful negation of the first part of the work. (An interesting sidelight is that as early as the draft of *Notes from the Underground,* Dostoevsky wrote a section in which the Underground Man was to see a Vision of Christ, which, it seems, was to have been the positive counterpart. For reasons of censorship, the section was deleted. The draft has not been preserved.)

After looking at the trinity of underground malcontents, it may be useful to examine the other constellations of Dostoevsky's heroes, the great personages of his large novels: Raskolnikov, Ivan and Dmitri Karamazov, Svidrigaylov, Stavrogin, Peter Verkhovensky.

The first three, Raskolnikov and the two Karamazovs, especially Ivan, are of course negators *par excellence,* in the grand style. Raskolnikov rejects traditional morality and "steps across" the conventional idea of what is crime, transgressing the law—religious, social, and moral—prohibiting murder. To show the wrongness of it, Dostoevsky works out the results of Raskolnikov's rejection: cut off from the sources of life, he dries out; and the antithesis, life itself, is dramatized by Dostoevsky, again, through a whole collage of visions: the Biblical story of the resurrection of Lazarus, the symbolism of water, vegetation and sunshine, the Siberian river, Easter, spring—and the love of Sonya.

It is these men, alongside the others who collectively help clarify Dostoevsky's central ideas, who are the rebels proclaiming the death of God, after which "everything is permitted" and Man-God comes into existence. In *Crime and Punishment* (1866), the drama (the oscillation from pole to pole, the tension between opposites) which in the Underground Man went on within one character's mental life now has expanded into sweeping across, committing murder, rejecting traditional ways of feeling and hence experiencing death in life—and his other antithetical self. Each of his selves is supported from the outside, attracted, and reflected by various other recollections, stories, objects, characters. The inner conflict of the rejector is half-externalized. In *The Brothers Karamazov*, the process has gone further. The struggle has expanded into strife between, and counterposing of, two whole sides, or world parties. A book within the novel is called "Pro and Contra." Ivan is split within himself; the division is paralleled by struggles within, and for, the children (Kolya, Ilyusha), within Zossima as a young man, Zossima's mysterious visitor, and Alyosha, with the entire novel being divided into antithetical diptychs: for instance, the sixth book, "The Russian Monk," replying to the fifth, "Pro and Contra." The action of the entire novel is necessary to see the full working out of the conflict.

What are the dominant dissatisfactions in these mature works of Dostoevsky, and what are the forms in which they are expressed? Ivan Karamazov, to take only one of the characters, repudiates the injustice of the world: innocent suffering, as exemplified in children. His is moral, cosmic repudiation. Its consequences are far-reaching: they lead to the "returning of the ticket"; in Ivan's view, the injustices are impossible to compensate for. They lead to a cancellation of traditional moral standards: "All is permitted."

When we turn our view from Ivan to other characters—especially the most positive ones, Alyosha, Zossima, and Myshkin—or to the objective events narrated in *The Possessed*, we find the dissatisfaction a ubiquitous one: everywhere there is evil and callousness; society is disintegrating, amidst arson, pretention, falsehood; indeed, it is "not a very nice town at all" [15] in which we are living. Dostoevsky's image of the 19th-century world is dark. His characters do not propose a gradual amelioration but appear to hope for a still further worsening which will eventually lead to a cataclysm. Only through still more evil, followed by a conflagration, will a cleansing, a rebirth, come about.

What is the characteristic literary form of Dostoevskian discontent? On a medium scale in *The Idiot* and *The Possessed*, on a grander, broader, and looser scale in *The Brothers Karamazov*, it is first the compilation of "anecdotes"—stories, examples, component parts—almost similar to our contemporary collages (newspaper clippings included), distributed among events in which the characters participate. They include the story of an onion in *The Brothers Karamazov*, the reminiscences of Zossima about his brother and his youth, tales told by the women coming to Zossima for advice—even Ivan's poem of the Grand Inquisitor, and his vision of the devil, the dream of Mitya of the "babe," examples of Turkish atrocities, Alyosha's vision of Cana, and many others. The expression of dissatisfaction thereby acquires great breadth: it is recurrent and general.

Secondly, the structure gains intensity through Dostoevsky's supplying us with great peaks, not only of rejection (and dejection)—such as Ivan's speeches—but also of the opposite: ecstatic joy. The raptures and loves of Alyosha, Dmitri, and Zossima balance and outweigh the agonies of Ivan; the joys of Shatov partly balance the despair of Kirilov and Stavrogin; Raskolnikov's gladness by his Siberian river contrasts with his earlier moments of gloom; Myshkin's flow of love, with the tinniness and speciousness of Petersburg and Pavlovsk life in *The Idiot*. In this regard—the interplay of agony and ecstasy—the works of Tolstoy, which in other respects have a different structure, are similar.

I suggest, then, that in the major novels of Dostoevsky, there are two basic forms of dissatisfaction—the mosaic of interpolated stories, or, to change the terminology, the collage of illustrative pictures, and the ecstasy of joy answering the outpourings of despondency and rejection.

Thus does Dostoevsky express his eagerness for cataclysm, the tension between denying and affirming—summed up in Lisa Khokhlakova's "Save me, I shall kill myself because I loathe everything" [16] on one hand, and in Zossima's brother's "Don't cry, mother, life is paradise and we are all in paradise" on the other. Catastrophe plus Vision are Dostoevsky's means. The world in which the Possessed are staging their revolt is indeed possessed in his view; there are devils in it which must be exorcised, not by the superficial deniers, not by nihilists—it is a hell which must be harrowed. The forms of inner conflict plus vision, in the Underground Man category of works, and of the collage of stories plus catastrophe versus vision (or Agony versus Ecstasy) in the others indicate the situation and the remedy.

In Tolstoy, discontented characters are as important as in Dostoevsky, but the objects and causes of their dissatisfaction are different. In addition, the narrator is often himself the chief voice of discontent. If in Dostoevsky the two groups of heroes are central—the Underground Man, the Ridiculous Man, and the pawnbroker on one hand, and Raskolnikov and Ivan Karamazov on the other—then in

Tolstoy there is but one line of such characters, running from Olenin in *The Cossacks,* in 1863, through Pierre in *War and Peace* and Levin in *Anna Karenina,* accompanied by a whole line of others, to Nekhlyudov in *The Resurrection;* and behind them, as their background, is the narrator with his important tones and techniques of speaking.

The trilogy *Childhood-Youth-Adolescence* (1852–57) in some ways parallels the place of *Poor Folk* in Dostoevsky's literary development. Irtenyev, Olenin, Pierre, Levin, and Nekhlyudov, different as they are, have in common that they are all, in different ways, seekers. They go along a certain line, searching for a goal—then abandon their achieved resting point and start again. One crisis stands out in their quester's progress. Life becomes meaningless; usually the facing of the fact of death throws the characters completely out of kilter. They are paralyzed; everything is purposeless, senseless.

In the *Childhood* trilogy, we have something similar if we merely outline or abstract the line of the interaction of the hero and his environment and his attitudes—his degree of acceptance (assimilation) versus his rejection (alienation)—but the tone, the atmosphere are quite different from that of the later works. Although the boy keeps growing up and there are several stages when he outgrows his milieu and his way of being part of it, he then shifts into an "older" stage, and the process of first adjustment, happiness, and then outgrowing repeats itself. The incidents which are the causes (or more accurately, the symptoms, indices) of his disillusionment and change are his encounters with death and grief, his discovery that other people do not know him and his family and that their consciousness is centered elsewhere, moving to the city, entering the university, becoming acquainted with students of a lower social class, failing examinations.

While there are these moments of the shattering of his belonging to his environment, however, the tone of the trilogy (except for the last few pages) is not dissatisfied or negative but the very opposite. It is an idyllic tone, and the trilogy is an idyllic work. Tolstoy makes it quite clear that he considers it natural and proper for a boy to outgrow the successive stages of his development, like a snake outgrowing and shedding his skin. Tolstoy considers the hero to be quite at home and acting naturally within each static state, and also within each period of learning and change. Both while he is in each stage of harmony and in disrupting it, he is doing what he ought to do. Hence the apparent paradox of an idyllic tone in a work of successive revolts—not a contradiction at all if one views both as quite natural.

Tolstoy presents, in the *Childhood* trilogy, a character entirely harmonized in a succession of Ideal Worlds, moving through stages of desirable disintegration to the next, again ideal, stage. This is the structural form in which, within the idyllic world of *Childhood*, we have a succession of dissatisfactions and failures.

An interesting contrast is *Hadji Murad*, Tolstoy's marvelous short novel written at the very end of his life (1901). There we find some parallels to *Childhood*. The main characters again are completely at home, accepting, at harmony with their environment. The Czar feels perfectly content in his milieu. Hadji accepts unquestioningly the standards of his nation and culture, as do Vorontsov in his aristo-cratic-military environment, the peasants within theirs, and all the ranks, civilian and military, Russian and Chechen, in theirs. Yet the effect (dominant tone) and structure are entirely different from *Child-hood*. This is due to the narrator and to the juxtaposition and anti-thetical positioning of the various scenes and of the two halves of the work—the Russian and the mountaineer. The Czar may be at home in his milieu, but the narrator mercilessly exposes his cruelty; the high officers are quite content, but the narrator reveals their hypocrisy, falseness, and stupidity. We have here a basic rejection of the atti-tudes of the chief Russian characters. They are self-satisfied and unquestioning; the narrator exposes them. The dissatisfaction is his. He is against them, against their mores, ways of thinking. In at-tacking them, he makes use also of the ancient device of "seeing through alien eyes." Hadji Murad moves amidst Russian society as an outsider—like the many 18th-century Chinese or Persian charac-ters in European literatures—and Tolstoy exploits the possibilities of ridiculing Russian ways by describing them as a freshly viewing alien observer, uncontaminated in his perception and interpretation by con-ventions, might see them.

If the structure of *Childhood* can be likened to a railroad train—linearly arranged scenes (in all of which Irtenev participates and grows up, the basic *Bildungsroman* form)—the narrative structure of *Hadji Murad* might be called a pyramidal peep-show mosaic, if that is not too ponderous a term. Tolstoy describes a slice of life among soldiers close to the front lines as one element in the mosaic. Then a message from them is sent to the next higher echelon, and he gives us a slice of life on that level, with the news about Hadji Murad and the discussion of it being only part of the action. We are given what precedes and follows—the entire context, with the affair of Hadji Murad only one of several focal points. The same procedure is re-peated until we reach the top of the pyramid, the Czar's day, in which Hadji plays only a very small part. Mainly we see the Czar at a ball, passing on various measures, revealing his ignorance, vanity, haste, and inhumanity. Thus as in a peep show, the reader is given successive detailed pictures, scenes, moving up and down the social pyramid of military and political power of Czarist Russia. The connecting thread is the decision about what to do with Hadji Murad and his sons, but in many of the scenes Hadji does not participate personally; he is only a subject of conversation and decision-making.

The vertical dimension—the change from lowly life, the peasant line-soldier, to the highest Czarist court—is emphasized strongly.

The joys of riding, being manly, brave, just, and young are also vigorously conveyed by Tolstoy, but the dominant effect is the protest against things as they are—against the power structure, the political and military establishment, and, under it all, against culture, against civilization.

Between these two works, the early *Childhood* and the late *Hadji Murad*, comes the series of Tolstoy's most important dissatisfied characters and narrators.

Pierre and Levin both pass through periods of complete alienation—being overwhelmed by the meaninglessness of existence. They come to a halt—paralyzed, basically dissatisfied with all life. Why live? What is the use of anything? They return to meaningful existence in various ways and find their high points in ecstatic moments, when intellection is weakened or disappears and the body moves rhythmically and almost independently of the mind (Levin mowing), or in moments of suffusion with love and perception of the unity of the natural order of things—including death, procreation, and the succession of generations, based on close family life. All this is too well known to need elaboration. Learning from the example of the most unalienated, completely assimilated man, Platon Karataev, Pierre is also reintegrated, his mood and spirit elevated.

Shorter works supply us with many examples supporting the two major characters, Pierre and Levin. The first difference between Dostoevskian dissatisfaction and these heroes' is that in Tolstoy the fact of death as the main jolt replaces Dostoevsky's characters' rebellion against injustice and God's order—with their attendant aspiration to become a Man–God who steps across.

There are several well-known passages describing the mental paralysis which is the first stage of dissatisfaction, or alienation, in Tolstoy's work, in his fiction as well as in his "confessions." Let us remind ourselves of only one—from the *Memoirs of a Madman* (1884):

> I took a pillow and lay down on the sofa. . . . I must have fallen
> asleep, for when I awoke I found myself alone in the room and it was
> dark. I was again as wide awake as I had been in the chaise. I felt

that to sleep would be quite impossible. "Why have I come here? Where am I betaking myself? Why and whither am I escaping? I am running away from something dreadful and cannot escape it. I am always with myself and it is I who am my tormentor. Here I am, the whole of me. Neither the Penza nor any other property will add anything to or take anything from me. And it is myself I am weary of and find intolerable and a torment. I want to fall asleep and forget myself and cannot. I cannot get away from myself!"

I went out into the passage. Sergey was sleeping on a narrow bench with one arm hanging down but he was sleeping peacefully and the man with the spot was also asleep. I had gone out into the corridor thinking to escape from what tormented me. But IT had come out with me and cast a gloom over everything. I felt just as filled with horror or even more so.

"But what folly this is!" I said to myself. "Why am I depressed? What am I afraid of?"

"Me," answered the voice of Death, inaudibly. "I am here."

A cold shudder ran down my back. Yes! Death! It will come— here it is—and it ought not to be. Had I been actually facing death I could not have suffered as much as I did then. Then I should have been frightened. But now I was not frightened. I saw and felt the approach of death, and at the same time I felt that such a thing ought not to exist.

My whole being was conscious of the necessity and the right to live, and yet I felt that Death was being accomplished. And this inward conflict was terrible. I tried to throw off the horror. I found a brass candlestick, the candle of which had a long wick, and lighted it. The red glow of the candle and its size—little less than the candlestick itself—told me the same thing. Everything told me the same: "There is nothing in life. Death is the only real thing, and death ought not to exist." [17]

The madman describes his way out of the paralysis:

It began by my going to church. I stood there through the liturgy and prayed well, and listened and was touched. Then suddenly they brought me some consecrated bread: after that we went up to the Cross, and people began pushing one another. Then at the exit there were beggars. And it suddenly became clear to me that this ought not to be, and not only ought not to be but in reality was not. And if this was not, then neither was there either death or fear, and there was no longer the former tearing asunder within me and I no longer feared anything.

Then the light fully illumined me and I became what I now am. If there is nothing of all that—then it certainly does not exist within me. And there at the church door I gave away to the beggars all I had with me—thirty-six rubles—and went home on foot talking with the people.[18]

The alienation is brought on by the confronting of death, one's own or someone else's or death in general. It is overcome, if at all, through somebody's example: by a stepping out of the world—a voluntary *Entäusserung*, to use Hegel's word marking the distinction from *Entfremdung*—or a rejection of the conventional, the world of trading, power, and social distinction, and an immersion in a genuine life of unself-seeking. Simple physical contact, such as that with the peasant Gerasim in Ivan Ilych's last hour, is the means and the goal.

The narrator also plays a very important role in conveying dissatisfaction in Tolstoy. Thus in *The Death of Ivan Ilych* (1886), Ivan is perfectly at home in his world, living conventionally, assimilatedly, studying, marrying, working, climbing the ladder of promotion, buying a house, furnishing it, quite like all others in his social group, unquestioningly, totally. Only toward the end, through his deadly disease, does he become alienated; he comes to see his whole life as having been false; he rejects it all, just before his death—except for a few things: physical contact with a simple, sympathetic human being, and love. The result is a scream and an ecstasy. Yet even earlier, the narrator had seen it all and showed it to the reader—from as rejecting a position as the latest, dying Ivan Ilych's. His satirical passages make this quite clear:

> Ivan Ilych's life had been most simple and most ordinary and therefore most terrible.[19]
>
> In the province he had an affair with a lady who made advances to the elegant young lawyer, and there was also a milliner; and there were carousals with aides-de-camp who visited the district, and after-supper visits to a certain outlying street of doubtful reputation; and there was too some obsequiousness to his chief and even to his chief's wife, but all this was done with such a tone of good breeding that no hard names could be applied to it. It all came under the heading of the French saying: "Il faut que jeunesse se passe." It was all done with clean hands, in clean linen, with French phrases, and above all, among people of the best society and consequently with the approval of people of rank.[20]
>
> He got up at nine, drank his coffee, read the paper, and then put on his undress uniform and went to the law courts. There the harness in which he worked had already been stretched to fit him and he donned it without a hitch: petitioners, inquiries at the chancery, the chancery itself, and the sittings public and administrative. In all this the thing was to exclude everything fresh and vital, which always disturbs the regular course of official business, and to admit only

official relations with people and then only on official grounds. . . .[21]

As soon as the official relations ended, so did everything else. Ivan Ilych possessed this capacity to separate his real life from the official side of affairs and not mix the two, in the highest degree, and by long practice and natural aptitude had brought it to such a pitch that sometimes, in the manner of a virtuoso, he would even allow himself to let the human and official relations mingle. He let himself do this just because he felt that he could at any time he chose resume the strictly official attitude again and drop the human relation.[22]

We find similar passages throughout *War and Peace, Anna Karenina,* and particularly—perhaps excessively—in *The Resurrection* (1899). They provide a background of insistent negativity. It is this continual undertone which more than anything else is responsible for Tolstoy's having been called *netovshchik*—from *ne-to,* not so, no— the nay sayer, the denier, the negative thinker. He has a sure eye for what is false in society. His target is not God's injustice or the injustice of the universe; it is the falseness of society. His works are full of passages in which the narrator, sometimes in the minutest detail, in many linguistic ways, criticizes, exposes, attacks. All his life, Tolstoy rejected one thing, moved on to something else, and rejected that. Even in literary art, his diaries for his last years (when he was in his eighties) show that he was dissatisfied with those forms of the novel which he had used, and he sought for new ways of describing and narrating.

This is the fundamental underlying form of his expression of discontent, against which he places the antithetical scenes of his questing characters' periods of paralysis followed by ecstatic insight into a nonrational harmony.

The forms of discontent of other Russian writers are quite different. Gogol and Lermontov are the two fathers of the Russian 19th century's literary expressions of dissatisfaction; some authors are outside of it altogether—for example, Aksakov, with his idyllic work about the days before the flood. We have a similar idyllic world in some of Goncharov, as in the Dream of Oblomov, while the bulk of his writings express discontent with different things, expressed by other means.

As I suggested at the start, it might be fruitful to contrast and compare Balzac, Flaubert, and others with Russian 19th-century writers— as well as periods of outstanding literary disaffection in other centuries, other countries—to see whether this theme leads to any significant conclusions about Western literature as a whole. We might find that there are other characteristic forms, structural organizations, allied to expressions of acute dissatisfactions, and be helped to under-

stand a little better some aspects of Civilization and Its Discontents—
and means of countering them—in our own days.

NOTES

1. *The Vintage Turgenev*, trans. Harry Stevens (New York, 1960), *I*, 207–208. The original Russian text may be found in I. S. Turgenev, *Sobranie Sochineniy v desyati tomakh* (Moscow, 1961), *III*, 159.

2. Trans. David Magarshack, p. 382. Original Russian is in F. M. Dostoevsky, *Sobranie Sochineniy v desyati tomakh* (Moscow, 1957), *V*, 383.

3. *Ibid.*, p. 382; Russian text: p. 383.

4. *Ibid.*, p. 383; Russian text: p. 384.

5. This point is developed in application to contemporary drama in Anthony Caputi, "The Shallows of Modern Serious Drama," *Modern Drama*, 4 (1961), 111–116.

6. Translated by George Gibian from F. M. Dostoevsky, *Sobranie Sochineniy, I*, 147.

7. Translated by George Gibian from a letter of February 22, 1854, from Omsk, to his brother Michael. F. M. Dostoevsky, *Pisma* (Moscow, 1928), *I*, 135–136.

8. *The House of the Dead*, trans. Constance Garnett (New York, 1959), p. 240. The Russian text is in F. M. Dostoevsky, *Sobranie Sochineniy, III*, 595.

9. *Ibid.*, p. 241; Russian text: pp. 595–596.

10. *Crime and Punishment*, p. 385; Russian text: *V*, 386.

11. *The Brothers Karamazov*, trans. Constance Garnett (New York, 1945), p. 717; F. M. Dostoevsky, *Sobranie Sochineniy, X*, 102.

12. Adapted from the quotation in Ernest Simmons, *Dostoevsky: The Making of a Novelist* (New York, 1962), p. 364.

13. Translated by George Gibian from F. M. Dostoevsky, *Sobranie Sochineniy, IV*, 133.

14. Translated by George Gibian, *ibid., X*, 384.

15. Translated by George Gibian from F. M. Dostoevsky, *Sobranie Sochineniy, IX*, 260.

16. Translated by George Gibian from F. M. Dostoevsky, *Sobranie Sochineniy, X*, 97.

17. *Ivan Ilych and Hadji Murad*, trans. Louise and Aylmer Maude (London, 1951), pp. 215–217. For the original, see L. N. Tolstoy, *Sobranie Sochineniy v dvadtsati tomakh* (Moscow, 1964), *XII*, 49–50.

18. *Ibid.*, p. 225; Russian text: pp. 55–56.

19. *Ibid.*, p. 11; Russian text: p. 65.

20. *Ibid.*, p. 14; Russian text: p. 68.

21. *Ibid.*, p. 27; Russian text: pp. 78–79.

22. *Ibid.*, p. 28; Russian text: p. 79.

Theodore Ziolkowski

The Crisis of the Thirty-Year-Old in
Modern Fiction:
Toward a Phenomenology of the Novel

Kafka's *Der Prozeß* begins with the awakening of its hero on the morning of his thirtieth birthday and ends, a year later, with his murder on the eve of his thirty-first birthday. At first glance this fact might seem to be no more than one of those singular but otherwise useless bits of literary trivia that are simultaneously the delight of pedantic professors and the despair of candidates for a degree in literature. For apart from the structural balance that it lends to the novel, the precise information regarding the hero's age does not seem to be particularly noteworthy. Critics generally point to the author's own crisis in his thirtieth year, thus obviating further discussion of the matter. Certainly Kafka's biography plays a role in the characterization of his hero which should not be overlooked: It is surely no accident that Josef K. is the same age as Kafka was when he wrote his novel. But if we look around further in the fiction of the times, there emerges a nagging suspicion that the age of the hero perhaps warrants more attention in some broader connection. For the important novels of our century are positively teeming with thirty-year-old heroes. When Franz Biberkopf is released from Tegel Prison in Alfred Döblin's *Berlin Alexanderplatz,* he is explicitly "a man at the beginning of his thirties." The three protagonists of Hermann Broch's trilogy *Die Schlafwandler*—Pasenow, Esch, and Hugenau—are all thirty in the volumes devoted respectively to each. Antoine Roquentin, who suffers from intolerable attacks of *nausée* in Sartre's novel, is a thirty-year-old, as are Meursault, the "stranger" of Albert Camus, and the little curate of Ambricourt in Georges Bernanos' *Journal d'un curé de campagne.* Malte Laurids Brigge is only twenty-eight at the beginning of Rilke's "prose book," but he too is in his thirtieth year during the greater part of his Parisian sojourn. And—to take a contemporary example—Oskar Matzerath concludes the memoirs of his Tin Drum days expressly on his thirtieth birthday.

Now, it is striking that the age of the hero is even mentioned—and in most of these cases explicitly emphasized. For often the precise age of the hero plays no role in novels and can only be calculated roughly from various hints in the text. So the simple verification of this similarity in age leads us to certain questions. For instance, is the age thirty in itself remarkable in the tradition of the novel? Going beyond literature, does the thirtieth year have any generally recognized typological significance that is relevant in this connection? Above all: Can we determine, despite all undeniable variety of theme, certain similarities among these novels that permit us to assume a common underlying attitude or structure? In other words: Is it possible to speak of a Novel of the Thirty-Year-Old that bridges, say, the philosophical abyss between the Catholicism of Bernanos and the atheism of Camus or Sartre? That affords a literary link between the speculative flights of Broch, the lyrical tone of Rilke, and the black humor of Günter Grass? Or are we dealing merely with a curious, but otherwise insignificant, coincidence?

I

The first question can be answered easily. If we consider some of the best-known fictional heroes of the 18th and 19th centuries, we soon realize that most of them share the sentiments of Schiller's Don Carlos, who cried out in despair: "Dreiundzwanzig Jahre,/ Und nichts für die Unsterblichkeit getan!"—which, by the way, is probably an echo of Alexander the Great, who according to a well-known legend was disconsolate because at twenty-three he had not yet conquered the world. Indeed, in the representative novels of the period, it turns out that very few heroes reach the relatively ripe old age of thirty. Novalis' Heinrich von Ofterdingen is twenty years old. Tieck introduces William Lovell as "a lively cheerful youth," and although his lively cheerfulness is of no great duration, he still doesn't become much older in the course of his three-year escapade. The standing epithet for Franz Sternbald is "young," and Graf Friedrich, who has just left the university, is scarcely older than Eichendorff himself when he wrote *Ahnung und Gegenwart*: namely, twenty-two. The Chevalier des Grieux has romped through the whole gamut of passions with Manon Lescaut—before his twenty-second year! Tom Jones' comic and tumultuous misadventures land him in the lap of wedded bliss before he becomes twenty-one. Stendhal's Julien Sorel and Balzac's Eugène de Rastignac, like Voltaire's Candide or Chateaubriand's René, are all in their early twenties.

In comparison with the blush of such tender youthfulness the protagonists of Jean Paul's *Flegeljahre*, Goethe's *Lehrjahre*, Benjamin Constant's *Adolphe* or Gottfried Keller's *Der Grüne Heinrich* strike us as creaking old-timers. Walt and Vult, namely, are twenty-four; Wilhelm Meister and Adolphe, at the end of their fictional careers, reach their twenty-sixth year, as does Heinrich Lee soon after his return to his home in Switzerland. In these novels, all of which conclude with the integration of the hero into the existing social structure, we find an exemplary confirmation of Hillaire Belloc's *Cautionary Tale* of Lord Lundy:

> It happened to Lord Lundy then,
> As happens to so many men:
> Towards the age of twenty-six
> They shoved him into politics.

It is hardly necessary to cite further examples because others would merely confirm the tendency we have already noted: In comparison with the typical hero of most older novels, the modern thirty-year-old displays a pronounced shift in age.[1] Now, if we take into consideration the fact that the tradition of youthful heroes is still vigorous in our own times—some critics have spoken of the "primacy of adolescence" in the 20th century,[2] and one needs only to think of Proust, Mauriac, Salinger, Golding, Böll, or Hesse to see how true it is—then the thirty-year-old hero distinguishes himself from the dominant fictional trend even within modern literature.

We can approach this anomaly most easily perhaps if we glance for a moment at some representative views regarding human age. For centuries, the thirtieth year has been regarded as the high point of a process of development culminating in the integration of the individual into the particular order of the world accepted at a given time.[3] Aristotle, for instance, designates the years from thirty on as the intellectual and physical zenith of life, while Isidore of Seville characterizes the age from twenty-eight to forty-nine as *firmissima aetatum omnium*. For medieval Christianity the thirtieth year marks the beginning of the *aetas canonica*, because Christ went forth at that age to proclaim his teaching. Similarly, the numerological calculations of the Romans and Germanic tribes yield this age as the fulfillment of man's preparation: according to the seven-year stages of the Romans, it was the twenty-eighth year, and according to the system of the Germanic tribes, the thirtieth year, in which the youth fully assumed the responsibilities of adulthood—what the Romans called *aetas legitima*. Everywhere we look, we note the same phenomenon: the years around thirty symbolize a turning point in human development, the integration into society, the goal of all previous education and training. It is the age at which a man—like François Villon—reaches firm conclusions about life and sets up his testament:

> En l'an de mon trentiesme aage,
> Que toutes mes hontes j'eus beues,
> Ne du tout fol, ne du tout sage,
> Non obstant maintes peines eues. . . .
> *(Le Testament, 1)*

Such a conception of the thirtieth year is possible only within the framework of a stable world order. As long as the world and its order remain intact, the thirtieth year constitutes the threshold to a Golden Age, to what Balzac in *La Femme de trente ans* called "ce bel âge de trente ans," defining it further as the "sommité poétique de la vie des femmes." But to have reached this peak implies at the same time the end of the fictionally interesting, tumultuous life that characterizes the years of youth. As soon as a man submits to the existing order of things, life offers little more that is really worth the telling. His further destiny is virtually predetermined by the function that he voluntarily assumes within the social structure. As long as the faith of the author in the order of his world remains unshaken, nothing can happen that might jeopardize the harmony attained by the thirty-year-old. Even if the hero perishes in his youth, at the end he ultimately acknowledges—like William Lovell or the Chevalier des Grieux—that he has destroyed himself through his own deviations, his own "Zerrissenheit," his own "désordres": but the sacred order is maintained and affirmed. Within the framework of such a stable reality, then, it is primarily the period of youth that offers material for the novelist, whose attention focuses above all on the critical struggles of his hero's years of apprenticeship. Thus, in dozens of novels from Grimmelshausen to Fontane, from Fielding to Henry James, we encounter in endless variation the formula of trials and tribulations, of "Irrungen, Wirrungen." The crises of the heroes may shift in nature according to the respective religious, philosophical, or social modes of the times; but the typical structure inevitably ends with the awareness of the mature hero that the existent order of the world is good.

It is within this framework that we should also assess the many negative utterances according to which the thirtieth year is not so much a turning point as it is an end point. Thus Montaigne writes: "Among all the fine human deeds that have come to my attention, by far the most of them—today as well as centuries ago—were achieved before the age of thirty." [4]   Or François Mauriac in his *Journal d'un homme de trente ans:* "It's too late now—since the war is over—to hope for anything else but the satisfactions of work in peace and quiet with the few people who don't annoy you. Not that you don't regret those whom you have missed forever. But it's too late. At thirty, one no longer switches his course in life." [5]   (At a time when the splendid tributes celebrating Mauriac's eightieth birthday still ring in our ears, this lament doesn't sound quite so pathetic.) Or listen to Reginald, the hero of Saki's stories, who "in his wildest lapses into veracity never admits to being more than twenty-two": "To have reached thirty," Reginald remarks with the characteristic heartlessness of the *fin de siècle,* "is to have failed in life." [6]   We could go on and on: from Thoreau, who grumbled in *Walden:* "I have lived some thirty years on this planet, and I have yet to hear the first syllable of valuable or even earnest advice from my seniors"; to Lord Byron's eloquent lament at the end of the first canto of *Don Juan.* But the negative attitude is summed up effectively by a slogan current on the Berkeley campus during the recent excitement there: "Never trust anybody over thirty!" [7]   What is expressed in all these partly melancholy, partly contemptuous observations is simply the other side of the same coin. For they all share, along with the more positive utterances, the basic belief that the thirtieth year constitutes a threshold, an axis in life; the sole difference lies in the fact that this negative conception expects nothing from life beyond thirty but peace and quiet, indifference, or—at worst—even dishonesty and betrayal. Yet the role of the thirty-year-old is still viewed from a point within a stable world order, even if that order is regarded by youthful rebels as not particularly desirable. Their very rebellion demonstrates their belief in its existence.

But if the system of belief that has given meaning to the symbolic threshold threatens to collapse, then the thirtieth year takes on a wholly new significance. This awareness is implicit, for instance, in the words of the twenty-four-year-old Ivan Karamazov:

> I've been sitting here thinking to myself: that if I didn't believe in life, if I lost faith in the woman I love, lost faith in the order of things, were convinced in fact that everything is a disorderly, damnable, and perhaps devil-ridden chaos, if I were struck by every horror of man's disillusionment—still I should want to live and, having once tasted of the cup, I would not turn away from it till I had drained it! At thirty, though, I shall be sure to leave the cup, even if I've not emptied it, and turn away—where I don't know. But till

I am thirty, I know that my youth will triumph over everything—
every disillusionment, every disgust with life.[8]

As the precursors of an essentially modern and problematic view of
life, Dostoevsky's heroes—like Ivan Karamazov, the twenty-five-
year-old "idiot" Prince Myshkin, or the twenty-four-year-old "underground man" (that is, during the narrative portion of the book)—
sense an impending hour of collapse and disintegration; but as the
heirs of a romantic narrative tradition, they are normally at an age
where their immense sense of life still supports them in the face of
despair—where, in other words, narrative action is still possible. Not
until the 20th century do we encounter certain documents that circle
with an almost masochistic fascination around the dilemma of the
man who has reached the symbolic year and sees stretching before
him, instead of the anticipated consolation of total affirmation, the
gaping horror of emptiness.

II

Today it is a commonplace of intellectual history to say that the
disappearance of a stable reality has become the central experience
of our century.[9] But who is capable of experiencing this disintegration tragically or even in a manner accessible of narrative representation? Surely not the rootless modern, to whom the patterns of relativism and pluralism are evident almost before he emerges from
childhood. No, the tragedy of disintegration manifests itself above
all in the man who was first scrupulously educated during his youth
to acknowledge an integral world order: who, so to speak, already
has a *Bildungsroman* behind him. Then when the symbolic moment
of affirmation arrives, the meaninglessness of the world is suddenly
unmasked, and the man finds himself compelled to doubt and question all the beliefs that he has inherited, experienced, or learned. The
thirtieth year has become, for better or for worse, a typological turning point, a symbolic *peripeteia*, that one reaches inevitably. But
instead of the bliss of fulfillment, only nothingness leers at the thirty-
year-old from beyond the threshold. Instead of affirming a given
world order, he finds that he must now examine anew the entire meaning of life that he has acquired so painfully in the course of thirty
years of experience and learning.

Let us consider as a first literary expression of this crisis a little
poem by Ogden Nash which, like all first-rate humorous poems, reveals in comic distortion the most important elements of the experience of a generation:

Unwillingly Miranda wakes,
Feels the sun with terror.
One unwilling step she takes,
Shuddering to the mirror.

Miranda in Miranda's sight
Is old and gray and dirty;
Twenty-nine she was last night;
This morning she is thirty.[10]

The chief elements in the experience of the thirty-year-old that clearly emerge here are: first, the sudden and unpleasant awakening; second, the disintegration of a familiar world in the face of a new reality (yesterday, beautiful—today, old and gray and dirty); and third, the urgent compulsion to self-scrutiny, however painful it may be.

If we make a leap in time from the dejected Miranda of Nash's poem to another lady who has experienced a similar awakening, we find precisely the same typological elements intensified to a state of despair that has nothing more in common with the "sommité poétique" that Balzac detected in the woman of thirty. I refer to the first paragraph of Ingeborg Bachmann's story "Das dreißigste Jahr":

> When a person enters his thirtieth year people will not stop calling him young. But he himself, although he can discover no changes in himself, becomes unsure; he feels as though he were no longer entitled to claim to be young. And one morning he wakes up, on a day which he will forget, and suddenly lies there, unable to get up, struck by harsh rays of light and denuded of every weapon and all courage with which to face the new day. If he shuts his eyes in self-defense, he sinks back and drifts away into a swoon, along with every moment he has lived. He sinks and sinks . . . and he crashes down into a fathomless abyss, until his senses fade away, until everything which he thought he was has been dissolved, extinguished and destroyed. . . . He casts the net of memory, casts it over himself and draws himself, catcher and caught in one person, over the threshold of time, over the threshold of place—to see who he was and who he has become.[11]

Here the typological experience is defined more precisely. The motif of self-scrutiny is transposed from the physical to the psychological realm: It is now a question of contemplating one's own past and of determining a new meaning for one's life. And this self-reflection is characterized further as a state that is lifted, as it were, out of time. For the person who—as the quotation continues—no longer simply exists from one day to the next, experiences in the symbolic moment of reflection a certain paralysis of time until, with a jolt of decision, he injects himself once again into the stream of time.

Precisely the same experience is mirrored in the words of another thirty-year-old of our time:

> It happens that the stage sets collapse. Rising, streetcar, four hours in the office or the factory, meal, streetcar, four hours of work, meal, sleep, and Monday Tuesday Wednesday Thursday Friday and Saturday according to the same rhythm—this path is easily followed most of the time. But one day the "why" arises and everything begins in that weariness tinged with amazement. "Begins"—this is important. Weariness comes at the end of the acts of a mechanical life, but at the same time it inaugurates the impulse of consciousness. It awakens consciousness and provokes what follows. What follows is the gradual return into the chain or it is the definite awakening. At the end of the awakening comes, in time, the consequence: suicide or recovery.[12]

We recognize the voice of the thirty-year-old Albert Camus. But here in *Le Mythe de Sisyphe* the dilemma is formulated even more radically than it was in Ingeborg Bachmann's story. The awakening to the absurdity of life—in other words, the awakening to the disintegration of a familiar reality—leads either back to a false existence or forward to death or to recovery. And the symbolic age for this awakening—in the essay as well as in the novel *L'Etranger*—is again the thirtieth year when, for the duration of the decision, time is suspended.[13] So there emerges from these documents—to which one could easily add others, such as the somewhat more complicated case of Alfred Andersch's autobiographical record *Die Kirschen der Freiheit* [14]—a clear-cut profile that permits us to speak of a modern typological significance of the thirtieth year that differs sharply from the traditional view, in which the chief element was affirmation.

The typological experience of the thirty-year-old begins with a shock of recognition and ends with a conscious decision. Between this absolute beginning and absolute end the thirty-year-old lives in a state of timelessness during which all action is paralyzed while the analysis of his own past and his own present existence moves into the foreground. It is the attempt to shape this experience fictionally that has produced the Novel of the Thirty-Year-Old. For it can be demonstrated that the same typological experience underlies each of the novels mentioned at the beginning. We can see this most clearly if we first consider five novels in which the form of the narrative coincides absolutely with the structure of the experience. In fact, the correspondence is so precise that the novel might be defined almost as the metaphorical elongation of the basic experience.

III

Der Prozeß, La Nausée, Le Journal d'un curé de campagne, Die Aufzeichnungen des Malte Laurids Brigge, and the three parts of *Die Schlafwandler* all begin with the sudden realization of the heroes that the world as they have previously known it has fallen apart. Josef K. learns one morning upon awakening that he is under arrest, and this fact, which jolts him out of the normal patterns of his existence, forces him for the first time in his life to give serious consideration to the question of his guilt or innocence. Roquentin's notes begin just as abruptly: "Quelque chose m'est arrivé, je ne peux plus en douter." He has noticed—and his nausea is the external symptom of the fact—that the reality he previously accepted now disgusts him. In the middle of a country lane Bernanos' little priest is suddenly paralyzed by the realization that his parish is being inwardly consumed by the "rot of despair," by *ennui*. A trip to Paris catalyzes a similar sensation in the case of Malte Laurids Brigge. "Is it possible," he asks in the famous introductory passage, "that people have as yet seen, recognized and said nothing real and important?" The separate parts of Broch's trilogy begin just as abruptly: August Esch, dismissed from his job because of a colleague's embezzlement, is compelled by this glaring unrighteousness to question his whole conception of cosmic justice; Wilhelm Hugenau's complete break with the old systems of value is symbolized on the first page by his desertion from the army. These beginnings, moreover, are anything but dramatic. As Camus emphasizes, it is precisely the triviality of the instigation that unmasks the absurdity of the world and shatters "the chain of daily gestures." [15]   But this abrupt beginning marks the entrance into a radically new situation—what Kafka was fond of calling the Archimedean point, from which conventional reality takes on a wholly new appearance.

The abrupt beginning is followed, for the duration of the novel, by a state of timelessness. In the third part of *Die Schlafwandler* Broch characterizes the time explicitly as a *Ferienzeit* ("vacation time"), the action as a *Ferialhandlung* ("holiday action"), and Hugenau himself drifts along during these six months "as though under a vacuum jar"—which is to say that his life is no longer subject to the normal categories of the world surrounding him. The same holds true for Josef K.'s period of arrest, in which the "paralysis of time" has often been noted. His alienation from the world is indicated, among other ways, by the fact that his private sense of time is completely out of touch with the mechanical time of the outside world: He always arrives too early or too late; he lets others wait or he waits for others who, like Beckett's Godot, never come; he slams the door on an unpleasant scene, yet when he returns, weeks later, the same scene is still being enacted, rigidified into what Northrop Frye has called a state of "refrigerated deathlessness." The critical month during which Roquentin searches for a valid and authentic attitude toward life is similarly lifted out of time: "Le temps s'était arrêté," he notes during the access of nausea in the famous scene under the chestnut tree. Likewise, Malte Laurids Brigge passes his Parisian months in a timeless state in which past, present, and future merge indistinguishably one into the other. He has as little sense for the exigencies of everyday life as does Bernanos' country priest.

Within the state of absolute freedom that is made possible by such a suspension of time, the heroes concern themselves with the characteristic questions imposed on them by the problematics of their respective authors. Thus Josef K. wrestles with the problem of his guilt, and Bernanos' country priest, with his crisis of faith. Roquentin wins his existential freedom from *mauvaise foi*, while Broch's heroes grope desperately for an ethical prop within the general disintegration of values. And Malte Laurids Brigge sets out in pursuit of the essence of things. But in each case the crisis of the thirty-year-old ends with a conscious decision that determines his future attitude toward the world. Roquentin discovers that he can overcome his nausea only by devoting himself completely to the existential encounter with the world and with himself. He discards his historical studies and decides to write a novel. "A moment would probably come when the book would be written, it would lie behind me; and I believe that something of its radiance would fall upon my own past." [16] Josef K., who is incapable of bearing the terrible freedom imposed by the acknowledgment of his own guilt, lets himself glide back into "bad faith" by denying that guilt—but this denial is nonetheless a conscious decision. [17] Bernanos' priest dies of his cancer—a disease that of course symbolizes the moral rot threatening him and his parish; but he dies with the affirmation of a renewed faith on his lips: "Tout est grâce." Broch's protagonists, as incapable as Josef K. of sustaining absolute freedom, decide unanimously to slip back into the false security of a partial system of values. And Malte Laurids Brigge commits himself so wholly to reality and "things" that he surrenders his own personality and is subsumed in the myths of his own notebooks. Without considering in detail the many complex problems of interpretation posed by the individual works, we can still see clearly from these sketchy outlines how the phenomenological structure of the novel is maintained in every case. Each novel begins on the very first page, almost in the first sentence, with a shock of awareness; they all end with a clear decision that leads the hero back out of the timelessness of reflection into engagement with life—either authentic or false. And in each case we are dealing with a thirty-year-old hero who, after years of accepting life quietly at face value, is jolted for the first time into questioning the meaning of this life.

In the other novels the typological experience is no less effectively present even though it may not coincide so precisely with the external structure of the work. In Günter Grass and Albert Camus—however greatly the stylistic exuberance of the one differs from the simple understatement of the other—we find a similar structural treatment of the basic experience. In both cases, namely, the story is narrated retrospectively during a period of imprisonment. As in Kafka's novel, it is the act of arrest that constitutes the shock of awakening and thus initiates the period of timelessness. But since here the arrest chronologically follows the events to be related instead of preceding them, as in Kafka's novel, the first page does not depict the abrupt awakening of the typological experience: Meursault's arrest is not mentioned until the beginning of the second half of his report; Oskar Matzerath describes his arrest in the last chapter of his book—which means, by the way, that here the abrupt beginning and abrupt end coalesce in an unusually effective conclusion. But this is what matters: Both reports stand nonetheless under the impact of the typological experience from start to finish because they are written as a response to the crisis of the thirty-year-old. In other words: Without the jolt of arrest, without the timelessness of imprisonment, it would have occurred neither to Meursault nor to Oskar Matzerath to reflect on his life and to seek to come to terms with it in writing. In both cases, therefore, we find all the characteristic elements of the typological experience although, for narrative purposes, the abrupt beginning has been shifted to the middle or the end and no longer coincides with the first sentence of the text.

Five months of prison seem to Meursault to be no more than a single enduring day, and, in general, he spends a lot of his time thinking about the new static aspect under which time reveals itself to him during his confinement.[18] On the first page of his report Oskar

Matzerath mentions the "stillness woven through white metal bars" in his cell, whose "equilibrium and serenity" is interrupted only once a week by the "violation" of visiting day.[19] Even in these superficially different novels, then, a suspension of time prevails from start to finish, and in this timeless state the decision of the heroes slowly matures. For Meursault, despite the meaninglessness that becomes apparent to him during his lonely mnemonic exercises in jail, it is a matter of affirming life on the last page: "I too, I felt ready to live through everything once again." [20] And Oskar Matzerath, who has learned through writing his own autobiography that his tumultuous Tin Drum life was in the last analysis nothing but a flight from responsibility, concludes in the last chapter: "Today I am celebrating my thirtieth birthday. At thirty, one is obliged to talk about the theme of flight like a man and not like a boy." [21] In both novels, a clear decision announces a totally new attitude toward life.

Alfred Döblin shows a further possibility of shaping the typological experience. In *Berlin Alexanderplatz* Franz Biberkopf's crisis is related only toward the end of the novel, in the last book. But it is this crisis that casts a proper light on everything that has gone before, for the meaning of the whole novel emerges only from Biberkopf's analysis of reality and his final decision. After the three hard blows that fate, as he thinks, has inflicted upon him, Biberkopf lands in the mental hospital, Buch. The insights leading to his nervous breakdown constitute the shock of recognition that reveals to him the naïveté of his previous conception of life. The stupor in which he passes his days is so remote from the temporality of the outside world that not even medical treatments penetrate his hermetic isolation. Only the ultimate concession that his stubborn attempts "to be respectable" (*anständig*) misled him to a false assessment of reality frees him from the past, thus opening the way for his decision to return into the world "with his eyes open."

In every case, then, the abrupt awakening of the thirty-year-old leads first into a timeless state of reflection and analysis of existence, which is finally ended by a conscious decision to act. Now, whether or not the experience of the thirty-year-old coincides absolutely with the structure of the book, each novel is constructed in such a way that the decision constitutes the high point of the narrative because it illuminates and explains all preceding action. For this reason death, whenever it occurs, is incidental and virtually forced onto the novel by external considerations. Josef K., Meursault, and Bernanos' country priest all die. But Camus doesn't consider it worthwhile to describe the death scene because the entire meaning of the novel is contained in Meursault's decision, and his execution thereby becomes almost irrelevant. For the same reason the little priest's death is mentioned almost in passing in a laconic appendix. Josef K.'s death is nothing but the external correlative of the more significant philosophical suicide that he has already committed through his decision in favor of *mauvaise foi*. In general, then, the life of the hero after his crisis is regarded as unimportant: In the light of his decision we are supposed to be able to predict his future behavior and attitudes. This point of view is expressed most clearly in the last paragraph of the first part of Broch's *Die Schlafwandler*, when the narrator takes leave of his hero with the following words: "Nevertheless after some eighteen months they had their first child. It actually happened. How this came about cannot be told here. Besides, after the material for character construction already provided, the reader can imagine it for himself." [22] Such an ending contrasts sharply with the conclusion of the traditional *Bildungsroman* or the novel of manners not only because certain facts conventionally considered of interest— births, deaths, marriages, and so forth—are ignored. But more important: Endings of this sort imply a radically different attitude toward the hero and the world. In the conventional novel it is the world order that consoles us with regard to the hero's future; whatever may come to pass, nothing more can happen to jeopardize the hero in a stable reality. Here, on the other hand, it is the hero in whom we have confidence; no matter what happens in a meaningless world, we know our man and know how he will react to any given situation in the future.

The same principle of total omission or relative foreshortening applies to the hero's earlier life. For in none of these novels is the adventurous story of youth told simply for its own sake, as is the case in the traditional novel. We experience the life of youthful action before the crisis, if at all, only in the radically relativized view of the thirty-year-old who has learned that his previous manner of comprehending and judging was completely false. Therefore his entire youth must be lived once again in his memory, as it were, if it is to have any value. This is implied when Bernanos' country priest is uncertain whether or not he actually recognizes the memory of his own youth: "because I was seeing it for the first time, I had never seen it before." [23] It applies even to *Die Blechtrommel*, which is inconceivable without the ironic tension that obtains between the thirty-year-old narrator and the autobiography that he recounts. And examples of a similar attitude toward the past can easily be multiplied in the works of Rilke, Sartre, and Broch, where the hero's life prior to his awakening merely supplies raw material for the new analytical powers of the thirty-year-old.

The suppression of the future together with the relativization of the past produces an almost explosive concentration in the narrative present. Hovering timelessly between past and future, the symbolic moment of analysis and decision is so psychically overcharged that most writers, to make this tension psychologically plausible, exploit the symbolic device of illness: thus Sartre, Rilke, Bernanos, Grass, Broch, and Döblin. For on the one hand illness provides a rational justification for the paralysis of time in the novel; the stay in the hospital or the isolation in one's own room releases the patient from the normal bonds of everyday life. On the other hand, it also affords a rich language of metaphor for the disintegration and inner decay of the traditional world: Consider, for example, the pervasive cancer symbolism of Bernanos, the macabre dermatological metaphors of Rilke, the brilliant surgical images of Broch. The depiction of the state of sickness, with its overlapping layers of time, is intensified finally by the frequent use of the first-person narrative: Five novels of the group are written in the form of notebooks or autobiographical records. In the other cases (Kafka, Broch, Döblin) the same effect of immediacy and internalization is achieved by other stylistic devices: interior monologue, visions, stream of consciousness, and so forth.

It is clear that the fictional shaping of the typological experience leads to characteristics of structure that distinguish these novels, as a group, from other novels. And what is perhaps equally striking: This form, this unique complex of structural elements, sets off these novels even in comparison with other works by the same author. Compare, for instance, the radical conclusion of *Der Prozeß* with the infinite spiral of Kafka's *Das Schloß,* or the concentrated experience of *La Nausée* or *L'Etranger* with the broad panoramic vistas of Sartre's *Les Chemins de la liberté* or Camus' *La Peste.* The Novel of the Thirty-Year-Old is simply the most adequate form for the shaping of this life-crisis and, as such, occurs most frequently in the 20th century—the century when an awareness of relativism and the disintegration of values has penetrated into the foreground of literary consciousness among many writers.

IV

But since the crisis of consciousness is by no means an exclusive prerogative of our time, but a typological experience that can crop up in any period, it seems to be a confirmation of the validity of our structure when we encounter it almost paradigmatically anticipated in the work of an older writer with an uncannily modern sense of being. "Up to his thirtieth year this extraordinary man could have passed for the model of a good citizen" is the second sentence of *Michael Kohlhaas*. Like his younger brothers in the 20th century, Kleist's hero is torn out of his habitual patterns at the beginning of the novella by an abrupt awakening: The world, which he has previously known as orderly and good, suddenly unmasks itself as arbitrary, shifting, and hostile. The novella begins, then, with an abrupt jolt of awareness and the hero finds himself, during the course of the concentrated narrative, in a state of suspension outside all conventional bonds: His wife has died, he sells his farm, sends his children away, and passes his year of vengeance in a timeless world of his own creation. The plot rushes along to the moment of decision when Kohlhaas has the choice of renouncing his legal claims and living in peace, or of obtaining justice at the cost of his own head. A thirty-year-old; closed form with an abrupt beginning; suspension of time and disintegration of the known world; and an absolute end in the critical decision. In Kleist's novella we find prefigured almost as in a model all the characteristic structural elements that we know from the modern novel of the thirty-year-old. But this striking parallel compels us in conclusion to consider the whole structure once again under a somewhat broader light.

Our investigation began with the observation that thirty-year-old heroes occur in a number of modern novels. While considering the possible reasons for this anomaly, we arrived at a basic typological pattern that all the novels of this group seem to have in common. Now—at the risk of diminishing the catchiness of the concept, but in the hope of increasing its phenomenological usefulness—let us waive the age thirty itself as a group characteristic. And right away several other modern novels come to our attention that reveal precisely the same structure although the hero is slightly older or younger. A conspicuous and familiar example in recent American literature is provided by Saul Bellow's *The Dangling Man*. Although Joseph is only twenty-eight, his experiences during the months while he waits for induction correspond point for point to the typological experience outlined above. The period of timeless dangling is precipitated by a draft notice, and during the months of waiting, Joseph's view of reality is so radically altered that he is forced, like Roquentin and Malte Laurids Brigge, to keep a journal in order to come to grips with the new reality he senses. His heightened perceptions bring about such a change that he is no longer the same man. "Very little about the Joseph of a year ago pleases me," he notes. "I cannot help laughing at him, at some of his traits and sayings." [24]   Bellow's Joseph responds to his crisis very much like his namesake Josef K. "To be pushed upon oneself entirely put the very facts of simple existence in doubt," he observes in one of his last entries. Unable to bear pure freedom, he longs to fall back into the patterns of a regulated security. "Hurray for regular hours!" he concludes on his last day of civilian life. "And for the supervision of the spirit! Long live regimentation!" Bellow's comic spirit saves his hero from the suicide of despair that claims two other modern thirty-year-olds: J. D. Salinger's Seymour Glass and the gigolo hero of Pierre Drieu la Rochelle's *Le Feu follet.*

In Heinrich Böll's *Billard um Halbzehn* the two male protagonists are well past thirty: On the day of the action one is in his middle forties, and the other is celebrating his eightieth birthday. But both for Heinrich Fähmel and his son Robert, it was an experience in their thirtieth year that precipitated the extended period of timeless detachment that is concluded, years later, by their simultaneous decision to assume the responsibility of *engagement* and to return to a life in reality.

At first glance Thomas Mann's *Der Zauberberg* seems to have few similarities with our structure, but if we look more closely, we see that Hans Castorp's seven-year sojourn on the magic mountain begins with an abrupt awakening to the new reality represented by life in the sanatorium; it continues during a period of pronounced timelessness and analysis of existence, all of which takes place with the heightened sensibility of sickness to the accompaniment of an elaborate rhetoric of fever images and tuberculosis symbolism; and it ends with the decision of the thirty-year-old hero to return from his mountain to the flatlands below, where World War I is raging. The same parallels can be established, finally, in Robert Musil's *Mann ohne Eigenschaften*, whose thirty-two-year-old hero takes what the author calls "a vacation from life" (*Urlaub vom Leben*—that is, timeless suspension) in order to come to terms with his own potentialities of existence.

What conclusions do these reflections permit us to reach? If we formulate our observations modestly, we can ascertain something like this: For centuries the thirtieth year has possessed a certain symbolic value as a crucial turning point in man's life. And in our own time the loss of a stable reality has emerged as the central experience of modern man. The thinking of our age has combined these two ideas in a typological experience with a distinct profile: abrupt awakening to the disintegration of the familiar world, paralysis of time during a period of analysis, and an abrupt ending in decision. The specific character of the crisis varies in accordance with the problematics of the individual author, but the phenomenological structure of the experience remains constant. It is this structure that certain writers have appropriated—whether consciously or unconsciously is irrelevant—in order to give fictional form to this life-crisis. Within the given structure there remains a broad area of freedom for the inventive genius of the author: The form of the novel can coincide wholly with the structure of the experience; the abrupt beginning can be shifted toward the middle or end of the novel; the duration of the crisis can be several hours or several years; the phenomenon of timelessness can be rendered symbòlically through illness or imprisonment; even the age of the hero does not need to be precisely thirty in every case (although it was the very frequency of this age that aroused our attention initially). But as long as the typological structure of the experience determines the form of the novel to a decisive extent, we are justified, I think, in speaking of the Novel of the Thirty-Year-Old.

On the one hand, we should not insist too categorically on our conclusions. There may be thirty-year-old heroes who have no such experience; there may be novels of crisis that make no use of the typological structure. And finally: Even when we have definitely established the fact that we are dealing with a Novel of the Thirty-Year-Old, we are still only at the beginning of any thorough analysis or interpretation of the work in question. But on the other hand, if we have detected in a given work this phenomenological framework, we do know a few basic things. We know that we are dealing with the fictional shaping of a very specific kind of crisis and are thus in a better position to analyze the nature of the crisis. We become alert, further, to important principles of structure: for instance, the distribution of the elements of the experience, the structuring of timelessness, the treatment of the past, the meaning of death, the function of sickness or confinement. And we are able, finally, to relate the work to others of its kind for the purpose of meaningful comparison—and in literary criticism there are also, unfortunately, meaningless comparisons! This is ultimately perhaps the principal conclusion of our considerations. This thirty-year-old, in his struggle for a new attitude toward reality, has shown himself to be so persistent and vehement that, wherever he appears, he virtually wrests the novel from the hands of its author in order to stamp upon it the unmis-

takable imprint of his own desperate features. Within the broad
spectrum of themes, motifs, and styles, the typological experience of
an age has produced its own characteristic structure. And with a
respectful nod toward the reservations noted above, we are justified,
I think, in calling it the Novel of the Thirty-Year-Old.

NOTES

1. This generalization applies, of course, only to those novels with a single
   hero—and not, for instance, to the novel of manners with several leading
   protagonists (e.g., Goethe's *Die Wahlverwandtschaften* or *Les Liaisons
   dangereuses* of Choderlos de Laclos).

2. Especially with regard to French literature. See Justin O'Brien, *The
   Novel of Adolescence in France* (New York, 1937).

3. I have gotten much of the following material from: Ulrich Helfenstein,
   Beiträge zur Problematik der Lebensalter in der mittleren Geschichte
   (Diss. Zürich, 1952).

4. "De l'Aage," *Oeuvres Complètes*, ed. A. Armaingaud (Paris, 1924), *II*,
   510: "De toutes les belles actions humaines qui sont venuës à ma con-
   noissance, de quelque sorte qu'elles soient, je penserois en avoir plus
   grande part, à nombrer celles qui ont esté produites, et aux siecles anciens et au nostre, avant l'aage de trente ans, que après."

5. (Paris, 1948), p. 24 (July, 1915): "Trop tard maintenant pour espérer
   autre chose, la guerre finie, que la joie du travail dans la solitude avec le
   peu d'êtres qui ne te froisseront pas. Non que tu ne regrettes tous les
   possibles à jamais manqués. Mais c'est trop tard. A trente ans, on ne
   s'aiguille plus."

6. "Reginald" and "Reginald on the Academy," *Reginald* (1904), *The Short
   Stories of Saki* (New York, 1937), pp. 4, 10.

7. This saying has become almost a national slogan since the disturbances
   in California. See the amusing article by John Fischer "Letter to a New
   Leftist from a Tired Liberal," *Harper's Magazine*, 232 (March, 1966),
   16–28.

8. *The Brothers Karamazov*, trans. Constance Garnett, p 273

9. See in this connection the significant study by Erich Kahler, "Untergang
   und Übergang der epischen Kunstform,". *Neue Rundschau, 64* (1953),
   1–44.

10. "A Lady Thinks She Is Thirty," *Verses from 1929 on* (Modern Library),
    p. 42.

11. *The Thirtieth Year*, trans. Michael Bullock (New York, 1964), p. 18.
    The German text—in Ingeborg Bachmann, *Gedichte, Erzählungen, Hör-
    spiele, Essays* (Munich, 1964), p. 67—runs as follows: "Wenn einer in
    sein dreißigstes Jahr geht, wird man nicht aufhören, ihn jung zu nennen.
    Er selber aber, obgleich er keine Veränderung an sich entdecken kann,
    wird unsicher; ihm ist, als stünde es ihm nicht mehr zu, sich für jung
    auszugeben. Und eines Morgens wacht er auf, an einem Tag, den er ver-

gessen wird, und liegt plötzlich da, ohne sich erheben zu können, getroffen von harten Lichtstrahlen und entblößt jeder Waffe und jeden Muts für den neuen Tag. Wenn er die Augen schließt, um sich zu schützen, sinkt er zurück und treibt ab in eine Ohnmacht, mitsamt jedem gelebten Augenblick. Er sinkt und sinkt . . . und er stürzt hinunter ins Bodenlose, bis ihm die Sinne schwinden, bis alles aufgelöst, ausgelöscht und vernichtet ist, was er zu sein glaubte. . . . Er wirft das Netz Erinnerung aus, wirft es über sich und zieht sich selbst, Erbeuter und Beute in einem, über die Zeitschwelle, die Ortsschwelle, um zu sehen, wer er war und wer er geworden ist."

12. Albert Camus, *The Myth of Sisyphus and Other Essays*, trans. Justin O'Brien (New York, 1959), p. 10. The French text—(Paris, 1964), p. 27 —runs as follows: "Lever, tramway, quatre heures de bureau ou d'usine, repas, tramway, quatre heures de travail, repas, sommeil et lundi mardi mercredi jeudi vendredi et samedi sur le même rythme, cette route se suit aisément la plupart du temps. Un jour seulement, le 'pourquoi' s'élève et tout commence dans cette lassitude teintée d'étonnement. 'Commence', ceci est important. La lassitude est à la fin des actes d'une vie machinale, mais elle inaugure en même temps le mouvement de la conscience. Elle l'éveille et elle provoque la suite. La suite, c'est le retour inconscient dans la chaîne, ou c'est l'éveil définitif. Au bout de l'éveil vient, avec le temps, la conséquence: suicide ou rétablissement."

13. Curiously, the age is not clearly stated either in the novel or the essay— in contrast to all the other works under consideration here. But in both cases it is clearly implied. The next paragraph of the essay continues, noting that men normally pay little attention to these events of everyday life: "Un jour vient pourtant et l'homme constate ou dit qu'il a trente ans. Il affirme ainsi sa jeunesse. Mais du même coup, il se situe par rapport au temps. Il y prend sa place." This striking association of the crisis with the age thirty can be no more accidental than Meursault's observation shortly before the end of the novel: "Dans le fond, je n'ignorais pas que mourir à trente ans ou à soixante-dix ans importe peu. . . ." It is reasonable to assume that the young narrator, who chooses the age seventy as a contrast, is himself about thirty. It is of further interest that Camus himself had not yet reached thirty when his two works appeared (1942). This might mean that, instead of using an autobiographical age chosen at random, he wanted to exploit the symbolic implications of the age thirty. That would explain the phrase: "l'homme constate *ou dit* qu'il a trente ans." It might be mentioned at this point that the age thirty has no necessary bearing on the age of the author, who is sometimes about thirty himself, but often much older.

14. This autobiographical report provides a perfect example for the crisis of the thirty-year-old. Andersch, to be sure, does not choose the age thirty for symbolic reasons; he is recording certain events of his life as they occurred. But the critical instant upon which the entire book is focused is, in the last analysis, his decision to desert from the German army—a flight into freedom that he made at age thirty. And this main episode ("Die Wildnis") reveals all the elements of the typological experience as we have analyzed it above.

15. *Le Mythe de Sisyphe*, pp. 26–27: "Toutes les grandes actions et toutes les grandes pensées ont un commencement dérisoire. . . . Le monde absurde plus qu'un autre tire sa noblesse de cette naissance misérable. Dans certaines situations répondre: 'rien' à une question sur la nature de ses pensées peut être une feinte chez un homme. Les êtres aimées le savent bien. Mais si cette réponse est sincère, si elle figure ce singulier état d'âme où le vide devient éloquent, où la chaîne des gestes quotidiens est rompue . . . , elle est alors comme le premier signe de l'absurdité."

16. *La Nausée* (Livre de Poche, 160), p. 250: "Mais il viendrait bien un moment où le livre serait écrit, serait derrière moi et je pense qu'un peu de sa clarté tomberait sur mon passé."

17. The question of Josef K.'s guilt and, by extension, the meaning of his death is, of course, a matter of interpretation on which critics differ. I regard him as guilty and unwilling to accept his guilt. But *both* schools of thought acknowledge a conscious decision on K.'s part: so the *structure* of the novel is upheld regardless of interpretation.

18. *L'Etranger* (Livre de Poche, 406), p. 119: "Lorsqu'un jour, le gardien m'a dit que j'étais là depuis cinq mois, je l'ai cru, mais je ne l'ai pas compris. Pour moi, c'était sans cesse le même jour qui déferlait dans ma cellule et la même tâche que je poursuivais."

19. *Die Blechtrommel* (Fischer Bücherei, 473/4), pp. 9–10: "Einmal in der Woche unterbricht ein Besuchstag meine zwischen weißen Metallstäben geflochtene Stille. . . . Solange sein Besuch währt—und Anwälte wissen viel zu erzählen—raubt er mir durch diesen Gewaltakt das Gleichgewicht und die Heiterkeit."

20. *L'Etranger*, p. 179: "Et moi aussi, je me suis senti prêt à tout revivre. Comme si cette grande colère m'avait purgé du mal, vidé d'espoir, devant cette nuit chargée de signes et d'étoiles, je m'ouvrais pour la première fois à la tendre indifférence du monde."

21. *Die Blechtrommel*, p. 484: "So nebenbei: ich begehe heute meinen dreißigsten Geburtstag. Als Dreißigjähriger ist man verpflichtet, über das Thema Flucht wie ein Mann und nicht wie ein Jüngling zu sprechen."

22. *Gesammelte Werke* (Rhein-Verlag, 1952), p. 170: "Nichtsdestoweniger hatten sie nach etwa achtzehn Monaten ihr erstes Kind. Es geschah eben. Wie sich dies zugetragen hat, muß nicht mehr erzählt werden. Nach den gelieferten Materialien zum Charakteraufbau kann sich der Leser dies auch allein ausdenken."

23. *Journal d'un curé de campagne* (Librairie Plon, 1964), p. 201: "En un éclair, j'ai vu ma triste adolescence—non pas ainsi que les noyés repassent leur vie, dit-on, avant de couler à pic, car ce n'était sûrement pas une suite de tableaux presque instantanément déroulés—non. Cela était devant moi comme une personne, un être (vivant ou mort, Dieu le sait!). Mais je n'étais pas sûr de la reconnaître parce que . . . oh! cela va paraître bien étrange—parce que je la voyais pour la première fois, je ne l'avais jamais vue."

24. *The Dangling Man* (Meridian Fiction, 9), p. 26.

III LITERATURE AND THE OTHER ARTS

Jean Hagstrum

The Sister Arts:
From Neoclassic to Romantic[1]

In 1652, writing about the epic poem, Pierre Mambrun, literary critic, Latin poet, and Jesuit father, said: "There is no one who has not been pleased with this comparison between poetry and painting." [2] Almost two hundred years later Leigh Hunt wrote: "It has been a whim of late years with some transcendental critics . . . to deny utterly the old family relationship between poetry and painting." [3] Between those dates two of the greatest artistic movements in Western culture rose and subsided. Did the Sister Arts of poetry and painting fare differently under neoclassicism and Romanticism, epochs so diverse in their basic assumptions, so unlike in their final achievements?

The 18th century, it may now be asserted dogmatically, was highly pictorialist in both poetry and criticism. Hildebrand Jacob, in 1734, expressed an almost universally accepted belief: "The nearer the *Poet* approaches to the *Painter,* the more perfect he is; and the more perfect the *Painter,* the more he imitates the *Poet.* . . ." [4] "Tous les arts," wrote Voltaire in one of his *Poésies mêlées* (Number 496)—

> Tous les arts sont amis ainsi qu'ils sont divins;
> Qui veut les séparer est loin de les connaître.

Under such tutelage, the 18th-century reader saw complete pictures where we detect only the most general visual hints.

> When Jubal struck the corded shell,
> His list'ning brethren stood around,
> And, wond'ring, on their faces fell.

Of that rather sketchy pictorial outline, made in Dryden's somewhat abstract first ode for St. Cecilia's Day, Joseph Warton wrote:

> This is so complete and engaging a history piece, that I knew a person of taste who was resolved to have it executed on one side of his saloon: "In which case, (said he,) the painter has nothing to do

169

but to substitute colours for words, the design being finished to his hands."

James Thomson, in *Summer,* wrote the following lines, which to the 20th-century reader seem only slightly to suggest visual personification:

> O vale of bliss! O softly-swelling hills!
> On which the power of cultivation lies,
> And joys to see the wonders of his toil. [11. 1435–37]

An unnamed contemporary critic responded as follows:

> We cannot conceive a more beautiful image than that of the Genius of Agriculture distinguished by the implements of his art, embrowned with labor, glowing with health, crowned with a garland of foliage, flowers, and fruit, lying stretched at ease on the brow of a gently swelling hill, and contemplating with pleasure the happy effects of his own industry.

In Prior's delicate society verse Cloe blushes over verses sung to Euphelia, who frowns because they were intended for Cloe:

> Fair Cloe blush'd: Euphelia frown'd:
> I sung and gaz'd: I play'd and trembl'd:
> And Venus to the Loves around
> Remark'd how ill we all dissembl'd.

Cloe, Euphelia, and the poet are in a drawing room or boudoir. But where is Venus? And who are the "Loves around"? An 18th-century reader would have known at once. Venus is represented on the wall or ceiling as speaking to the winged cupids that constitute her train.[5]

Today we tend to find in 18th-century poetry only the lightly musical or the heavily didactic. But properly trained to see as we read, we find in the enlarging images of Dryden's great odes the baroque of Counter-Reformation Europe—of Rubens and Guercino. In Pope we find not only a rococo or a minuet style but both heroic landscape and a modified baroque that specifically invokes Bernini. In Thomson we see, not a timid precursor of Wordsworth and Wilson, afraid to speak out, but a late and somewhat overblown expression of the mythologized nature in 17th-century landscape. Collins we relate to the emblematic allegories of both book and canvas, and in Gray we find inescapable the large tableaux of the new historical school that was throwing English light on English walls.

How did painting and poetry—still, and always in this essay, conceived of together as the Sister Arts—fare in the Romantic period?

Poorly, we say inevitably, if we look only at the main contours of the landscape or at German aesthetics, at Neoplatonic thought or at Coleridge the critic. The Lockean 18th century made beauty and the visual virtually coterminous.[6] But the Romantics, substituting for the reflecting mirror of mimesis either the candle of the Lord or the interior lamp of private vision, attacked what Coleridge called "the despotism of the eye."[7] Under impulses from German criticism—but also from Burke, who tried to establish the sublimity of obscurity and of half-lights—music replaced painting as the most analogous art. Remote from nature, necessarily abstract in its configurations, fluid and suggestive in its movements, music became not only a sister of poetry but its Platonic ideal—a supersensuous entity to which all the arts turn, as the sunflower turns to the sun. Music is the condition to which all art constantly aspires. At its most volatile music rarefies into the intense inane; at its least it freezes into architecture. Music, better than any other art, challenges the "bounds of the picturable"[8] that Coleridge disliked. Music can free the imagination from its bondage to the eye.

Such a view is itself aesthetically satisfying and has, besides, the merit of being true for important parts of the Romantic whole. But it also has a tendency to become a unitary and exclusive interpretation of Romantic verse. Its philosophical and historical limitations must therefore be confronted, lest it distort both our vision of the poetry and our view of the period. The most serious of these limitations is that the philosophy I am attempting to refute is not equipped to account for three of the greatest achievements of the Romantic period in England: (1) the criticism of Hazlitt, in which the arts of poetry and painting are treated with almost equal emphasis and equal genius and in which each art endows the other with important and fructifying values; (2) the canonical—that is, the engraved and colored—poems of William Blake, a painter hyphen poet (not merely a poet and also a painter), who united the Sister Arts more closely than they had ever been united before and whose form of artistic expression consisted of word, picture, and abstract design in closest collaboration; and (3) the poetry of John Keats, which is not only sensuous in the vaguely general way it is usually described but is specifically the expression of a pictorialist vision. Blake I have discussed elsewhere,[9] and Hazlitt, who cannot here be given the separate treatment he richly deserves, will help lead us into the pictorialist vision of Keats, our chief witness against the pre-emptive view that in the early 19th century *ut musica poesis* replaced the venerable *ut pictura poesis*.

In one other respect the "musicalist" view of Romantic poetry and criticism is impoverishing. Walter Pater, who believed that "all art constantly aspires towards the condition of music," also believed in the phenomenon of *Anders-streben,* by which each art strives to transcend the limits of its own distinctive medium, trying to obliterate all distinctions between matter and form and to "present one single effect to the 'imaginative reason'." [10] But why only *one* condition or *one* single effect? Similarly, Henri Focillon believes in the "law of technical primacy in the arts": under that law all the arts of a given period fall under the dominating technique of one of them.[11] But such a restrictive law can hardly account for the effects of a single richly resonant poem, to say nothing of the large and shifting panorama of the entire period. The "Ode to Autumn," for example—a poem we shall confront in concluding this essay—is at once natural, painterly, and musical. It will yield its complexities to no simple or unitary doctrine of poetic value.

It is only at the close that I confront the complex diversities of Romantic poetry. My chief purpose is to argue for the presence in its richly diverse totality of literary pictorialism or, as it is more agreeably referred to, the Sister Arts. That tradition has been more or less active in Western culture since at least the time of Homer. No modern period has been entirely free of its influence, even our own day. The signs of its presence (five in number) have sometimes all appeared in the career and work of a single poet like Keats and sometimes—as in baroque France—all in a single epoch. (To each of these five criteria [save one] I am able to give a fashionable foreign tag.)

1. That famous phrase from Horace, *ut pictura poesis* (as a picture, so a poem) is, stated or implied, a sign of pictorialist thought. It encourages criticism to draw analogies from painting in describing poetic effects and encourages poetry to imitate the Sister Art of painting.

2. A pictorialist poet will usually write verses about art objects, real or imaginary. At least he as done so from Homer to Keats, from the shield of Achilles in the *Iliad* to the *Ode on a Grecian Urn.* That kind of verse has sometimes been called *ekphrastic* (after the Greek word for speaking out), since the art object, though silent, is given a voice by a poet. I have called such poetry "iconic," after the example of a famous rhetor of late antiquity, whose specialty it was to travel about and describe paintings.

3. Pictorialist poets tend themselves to be painters, or to associate with painters, or to visit museums, or to collect engravings—in short, to use all possible means to create what André Malraux has called a

personal *musée imaginaire*, which can be carried around in the head.

4. The pictorialist tradition—and it is here that foreign vocabulary deserts me—can easily be mediated by previous poets, without benefit of direct contact with visual arts and artists. The pictorial effects of Sidney's *Arcadia* may have come from the Greek romances of late antiquity.

5. All pictorial poetry must have moments that reduce narrative and logical movement to *stasis*—a stasis that is not merely visual but also picturable; a stasis that directly quotes or indirectly recalls particular works or schools of visual art. In relation to paintings or schools of painting these static moments can be obvious or subtle. Their particulars can come from a single source or from many sources. But the effect of picture-like stasis is inescapable to the trained reader.

These five signs of pictorialist poetry—*ut pictura poesis*, iconic verse, the *musée imaginaire*, the presence of an antecedent literary tradition that is also pictorial, and verbal *stasis*—will be in our mind, though not in schematized form, as we consider Byron and Shelley, Coleridge and Wordsworth, and, with greater fullness, the poetry of John Keats.

Byron exclaimed over the Uffizi and Pitti galleries of Florence— with the effusiveness one would expect, especially over those canvases that portrayed, as he called them, the "mistresses" of Raphael and Titian. He apparently idolized Canova the sculptor, and he liked the works of Domenichino and Guido Reni in Bologna. In *Don Juan* he briefly and conventionally characterizes Salvator Rosa, Vernet, Claude, Rembrandt, Caravaggio. Nevertheless, he consistently shows, surprisingly, the lack of an effectual *musée imaginaire* of paintings that he can draw on as a poet. It is somewhat otherwise for sculpture, since only Shelley among the Romantics surpassed him in the number of allusions to statues. But can we call Byron's preoccupation with statuary a vital taste? He remained hostile to the Elgin Marbles and clung to those enervated idols of previous generations, the *Apollo Belvedere* and the *Venus dei Medici*. Such conventional taste one could forgive, had the poet made good verse of what he liked, for many a fine poetic purse has been made of a sow's ear. But the *Venus dei Medici* is as slack in Byron's verse as she is in her mother marble. The *Dying Gladiator* provokes angry but unvisual rhetoric. Canova's statue becomes "the Helen of [Byron's] heart"; but really it is the cold head that creates the tired conceit she inspires. Byron the rhetorician cannot seem to sustain a pictorial stasis, and his eye moves rapidly away from the object that should hold it fast until the visual-poetic meaning has been yielded.[12]

Shelley wields the chisel but not the pencil. In painting, which he had abundant opportunity to see, how tame and conventional his taste is! He loves Guido Reni; but Michelangelo offends him, and he hates the vigorous Domenichino. Does he distrust all visual energy and feel at home only with the languorous? It is fortunate that he seldom tried the pictorial, for he would have created women with white arms lifted through the shadowy stream of their loose hair—poetical versions of the simpering white allegories of Angelica Kauffmann, Lady Diana Beauclerk, Richard Cosway, or Thomas Stothard. Shelley's statues are better than that, since Parian marble (beautiful in its whiteness, with its "azure veins") and "shapes of living stone" in "white tranquillity" singing songs of freedom brought to him the liberating vision of ancient Greece. But when art is not Greek, it is dead. Architecture, with its frozen or bloody altars, suggests dead or tyrannical priestcraft and the worship of the "fiend-God," "Almighty Fear." Painting represents either moribund convention or decorated despotism.[13]

Yet Shelley's pages are full of pictorialized allegories. These represent his adaptation of the pictorialism of his poetical predecessors. Dante guided him in the *Triumph of Life*. The opening of *Alastor* recalls the picturesque of Thomson. Homer provides the picture of the Eagle and the Serpent in the *Revolt of Islam*.[14] And Collins has helped to shape the tableau that introduces the *Daemon of the World*.

Hazlitt heard Coleridge speak "eloquently and feelingly of pictures where the subject-matter was poetical and where 'more was meant than met the eye'."[15] What was that "more"? For Coleridge the critic it must have been a revelation of that state anterior to artistic expression in any medium—the creating life of the imagination in which all true artists partake. Raphael's *Galatea* illustrated the "perfect reconciliation" of "FREE LIFE" and "the confining FORM." Late medieval and early Renaissance art, Michelangelo, Raphael, even Titian and Correggio, constituted Christian art, produced under the pressures of "a divine philosophy." But Bernini—and one assumes also the entire high baroque and the eclectic 17th century—were impelled by the aggregative fancy alone, not by the esemplastic imagination.[16]

For Coleridge painting can illustrate aesthetic theory, but it cannot be said to engage in vital commerce with poetry. Coleridge's own imagery reflects his beliefs about nature, but reveals no obvious or fructifying contact with the Sister Art. Nature in Coleridge's poetry is always in motion, as if to show the omnipresence of the living, interinanimating I AM: leaves tremble, wind blows to create music on hanging harps, light shimmers, the setting sun softly unites the landscape with the sky, frost and fire paint evanescent forms, clouds move and change in color and shape, pools are mirrors only briefly, for their surface is soon ruffled by extraneous motion. Painting and sculpture are too static to convey the phantasmagoric commerce between mind and matter, as nature becomes thought and thought becomes a new nature. The maiden Lewti lies under a leafy labyrinth in a posture and setting that one could call Titianesque—except that breezes blow, nightingales sing, white swans and the lady's white bosom heave together in time with the gently swelling wave. All Coleridge's pictures—and they are none the worse for that—dissolve into motion, music, or thought.[17] Leaving judgment of value aside and thinking only of definition, one must agree with Henry Nelson Coleridge that his father-in-law "does not belong to that grand division of poetry and poets which correspond with painting and painters." [18] Coleridge's vital nature had to move as nothing in plastic art can move. The pictorial was static, bounded, idle—"as idle as a painted ship upon a painted ocean."

In discussing Wordsworth, Coleridge gave no hint that his friend was in the slightest degree concerned with or influenced by any visual art whatever. But Hazlitt declared that Wordsworth liked Bewick and Waterloo—the woodcuts of the first and the sylvan etchings of the second—and that he used to enlarge with fine enthusiasm on Nicolas Poussin's landscapes. In Rembrandt, so Hazlitt asserts, Wordsworth saw a close analogy to his poetry, particularly in the painter's ability to transform, by the use of light and shade, a common into an ideal object. Wordsworth, we are told, invoked Titian's *Bacchus and Ariadne* to shame the lack of sensuous and painterly detail in Dryden's *Alexander's Feast*.[19]

Who is right, Hazlitt or Coleridge?

At first, in the light of our own preconceptions about Wordsworth, we are inclined to say that Hazlitt, the lover of painting, has surely created Wordsworth in his own image. The few expressions in the prefaces that recall pictorialist criticism are only a conventional residue in the phraseology. By his own confession, Wordsworth began his career ignorant of painters and painting. After years of friendship with Sir George Beaumont, and under pressure to know something about an art that was achieving unprecedented triumphs in England, Wordsworth ended his career with solemn, general, and fashionable pontifications about painting.[20]

The poetry bears out, to begin with, our first impressions. Describing the visionary power as a fleeting, shadowy exultation, Wordsworth writes:

I would walk alone
Under the quiet stars, and at that time
Have felt whate'er there is of power in sound
To breathe an elevated mood, by form
Or image unprofaned. [*Prelude,* II, 302–306]

The paradox is deep—or would have been to the 18th century. A *visionary* gift "unprofaned" by "form or image"! For all his critical insistence on looking steadily at the object, the poet very frequently, as Professor Pottle. has seen, blurs the edges of his images until they waver and disappear.[21] Most of the sonnets are Miltonic in more than form. The images are general and enlarging and musical, not visually concrete. A soul is like a star, the sun is broad. The shepherd Michael's own special power, like that of his creator, is auditory: he responds to the sounds of nature—the wind in rock and tree—more than to its sights. Wordsworth did write a few iconic poems, but two of these, the ones on King's College chapel, Cambridge, end in a burst of organ music, and the eye has not been held fast to the object.

But before we conclude, from the absence of *ut pictura poesis* in his criticism, of truly iconic verse in his canon, and of an operative *musée imaginaire* in his mind, that the poet is unpictorial, let us remember one other source of pictorialism, the one present in Shelley—the pictorialist achievement of antecendent poets. If we do, we discover one more tradition that Wordsworth inherited and reanimated. One sign of this influence is the poet's tendency to be inscriptive—to create the fiction of engraving his lines, as though in permanent form, on tombstone, tree trunk, bench, seat, and also as though to address the passing traveler.[22] Even when this fiction is not insisted upon, there is a desire to make the scenes permanent or stable, so that they will return or can be returned to. Thus they will live in the mind as palpable, solid realities, not as wisps of disappearing smoke. So *Tintern Abbey* begins with a paintable scene. Cliffs, the sycamore, orchard tufts, the one green hue, the hedge rows, the farm, and the rising smoke compose a landscape. And this pictorial composition holds the thought fast in "beauteous forms," in "lovely forms," all the details held fast in "their colours and their forms." Even when scenes are not fully composed, motion sometimes slows to stasis. The leach-gatherer is motionless as a cloud; Michael's cottage, "The Evening Star," stands solid and silent and immovable on its high place. Wordsworth's need in poetry to achieve hard and changeless plastic form provides an insistent contrast to the more vibrant and tremulous verse of Coleridge.

That need may have grown with the debilitating years, but it was at least partially met by traditional means in some of Wordsworth's best poems. In 1807, when he was begining to feel the power of moral abstractions, the pictorialist tradition is present, even though it never dominates. That tradition, you may recall, saw ideal forms as sculptures or as pictorial allegories. The only way to feel the force of Wordsworth's vision of the benignant but "Stern Lawgiver" Duty is to remember the smiling Aurora leading her train through nature and touching the flowers to laughter and life as day returns to earth. That image, which had dominated 18th-century nature poetry, was perhaps best known in Guido Reni's painting—a painting much loved in England, which Thomson and Collins had both adapted to verse and which Wordsworth admired at the age of 73.[23]

> Stern Lawgiver! yet thou dost wear
> The Godhead's most benignant grace;
> Nor know we anything so fair
> As is the smile upon thy face:
> Flowers laugh before thee on their beds
> And fragrance in thy footing treads;
> Thou dost preserve the stars from wrong;
> And the most ancient heavens, through Thee, are
>   fresh and strong.

About the same time that Wordsworth began painting allegorical figures to embody the idealized abstractions that he hoped would guide his life, he produced one of the finest iconic poems in the language— iconic it may be called because it presents the poet contemplating a painting, Sir George Beaumont's *Peele Castle in a Storm*. The poem, in fact, includes one scene and two paintings: the castle by a stormy sea on the painter's canvas, a symbol of Wordsworth's emotion after his brother's death in another angry sea; the real scene of Peele Castle, in the perfect calm that Wordsworth remembered years before; and the picture the poet now imagines himself as painting of that scene—close to the calm nature he had known but also imbued with "the light that never was on sea or land." These three moments of *stasis* subtilize the iconic conventions into a work of visual beauty and of deep but controlled feeling. A real painting is compared with an imaginary painting. The eye is held to the appropriate object until its proper emotion is released and re-created. Nature is compared with art, and the poet and the painter collaborate to make a universal symbol of lost and irrecoverable Arcadian bliss. For Wordsworth's own creation—his "painting" that exists only in the poem (the painting that would have reproduced the perfect calm of the "Mighty Deep" as the "gentlest of all gentle Things")—was a work of both "the Painter's hand" and the Poet's dream. Seldom have the conventions of iconic poetry been so faithfully reflected and so triumphantly enriched.

Of the criteria we laid down at the outset for pictorialist poetry, Keats—alone of the major Romantics—embodies all five. These we shall apply—somewhat more schematically than for the other poets and in an ascending order of importance—to the career and achievement of John Keats.

1. *The pictorialist inheritance from other poets*

The pictorialized allegory of Collins and Thomson, present in Wordsworth and Shelley as a major strain, appears also in Keats, although its presence is overshadowed by more direct forms of pictorialist expression. The Apollo of the ode sits in a state that recalls Ovid and Collins. "Melancholy" concludes, like an ode of Collins, in an allegorical temple, where a veiled goddess is at her shrine, surrounded by her "cloudy trophies," and Joy appears like a figure from a book of icons, "his hand ever at his lips/Bidding adieu." "The Ode to Psyche" addresses the poetic imagination in a way that recalls the Miltonic allegories of the Wartonian school.

2. Ut pictura poesis *in criticism*

Keats opened his critical mind only in private letters, and so he remained an amateur. But though unsystematic, brief, and offhand, his criticism can be intense and luminous, and the light that it sheds on our subject reveals a dedication to the immemorial values of *ut pictura poesis*. What Hazlitt called "gusto" and Keats, "intensity" both refer to qualities that are fundamentally pictorial and only derivatively literary. Hazlitt's "gusto" refers primarily to the living, veined, white flesh of a Titian nude. Benjamin West's "Death on a Pale Horse" invokes, negatively, Keats's requirement of intensity: "It has," he writes, "nothing to be intense upon; no woman one feels mad to kiss, no face swelling into reality—The excellence of every art is its intensity. . . ." [24] Sometimes Keats's enthusiasm for visual art surpasses even his love of literature. Of a book of prints from the fresco of a church in Milan, he declared: "I do not think I ever had a greater treat out of Shakespeare." [25] From the many pictures he admired and analyzed with Leigh Hunt, he seems to have derived another critical principle, which he calls "stationing" or "statuary" and which, in its essence, is related to what we have called "stasis." Of Milton's imagery Keats wrote: "Milton in every instance pursues his imagination to the utmost. . . . He is not content with simple description, he must station—thus here, we not only see how the Birds *'with clang despised the ground,'* but we see them *'under a cloud in prospect.'* So we see Adam *'Fair indeed and tall—under a plantane'*—and so we see Satan *'disfigured—on the Assyrian Mount.'* " [26] Such, in different language, is *ut pictura poesis.* Keats's "stationing" is a demand that poetic description be given composition and stasis—that it achieve the position and palpability of pictorial expression.

3. *Iconic verse*

Keats wrote four poems about real or imagined art objects, two on the Elgin Marbles and two on urns. In each case the chronologically later one is not only superior to the first but a triumph of its kind. The "Ode on a Grecian Urn" has been endlessly discussed, but it has seldom been viewed for what it is—an iconic poem.[27] It uses conventions that for centuries had governed that genre of verse. Art at once captures and transcends nature. A silent object speaks. The poem, like an actual urn, has at its base an epigrammatic inscription ("Truth is Beauty") that addresses the reader. Cold material receives the impress of warm life, which is immortalized as it freezes to form. Like all good iconic poetry, Keats's defies the doctrine of Lessing that poetry is temporal and statuary spatial. For Keats reminds you of the marble of the urn in almost every line—"Cold Pastoral," "brede/Of marble men and maidens"—and his own words are themselves carved out of marble, as it were—slowly, deliberately, in defiance of the tooth of time until they too achieve the "fair attitude" of the urn itself. Henry Moore, thinking of the narrative achievements in hard stone of a Rodin or a Bernini, declared that "Truth to material should not be a criterion of value in a work of art." [28] If a great baroque sculptor can make the movement of narrative poetry a major aesthetic aim, a pictorialist poet, conversely, will attempt in words the stasis of plastic art. Keats's bride of quietness is a lapidary creation.

4. *The* musée imaginaire

Keats's pictorialist poetry rests on the bright, coherent, and intensely personal *musée imaginaire* he carried about in his head. That museum Keats's painter and critic friends helped him create, and it is to their credit that they introduced him to art that surpassed their own. Severn did not impose on Keats's imagination the canvases that kept him a struggling painter but took his friend to the British Institution to see Titians, Claudes, and Poussins. Haydon's canvases the young poet professed, incredibly, to admire, but the important matter was that it was Haydon who introduced Keats to the Elgin Marbles. Leigh Hunt's own criticism may be flaccid, but his *soirées* were not, when Keats was intoxicated by his friend's "reading" of mythological paintings.

> Thus I remember all the pleasant flow
> Of words at opening a portfolio.[29]

Those evenings, which Keats also described as "joco-serio-musico-pictorio-poetical," [30] had this immediate result for Keats's first volume of poetry in 1817: as Ian Jack has well said, "Half the poems in the volume have the air of having been written after a visit to Hunt. . . ." [31] Most of all it was Hazlitt, a critic of painting fully as much as of poetry, who became the *miglior fabbro* of Keats's imaginary museum. The poet found Hazlitt's "depth of taste" one of the three things to rejoice at in his age.[32]

5. *Pictorial stasis in poetry*

It is a rule in pictorialist verse that time must have a stop—or very nearly. In Keats's poetry such stasis is pervasive. The deep-browed Homer of the sonnet on Chapman is statuesque, and stout Cortez and his men gazing at the Pacific are "stationed"—to use Keats's own term—in a history painting. A Claude-like vista is suggested by the poet's standing alone "on the shore/Of the wide world" as fame and love sink with the setting sun to nothingness. The "Eve of St. Agnes" moves from tableau to tableau of Gothic art: the dead, the angels, and the casement arches are in sculpture; the window, in heraldic stained glass; the crimson cloth, the golden dishes, and the silver baskets, in the still life of medieval tapestry; and Madeline kneels, like the Virgin in an illuminated Book of Hours.

In the longer poems—*Sleep and Poetry, I Stood Tiptoe, Endymion*, and the two *Hyperions*—it is the mythological landscape of the 16th and 17th centuries that slows the narrative movement to pictorial stasis. It is important to see that Keats's is in fact the mythological and heroic landscape of an earlier epoch and not the kind of landscape fashionable in his own day. Try as he would, Keats was not long attracted by the woodland picturesque, by the mountain sublime, or by the wild nature of Capability Brown. His was a landscape with architecture—a pagan temple or a castle on a hill with windows opening on a vista of water or valley. Nature was a "leafy luxury" that formed wreathed and rosy sanctuaries or a roof of boughs or creepers that entwined pools, fountains, and statues on pedestals. Above all, it was a peopled landscape, in which nymphs, cupids, gods, goddesses slept on the ground, peeped from trees, moved in ceremonial procession, or performed some rite described by Ovid. Keats painted nature with men and gods: heads with laurel chaplets, white arms, veined feet, snowy shoulders—all against the green and blue of forest and sky.

To that landscape Keats may now and then have added a detail from the mythological dictionaries of Bryant, Spence, or Lamprière, as many scholars have suggested. But it is closer to the facts—and more pleasant—to believe that Keats's landscape was a vision mediated to him by the strikingly parallel mythologies of Claude Lorrain, Nicolas Poussin, and Titian.

PLATE I The only painting of Claude that Keats referred to by name [33] has no direct relevance to any of his poems, except the one in which he describes it briefly. The castle in Claude stands, as Keats says, upon a rock on the border of a lake, but it is not "nested" in trees, although trees stand at its back; nor is it a "golden Galley all in silken trim" that approaches the castle, but a rowboat, barely visible, with two oarsmen. On Claude's canvas it is Psyche who sits in a contemplative pose, and the castle is the royal palace of Amor, to whose vicinity she has been transmitted by magic. The title by which Keats refers to the painting, *The Enchanted Castle*, dates from Woollett's engraving of 1782. [34] In the spirit of that title Keats refers to the building as "a Merlin's Hall, a dream." That association of Claude's building and dreamlike magic is, as we shall see, important.

PLATE II Claude loved to paint castles on frowning hills overlooking water; but he also liked Grecian temples on smaller, more civilized hills—slopes on which people in subdued light performed their ancient rites. In the *Landscape with Mount Parnassus* an old river god reclines apart from the group in a traditional pose, one hand resting on his emblematic urn, the other holding an almost imperceptible "scepter." Keats's old Saturn, "quiet as a stone," is not an exact replica of Claude's figure, but the lonely god of the *ancien regime*, in melancholy separation from his successors, is in the setting and spirit of Claude:

> Upon the sodden ground
> His old right hand lay nerveless, listless, dead,
> Unsceptred; and his realmless eyes were closed;
> While his bowed head seem'd list'ning to the Earth,
> His ancient mother, for some comfort yet. [35]

PLATE III Claude, like most mythologists of the Ovidian school, presented figures of gods or mortals sleeping on the ground—a motif that entered Keats's imagery again and again, even in his personifica-

PLATE I *Claude—Landscape with Psyche and the Palace of Amor (Courtauld Institute of Art, by permission of the Trustees of T. C. Loyd, Lockinge, Wantage, Berks.)*

Plate II *Claude—Landscape with Mount Parnassus (National Gallery of Scotland)*

PLATE III   *Claude—Narcissus and Echo* (*National Gallery, London*)

tions.   Poesy is Might, for example, who lies "half-slumb'ring on its own right arm," [36] the favorite position of sleeping gods or men in a mythological scene.   More even than *The Enchanted Castle*, the painting now in the National Gallery, London, entitled *Narcissus and Echo* has an air of enchantment, with its distant castle, its dark water, its landscape misty in the subdued light, the mythic figures almost a part of nature itself.   Hazlitt found that the trees of Claude, which were "perfectly beautiful," also had a "look of enchantment"; in fact, Claude's entire landscape seemed unreal, "as if all objects were become a delightful fairy vision . . ." [37]—a view of Claude shared even by Sir Joshua Reynolds, who said that Claude Lorrain "conducts us to . . . fairy land." [38]   May not Keats's vision, then, be termed Claudian when he sees "magic casements" that open on the "foam/Of perilous seas, in faery lands forlorn"? Such, at least, was the kind of language his period used of the landscapes of Claude.

To Hazlitt Claude was the most magical of painters; Poussin, the most "poetical." [39] "Poetical" was a standard term in art criticism to refer to paintings that told a story or presented ideas. Poussin as "poet" was not therefore a simple landscapist; he was not a portrayer but a lord of nature, who shows us what nature has been and what it can be. Poussin's landscape is nature cultivated by man—not, however, by his plow and harrow but by his future dreams and by his ancient recollections.

Poussin's heroic-mythological landscapes may be even closer to Keats's than Claude's. Two of Poussin's *Four Seasons* (Louvre) have Keatsian details: in *Summer*, Ruth the gleaner appears, kneeling before Boas in a setting that is dominated by a large field of alien corn. Poussin's *Autumn*, like Keats's, has another gleaner, who keeps "Steady [her] laden head across a brook." Poussin, more often than Claude, placed a sleeping nude in the grass. His *Sleeping Venus* in Dresden has a pouting mouth; one of Keats's sleepers—a male—has "a faint damask mouth" in "slumbering pout." The same sleeper in Keats lies facing the spectator—"Sideways his face repos'd" beneath four lily stalks above his head. Exactly the same number of tiny white flowers blossom over the head of Narcissus as he sleeps facing the spectator in Poussin's *Echo and Narcissus* in the Louvre. In the Munich *Midas and Bacchus*, Venus sleeps with "one white arm" (to quote Keats exactly) thrown over her head. A pout from one canvas, a sleeping posture and a flowery coronal from another, and an arched arm from a third—such details as these Poussin's sleepers contribute to Keats's scene.[40]

PLATE IV *The Kingdom of Flora,* now in Dresden, Keats "quotes" more than perhaps any other canvas.[41] In "I Stood Tip-toe" (ll. 96, 102) a maiden's gown fans away the down of the dandelions she walks over; she herself has "half-smiling lips, and downward look"; and Apollo appears on the pedestal (in Poussin it is Pan). In an "Imitation of Spenser" (l. 36) Keats refers to "all the buds in Flora's diadem." In a verse epistle to his brother George he describes a poetic trance in which he sees white coursers paw and prance "in air." In *Sleep and Poetry* (ll. 125–154) he "sees afar":

> O'ersailing the blue cragginess, a car
> And steeds with streamy manes—the charioteer
> Looks out upon the winds with glorious fear:

PLATE IV *Nicholas Poussin—The Kingdom of Flora*
(*Staatliche Kunstsammlungen, Dresden*)

And now the numerous tramplings quiver lightly
Along a huge cloud's ridge . . .

Later, "a lovely wreath of girls appears/Dancing their sleek hair into
tangled curls," as the "driver of those steeds is forward bent/And seems
to listen. . . ."

Coleridge quoted "an illustrious friend" in the *Biographia Literaria*,
who said that "our very signboards . . . give evidence that there has
been a Titian in the world."⁴² So does Keats's poetry. Again, it is
not impossible that Hazlitt may have been one of the instructors of
the poet's taste—Hazlitt, who once exclaimed of Titian, "I have wor-
shipped him on this side of idolatry," and who called the painter "the
greatest genius for colouring that the world ever saw." In commenting on the paintings reproduced in Plates VI–VIII, Hazlitt goes beyond
lyrical praise of their color, their charm, and their rich distilled per-
fumes: His criticism extracts from these canvases those details that
constitute Keats's landscape: "the snowy feet of the naked nymphs
in the water," "the snowy ermine-like skin," "the delicately formed
back," the "bright" scarves—above all the "delicious" "texture of/the
flesh."⁴³ In 1590 G. P. Lomazzo praised "la temperanza singolare di

Tiziano." [44]   In two centuries the emphasis had changed.   It was not temperance that Erasmus Darwin admired, but "glowing limb, . . . flowing hair,/Respiring bosom, and seductive air." [45]   It was not temperance that Fuseli attempted to imitate, that Hazlitt referred to as "prodigious gusto," and that Keats would have named "intensity."

PLATE V   Keat's landscape, like Titian's, has many a "dimpled hand."   In one, "two sweet sisters" appear

> Bending their graceful figures till they meet
> Over the trippings of a little child.[46]

PLATE VI   Titian's *Diana and Callisto,* in which Hazlitt saw "a charm . . . which no words can convey," is a Keatsian landscape, with its nudes, its sculptured altar and statue, its canopied trees.   It presents Diana as Keats saw her—in a shady bower, near a stream or fountain, being dried after her bath.

PLATE VII   Titian's *Diana and Actaeon* Keats describes directly:

> See, in another picture, nymphs are wiping
> Cherishingly Diana's timorous limbs;—
> A fold of lawny mantle dabbling swims
> At the bath's edge, and keeps a gentle motion
> With the subsiding crystal. . . .[47]

PLATE V   *Titian—The Three Ages of Man (National Gallery of Scotland, Courtesy of the Duke of Sutherland Collection, on loan to the National Gallery)*

PLATE VI *Titian—Diana and Callisto (National Gallery of Scotland, Courtesy of the Duke of Sutherland Collection, on loan to the National Gallery)*

The man who allowed his imagination to linger over the details of Titian's scene may well have identified himself with one of its chief actors, Actaeon, who with direct gaze looked on mythic beauty bare. Shelley, with exquisite appropriateness, when praising the dead Keats in *Adonais* (ll. 275–76), casts himself in the very same role—as one who

> Had gazed on Nature's naked loveliness,
> Actaeon-like. . . .

PLATE VIII Titian's *Bacchus and Ariadne* was called "much celebrated" by Joshua Reynolds, was praised by Hazlitt for the "prodigious gusto" of its colors, was a great favorite of Haydon, and was allegedly used by Wordsworth to embarrass Dryden for his lack of

PLATE VII *Titian—Diana and Actaeon (National Gallery of Scotland, Courtesy of the Duke of Sutherland Collection, on loan to the National Gallery)*

sensuousness in *Alexander's Feast*.[48] The painting was also much in Keats's mind. He loved a vintage scene, a group of Bacchic revelers moving down a hill, the faces aflame with sun and wine. Keats's figures often come riding in chariots or carts, drawn, as here, by the pards of Bacchus or by the "four maned lions hale" of Cybele. Keats admired a lovely nymph holding her "white hand toward/The dazzling sun-rise," and he remembered

> the swift bound
> Of Bacchus from his chariot, when his eye
> Made Ariadne's cheek look blushingly.[49]

PLATE VIII   *Titian—Bacchus and Ariadne (National Gallery, London)*

Keats created his landscapes of materials borrowed from three painters working in one genre. Paintings in that genre—a genre native to Venice and created about 1500—were called *poesie* and were themselves drawn from Ovid's mythologies. A pictorialist poet like Ovid thus inspired a poetic painter like Titian, who in turn inspired a pictorialist poet like Keats—a cycle of mutual admiration and influence between the Sister Arts.

Keats, the most insistently pictorialist of any Romantic poet and one of the finest flowerings in any soil of the centuries-old and European-wide tradition of the Sister Arts, is also a poet of the deepest musical resonances. At the home of Leigh Hunt, where so many of his visual impressions were born, he

> Was warm'd luxuriously by divine Mozart;
> By Arne delighted, or by Handel madden'd.[50]

The alternation in Keats's aesthetic education of the painterly and the musical is reflected in his maturest poetry. In the "Ode on a Grecian Urn" it is the visual that dominates, and the musical is consciously subordinated to it. The heard melodies cannot vie with those unheard, and the poem pipes "to the spirit ditties of no tone." In the pendent "Ode to a Nightingale" the reverse is true. Sound dominates, and the value of sight is subordinated and even denied. The poet "leave[s] the world *unseen*" in a flight that deserts Titian for "embalmed darkness," where the voice of an immortal bird tolls like a bell.

> Away! Away! for I will fly to thee,
> *Not* charioted by Bacchus and his pards,
> But on the *viewless* wings of Poesy.

Keats's greatest achievement, the ode "To Autumn," is a combination of the two modes of painting and music, with the addition of a third, natural description. Each of the three dominates a stanza: nature the first, painting the second, and music the third. Two of these, the natural and the pictorial, seem to have figured in the inspiration of the poem. Hazlitt saw in Titian's *Actaeon Hunting* a "brown, mellow, autumnal look." [51] Keats wrote of the autumn of 1819: "How beautiful the season is now. . . . Dian skies—I never lik'd stubble-fields so much. . . . Aye, better than the chilly green of the Spring. Somehow a stubble-plain looks warm—in the same way that some pictures look warm—This struck me so much in my Sunday's walk that I composed upon it." [52] What he composed was the ode "To Autumn," whose second stanza embodies the pictorial element of the original inspiration. Autumn is sharply personified and is carefully "stationed" in four fully paintable poses as she sits, sleeps, bears her burden, or watches, drop by slow drop, the last oozings of the cider press:

> Who hath not seen thee oft amid thy store?
>   Sometimes whoever seeks abroad may find
> Thee sitting careless on a granary floor,
>   Thy hair soft-lifted by the winnowing wind;
> Or on a half-reap'd furrow sound asleep,
> Drows'd with the fume of poppies, while thy hook
>   Spares the next swath and all its twined flowers:
> And sometimes like a gleaner thou dost keep
>   Steady thy laden head across a brook;
>   Or by a cyder-press, with patient look,
>   Thou watchest the last oozings hours by hours.

Keats luminously refutes, first, those literary historians who find that literary pictorialism died with the 18th century and, second, those aestheticians who assert either that art must remain true to its material or that one art must in any given age be dominant or that all art always aspires to the condition of one other art. For Keats is poet, painter, musician, natural observer all in one. In his best moments he achieved the perfection of style that Schiller dreamed of: "Poetry in its most perfect development must, like musical art, take powerful hold of us but at the same time, like plastic art, surround us with quiet clarity." [53]

NOTES

1. The present article, which was written two and a half years ago, anticipates much of the argument of Ian Jack's new book, *Keats and the Mirror of Art* (Oxford University Press, 1967). I should say that although I have known of Mr. Jack's study and have relied on the article that I acknowledge later on, my article was prepared without the benefit of Mr. Jack's complete researches, just as his book was prepared without any help from me. I trust the reader will note our differences and understand that any similarities of argument arise from absolutely independent consideration of the evidence.

2. *Dissertatio peripatetica de Epico carmine*, p. 41.

3. *Imagination and Fancy* (1st ed., 1844) (London, 1883), p. 91.

4. *Of the Sister Arts: an Essay*, p. 380.

5. The references in this paragraph come from Jean H. Hagstrum, *The Sister Arts* (Chicago, 1958), pp. 131, 147, 267.

6. "The term Beauty, in its native signification, is appropriated to objects of sight." Henry Home, Lord Kames, *Elements of Criticism* (1st ed., 1762) (Edinburgh, 1788), p. 196.

7. See M. H. Abrams, *The Mirror and the Lamp* (New York, 1958), p. 160 and also pp. 50–51, 94.

8. *Biographia Literaria* ("Everyman's Library," [1962]) p. 157.

9. *William Blake, Poet and Painter* (Chicago, 1964).

10. "The School of Giorgione," *The Renaissance* (London, 1928), pp. 131, 132, 135. At the beginning of the essay Pater concedes that each art has "its own peculiar and untranslatable sensuous charm, . . . its own special responsibilities to its material" (p. 128).

11. *The Life of Forms in Art* (New York, 1948), p. 10.

12. On Byron, see Leslie A. Marchand, *Byron A Biography* (New York, 1957), II, 690, 790; Stephen A. Larrabee, *English Bards and Grecian Marbles* (New York, 1943), pp. 151ff., 161, 171; dedication to Canto the Fourth of *Childe Harold's Pilgrimage* and also IV, xlix, cxl, clxi; *Beppo*, xlvi; "On the Bust of Helen by Canova"; *Don Juan, XIII*, lxxi–lxxii.

13. Larrabee, *op. cit.*, pp. 190, 195; *Letters of Shelley*, ed. Frederick L. Jones, *II*, 49–53, 80–81, 93, 112; *Daemon of the World, I*, 12–17, *Revolt of*

Islam, 11, 919–920 (*II*, xxix), 2268–2269 (V.li.6); *Prometheus Unbound, III*, iv. 164ff.; *Ode to Liberty,* iv, 57–58; v. 74.

14. *Iliad,* xii, 200 ff.; *Revolt of Islam, I*, viii.

15. "Memorabilia of Mr. Coleridge," *The Atlas,* Mar. 22, 1829, in *Complete Works,* ed. P. P. Howe (London, 1930–1934), *XX*, 217.

16. *Biographia Literaria,* ed. John Shawcross (Oxford, 1907), *II*, 235; *Collected letters of Coleridge,* ed. E. L. Griggs (Oxford, 1956–), *IV*, 569, 759.

17. See esp. "Lewti," 11, 65–75, "The Eolian Harp," "The Picture or the Lover's Resolution," 11, 68–110.

18. *Quarterly Review,* Aug., 1834.

19. "Mr. Wordsworth," *Spirit of the Age, Complete Works, XI*, 92–93.

20. *Early Letters of William and Dorothy Wordsworth,* ed. Ernest de Selincourt (Oxford, 1935), pp. 396, 401–402, 424; *Letters . . . : The Middle Years* (Oxford, 1937), *II*, 467–468, 861.

21. Frederick A. Pottle, "The Eye and the Object in the Poetry of Wordsworth," *Wordsworth Centenary Studies,* ed. Gilbert T. Dunklin (Princeton, 1951), p. 38.

22. See Geoffrey H. Hartman, "Wordsworth, Inscriptions, and Romantic Nature Poetry," *From Sensibility to Romanticism,* ed. Frederick W. Hilles and Harold Bloom (New York, 1965), pp. 389–413.

23. *Letters . . . : The Later Years,* ed. de Selincourt, *III*, 1123; Hagstrum, *The Sister Arts,* pp. 260, 278, 305, and Plate XXIV.

24. To George and Tom Keats, Dec. 21, 1817.

25. To George and Georgiana Keats, Dec. 1818–Jan. 4, 1819.

26. Marginalia on *Paradise Lost, VII*, 420–423, *Poetical Works and Other Writings,* ed. H. Buxton Forman (New York, 1939) *V*, 303–304.

27. Leo Spitzer has understood the *kind* of poem Keats wrote. See *Comparative Literature,* 7 (1955), 203–225, and Hagstrum, *The Sister Arts,* pp. xix, 23, 73, 75, 88, 119, 161.

28. As quoted by Rudolf Wittkower, *Bernini* (London, 1955), p. 1.

29. *Sleep and Poetry,* 11, 337–338.

30. As quoted in Aileen Ward, *Keats* (New York, 1963), p. 79.

31. *English Literature 1815–1832* (Oxford, 1963), p. 106.

32. To Haydon, Jan. 19, 1818.

33. *The Letters of John Keats,* ed. Hyder Edward Rollins (Cambridge, Mass., 1958), *I*, 263. See *Ibid., I*, 260, n. 8. *Epistle to John Hamilton Reynolds,* 11, 26–60.

34. Marcel Röthlisberger, *Claude Lorrain* (New Haven, 1961), *I*, 384–387.

35. *Hyperion, I*, 17–21.

36. *Sleep and Poetry,* 1, 237.

37. "On Gusto," *The Round Table, Complete Works, IV*, 79.

38. Discourse 13.

39. "On a Landscape of Nicolas Poussin," *Table Talk, Complete Works, VIII*, 171.

40. *Sleep and Poetry,* 1, 68; *Endymion, II*, 393–409.

41. Ian Jack is the first to have seen fully and precisely the influence of Poussin's painting on Keats. See " 'The Realm of Flora' in Keats and Poussin," *Times Literary Supplement* (London), April 10, 1959.

42. ("Everyman's Library," 1962), p. 105.

43. *Complete Works, X,* 27, 32, 72, 270.

44. *Idea del tempio della pittura* (Rome, 1947), p. 70.

45. *Temple of Nature,* iii. 299–300.

46. *Calidore,* 1, 93; *Sleep and Poetry,* 11, 367–369.

47. *Sleep and Poetry,* 11, 372–376.

48. Reynolds, Discourse 8; Hazlitt, *Complete Works, XI,* 92; *Letters of John Keats, II,* 284, n. 34.

49. *Sleep and Poetry,* 11, 334–336, 366–367.

50. *Epistle to Charles Cowden Clarke,* 11, 110–111.

51. "On Gusto," *The Round Table, Complete Works, IV,* 78.

52. Letter to Reynolds, Sept. 21, 1819.

53. *On the Aesthetic Education of Man,* trans. Reginald Snell (New Haven, 1954), p. 105.

IV | PRACTICAL CRITICISM II: POETICS

Harry Levin

Shakespeare in the Light
of Comparative Literature

Goethe had the grace to mark one of his returns to a favorite subject with the caption *Shakespeare und kein Ende*. For that forthright expression, with its Teutonic admixture of reverence and despair, J. E. Spingarn could propose no happier English translation than "Shakespeare Ad Infinitum." Evidently we are entering a domain where familiar shapes are subjected to sea changes. Of the making of books or speeches or essays concerning Shakespeare, the end is nowhere in sight. As we move into the fifth century of the Shakespearean epoch, that dénouement seems farther away than it can ever have seemed before. Reckonings of performance and publication on a world-wide scale are taken yearly by the *Shakespeare Survey* in England, the *Shakespeare Jahrbuch* in Germany, and the *Shakespeare Quarterly* in the United States. There is even, along with newsletters devoted to breathless bulletins about Scott Fitzgerald and other near-contemporaries, a *Shakespeare Newsletter*. Clearly it is not Shakespeare whose existence needs to be justified at this point. Rather it is comparative literature which must abide our question, and perhaps my caption would make more sense if it were reversed to read: "Comparative Literature in the Shadow of Shakespeare."

Whether comparative literature remains a marginal discipline, as it has been until quite recently, or becomes—as some of us feel encouraged to hope—a central one may conceivably hinge upon its capacity to deal with artists of larger stature than Madame de Staël. Not that I would presume to challenge the jurisdiction of the English department over its most highly valued treasure; but the very circumstances of language, culture, and history that made Shakespeare so English a phenomenon could not be fully appreciated without overstepping his native boundaries. There are times when we must relinquish the pedagogical microscope for the telescopic view—or, to put it more bluntly, ask ourselves Kipling's question:

> What shall they know of England
> That only England know?

Nor is the field of comparative literature as much of an innovation as its elliptical name and its current spread might seem to suggest. Its critical practice can be traced back as far as that famous Greek treatise *On the Sublime*, which not only compares Demosthenes with Cicero but cites a passage from the Pentateuch, thereby bringing the Old Testament within the range of Greco-Roman literary criticism. It is within this larger frame of reference, further enlarged by nearer and by more distant ranges of literature, that we must seek an ultimate place for the greatest masterpieces.

When Thomas Fuller looked back across a generation, from the mid-17th century to Shakespeare's lifetime, he compared Shakespeare with three classical authors: Ovid in poetry, Plautus in drama, and Martial in the warlike sound of his surname. Fuller's quasi-military parallel is no more extravagant or extraliterary than some of the far-fetched comparisons that now and then find their way into our scholarly journals. Some of these are worthy of Shakespeare's Welsh captain, Fluellen, when he eulogizes Henry V by comparing him with Alexander the Great:

> There is a river in Macedon, and there is also moreover a river in Monmouth. It is called Wye at Monmouth; but it is out of my prains what is the name of the other river. But 'tis all one; 'tis alike as my fingers is to my fingers, and there is salmons in both. . . . I speak but in the figures and comparisons of it.

Such reasoning compels us to agree with the lately installed Professor of Comparative Literature at the Sorbonne, M. Etiemble, who has so emphatically proclaimed in the title of his inaugural pamphlet: *Comparaison n'est pas raison*. No, comparison is not the same thing as reason; and if the fortuitous jingle in French has aroused false hopes, it has pointed the way to undeceptions; whereas in English we have known all along that, with humanistic subjects, the logic is not necessarily inherent; if there is to be methodological rigor, we ourselves must achieve it.

Shakespeare's master of malapropisms, Dogberry, warns us that comparisons are odorous, if not odious. And Falstaff denounces Prince Hal, after a bout of unsavory similes, for being "the most comparative, rascalliest, sweet young prince." Whether the "comparative" goes with the "sweet" or the "rascalliest" is impossible to determine with any certainty. The kindliest attitude toward our present concern that we could wrest from Shakespeare would probably be no more encouraging than an amused tolerance. Yet relevant comparison may be—must be —an instrument of analysis and a criterion of evaluation. Shakespeare had to undergo a certain amount of invidious comparison with Ben Jonson and others before he was found to be *primus inter pares,* and with leading writers of other countries before he was declared to be incomparable. Paragons would not attain their unique positions without benefit of the comparative process—a process exemplified by Samuel Johnson's announcement that the excellence of Shakespeare's works was "not absolute or definitive, but gradual and comparative." Since Shakespeare lived about two centuries before literary history had been systematized, and incidentally nationalized, the original effort to place his work was framed by a double perspective: on the one hand, his English contemporaries and predecessors, and, on the other, the ancient classics.

The compilation of Francis Meres, *Palladis Tamia, or Wit's Treasury,* published in 1598, is often adduced as a terminal date for the number of plays it lists. More ambitiously, it strove to be an intellectual survey of its era, albeit somewhat Procrustean in its approach, and proceeded to "a comparative discourse of our English poets with the Greek, Latin, and Italian poets." Its method was to demonstrate, by all too specific analogy, item for item, that the English moderns could match the achievements of the ancients. Hence it could be retrospectively viewed as a preliminary skirmish in what, a hundred years later, developed into the Battle of the Books. Meres, like Fuller afterward and many of Shakespeare's earlier admirers, set much store by his erotic poems: "The sweet, witty soul of Ovid lives in mellifluous and honey-tongued Shakespeare." Among Meres's other analogues the most important, because they were jointly applied to Shakespeare alone, signalized two different counterparts for his dramaturgy: "As Plautus and Seneca are accounted the best in comedy and tragedy among the Latins, so Shakespeare among the English is most excellent in both kinds for the stage."

In an early display of versatility, he had ranged the spectrum from *The Comedy of Errors* to *Titus Andronicus.* His repertory would be described by Polonius: "Seneca cannot be too heavy, nor Plautus too light." Elsewhere the Elizabethans paid lip-service to the Greeks; but, as is evident here, their models were Roman. Ben Jonson's condescending reservation, that Shakespeare had small Latin and less Greek, has misled many readers less learned than Jonson—or, for that matter, than Shakespeare. Scholars have employed much learning to take the measure of Shakespeare's relative ignorance and have more or less concluded that he knew no Greek at all, but that—measured by our unhumanistic standards—he had a fair background in Latinity. It is sometimes regretted that he had no acquaintance with Aeschylus and Sophocles. Yet imitation of consummate masters tends to produce lesser works, while writers of the second rank may serve as stimulating examples to be transcended. Obviously, it is more rewarding to study the influence of a minor on a major writer than to retrace a chain of causation which begins with unmatched brilliance and trails off into epigone mediocrity. The emulation of Shakespeare has had a debilitating effect upon all later attempts at poetic drama in English.

How the silver decadence of Seneca contributed to the golden flowering of drama in the 16th and 17th centuries—the paradox of abundant vitalities springing belatedly out of constricted agonies—is the impressive topic of a recent symposium, *Les Tragédies de Sénèque et le théâtre de la Renaissance,* edited by Jean Jacquot. Rather verbosely combining metaphysics with melodrama, not unlike that popular pessimist of our own day, Jean-Paul Sartre, Seneca offered his readers and hearers a paradigm for a dramatic relationship between the individual and the universe. Shakespeare deepened this relationship by shifting his emphasis from the turbulence of the universe to the consciousness of the individual. The observance of Senecan conventions helped to shape his tragic form; but, since his five-act structure was superimposed, it led toward unclassical complications. The structural norm for modern plays would seem to be three acts rather than five; and it could be argued with support from such theatrical technicians as Freytag and Granville Barker—it has indeed been argued by W. J. Lawrence—that Shakespeare, left to his natural devices, might have evolved a three-act play along more straightforward lines.

To attain the canonical five acts, the main plot had to be eked out with subordinate plots. This brought in a good deal of indigenous matter, whose origins could be sought in folklore and ritual rather than in more literary sources and consequently have been overlooked until not long ago. However, the tendency of comic interludes to parody the more serious episodes may be the most distinctive and deeply rooted characteristic of the English stage. The sudden transitions from tragic to comic and vice versa, which outraged classicists and emboldened romanticists, were deliberate effects, not random jumbles. They were based upon a new aesthetic of contrasts, appropriate to a climate which favored hybrid growths, and not upon the old unities, which had never been so firmly fixed as their proponents contended. The resulting intermixture of styles, under Shakespeare's full control, carried poetry closer and closer to the immediacy of reality— as innovating poets have attested, from Victor Hugo to Boris Pasternak. But with such witnesses we anticipate Shakespeare's bequest, whereas our initial glance should be directed toward his heritage.

If he has come to belong—as Benedetto Croce affirmed—to the common patrimony of culture, it should likewise be acknowledged what a rich inheritance came his way. The negative fact of not having studied Greek or even attended a university matters much less, in the long run, than the positive fact of having lived in a period which attached its highest values to books, the arts, and the pursuit of knowledge. An occasional slip or anachronism dwindles into insignificance before Shakespeare's ready command of so many professional vocabularies. He conjured with the apposite Latin tags, more especially in the early plays. He understood French well enough to risk a bilingual scene or two, not to mention a risqué joke or two, in *Henry V*. Some of his characters smatter a *lingua franca* of Italian, Spanish, and strange locutions from outlandish dialects. We roughly understand what Pistol means when he rants, *"Si fortune me tormento, sperato me contento."* And we are just as baffled as Parolles by the "terrible language" of his tormentors, sheer double talk and yet a demonstration of Shakespeare's linguistic virtuosity: *"Oscorbidulchos volivorco."* Above all, he could draw upon series of translations which relayed the *belles lettres* of the Continent to him with all the creative impetus of their age.

In the large assortment of reading that scholars have pieced together through internal evidence, two major writers stand out as kindred minds: Plutarch, the Greek biographer of the Romans, translated by the Frenchman Amyot and retranslated by the Englishman North, and Montaigne, the French psychologist of the self, whether or not in Florio's translation. Shakespeare could hardly have chosen better guides to human relations and to introspection. No English writer, apparently, meant so much to him. He had to be a wide reader in order to pick up his subjects in some of the far-flung places where he encountered them. The rule holds true that he seems less inspired when his source was another major writer: Consider Chaucer, for instance, and *The Two Noble Kinsmen*. *Troilus and Cressida*, where Homer stands behind Chaucer with Chapman between, may constitute an exception. But it may be observed that Shakespeare's chief masterworks, except for *King Lear*, were not derived from English originals. (*King Lear* is primarily Celtic, of course, and *Macbeth* is on the border in more ways than one.) There may have been more artistic challenge for him in dramatizing a slight or obscure *novella*. In any case, genetics are always more interesting when they involve crossbreeding.

The game of source hunting is still worth playing when we can learn something from it about Shakespeare's technique of adaptation, and particularly when it illuminates the means by which imagination renews itself, the permutation and transmutation of themes. Old-fashioned believers in original genius have been duly shocked by Shakespeare's habits of composition, forgetting that the Aristotelian word for plot was *mythos* or that Henry James himself scanned the *Times* and listened to gossip for his *données*. Nothing can be created by human beings *ex nihilo:* such is the lesson so harshly imparted by *King Lear*. When painters were cut off from mythology and forced to dream up their own subject matter, rather than simply to depict what patrons had commissioned, they turned to impressionism, expressionism, and abstraction. The pressure on playwrights to invent their own stories out of their heads has latterly been pushing them farther and farther toward the cultivation of novelty for its own sake, or else throwing them back upon the haphazard resources of their subjective selves. Conversely, more traditional writing rests on the shared experience of mankind, as digested into narrative and expressed through varying forms.

Count Gozzi, generalizing from his association with the *commedia dell' arte,* observed that there were no more than thirty-six dramatic situations. Schiller thought there ought to be more than that, according to Goethe; but when Schiller tried to enumerate them, he could not account for so many. We need not conclude that Shakespeare's artistry was reducible to the thirty-six categories ticked off in Polti's easy handbook of playwriting. Folklorists refine the enumeration by recognizing as many as 10,000 motifs. The aesthetician Etienne Souriau has devoted a mind-extending book to 200,000 dramatic situations. The point is that these are finite, however numerous; there are just so many combinations, though they may be recombined and modified to give the impression of infinite variety; and we may leave the tabulation to our colleagues' computers. The raw material, the basic fabric, which Shakespeare liked to call "stuff," has a life of its own which can be charted by what used to be called *Stoffgeschichte*. We may well prefer to regard his treatment of a given theme as definitive, yet we shall appreciate it better for an awareness of the variations that have been played upon it: the underplot of *The Merchant of Venice,* for example, and the story of the three caskets in ancient and modern, Oriental and Occidental lore.

The tale of Romeo and Juliet is traceable, through the poem of Arthur Brooke that Shakespeare used, to a collection of Italian tales by Matteo Bandello. Since it was independently used by Lope de

Vega for his tragicomedy, *Los Castelvines y Monteses*, it affords us an unparalleled opportunity for the controlled observation of what differentiates Shakespearean tragedy from the Spanish drama of the Golden Age, where the focal interest dwelt upon the families, the formalities, and the happy ending. From a broader standpoint, the basic motif of the tryst in the tomb is a Renaissance incarnation of the classic myth about Pyramus and Thisbe, which Shakespeare had read in his Ovid and burlesqued in his *Midsummer Night's Dream.* Furthermore, on the very highest plane of generality, Romeo and Juliet have common features with, and striking divergences from, Tristan and Isolde and many another pair of star-crossed lovers whose love is consummated by death. The organic totality of literature itself, insofar as it can be comprehended through its dynamic processes and its related configurations, must—in the last analysis—prove greater than any single author, even one who is generally acknowledged to be the greatest.

Thematic studies have much light to throw on characterization, as well as plotting. Critics of the late 18th and 19th centuries—periods when prose fiction flourished more than stage drama—tended to read Shakespeare's plays as if they were novels, identifying closely with the characters, and looking for more intimate details and more elaborate continuities than the dramatist had needed to supply. Twentieth-century criticism has endeavored to restore the balance by methods that the trenchant American scholar-critic, E. E. Stoll, termed "historical and comparative." These entail some danger of reduction: to reduce a character to his prototype—Falstaff, say, to the *miles gloriosus* of comic tradition—is to undermine his individuality. But, perceptively handled, they foster discernment: to discern the archetype from which a character gains his strength, as Gilbert Murray did in his essay "Hamlet and Orestes," is to show how literature gains its subliminal effects. Hamlet, for descriptive purposes, invokes several figures of mythology: Hyperion, Pyrrhus, Vulcan, Hercules (it remained for the Freudians to bring in Oedipus). Hamlet has himself walked out of his part into the sphere of mythological personification, like Falstaff, Othello, or Shylock, with their respective tutelary attributes.

Thus Turgenev could localize a self-conscious personage as "A Hamlet of the Shchigri District," and could set up his own antithesis between Hamlet and Don Quixote as the alternative confronting all Russian writers and their protagonists. Tolstoy's Prince Andrey is Hamlet-like, his Pierre is Quixotic; Turgenev himself is a Hamlet, Dostoevsky a Quixote. Tolstoy's stubborn resistance to Shakespeare was a poignant irony, since he is one of the few observers of his fellow men who has manifested a comparable breadth of sympathy. George Orwell has explained the contretemps by pointing to the tormented destiny that ended by casting Tolstoy in the role of Lear. The very need of the Russians to come to terms with Shakespeare, or else to fight him off, registers the extent of his diffusion and assimilation. Their Shakespearean scholar, Mikhail Morozov, informs us that *Othello* alone has been played in sixteen Soviet languages. Shakespeare was introduced into Russia under the imperial auspices of Catherine the Great, who—in adapting *The Merry Wives of Windsor* —adapted the staple of Falstaff's diet, sack, by substituting a homely local beverage, quass. That may be a trivial detail, yet it illustrates the crucial distinction between what is universal in Shakespeare's appeal and what is merely particular: the universality of thirst and the particularities of the endemic potables for quenching it.

Shakespeare's international ascendancy is not unrelated to the peculiar cultural and linguistic position of England, notably its interdependence and interplay with the Romanic and Germanic cultures and languages. Here two books, both written about two generations ago, both of them pioneering contributions to comparative literature, have served as guideposts and remain object lessons: *Shakespeare en France sous l'ancien régime* by Jules Jusserand and *Shakespeare und der Deutsche Geist* by Friedrich Gundolf. The contrast between them aptly mirrors the divergent fortunes of Shakespeare in France and Germany. Jusserand, a scholar by avocation and an Academician by predilection, was a diplomat accredited to England and to the United States. Gundolf was a professor at Heidelberg, more concerned with letters than with philology, and in close touch with the poetic circle of Stefan George. His study is philosophic and lyrical; Jusserand's is urbane and anecdotal; taken together, they virtually personify the variance between *Geist* and *esprit*. If Jusserand's is a fairly shallow book, it is because the contacts between Shakespeare and France were comparatively superficial during the two centuries to which his investigation is limited.

These are filled in with social documentation and rounded out with national generalizations, which are both shrewd and amusing; but the confrontation was strongly antipathetic, from the earliest allusions to the revolutionary epoch. Such a mutual repulsion has its significance for the history of taste, to be sure; and there have been English neo-classicists, notoriously Thomas Rymer, who were much more pig-headedly anti-Shakespearean than Voltaire. Voltaire's case is a complex one, which has been thoroughly investigated by later students and which is amply articulated through his collected works, since he kept returning to Shakespeare obsessively. Starting from a youthful enthusiasm for all manifestations of English liberalism, it turned into a sense of rivalry after he had aided Shakespeare to win a hearing in France and culminated in a jealously nationalistic antagonism when Shakespeare was being hailed as a god of the theater. If the admiration and the reservation were balanced in Voltaire's catch phrase, "a barbarian of genius," then he put his hand upon the scales when he added that Shakespeare had more barbarism than genius.

This was a triumph of culture over language, though it would be hard to say which culture over which language. With ironic symbolism, Voltaire's chair at the Académie Française was filled upon his death by Jean-François Ducis, who was best known for his adaptations of Shakespeare. These are all the more remarkable because Ducis was utterly unacquainted with English, though he claimed to derive inspiration from portraits of Shakespeare and David Garrick on his writing-desk. The version of Ducis most performed and admired was his highly classicized Hamlet. Therein the ghost is decorously mute; the prince swears revenge on an urn containing his father's ashes; and the play is dedicated, in a tearful epistle, to the ashes of the playwright's father. The old king, it transpires, has been killed in a crime of passion by none other than his queen, who finally kills herself. Her accomplice, Claudius, is the father of Ophelia—inasmuch as Polonius is no more than a Racinian confidant—so that this Hamlet, like the heroes of Corneille, is faced with a clear-cut choice between his love for the heroine and his own family's honor. It requires no further manipulation of the plot for him to survive the carnage and mount the throne.

Well, it should not surprise us that every nation beholds its visage in Shakespeare's mirror. On the other side of the Rhine, after Goethe had re-created a Hamlet in the neurasthenic image of Wilhelm Meister, the radical poet Freiligrath would declare: *"Deutschland ist Hamlet!"* It will be conceded that, though the role has been more happily acted and the identification is far from complete, certain affinities have been stronger in Germany. Hence Gundolf had a richer and more sympathetic body of testimony to cover than Jusserand. At the outset, the German critic felt compelled to redefine the concept of influence—which has functioned as so jejune an entry on the ledgers of comparative literature—in terms of its etymological derivation, *Ein-fluss*, the inflow of a vitalizing current which changes the whole nature of the mainstream. He went on to show how that fusion had enabled German literature to free itself from the long French Dom-

inance and how characteristically its emerging spokesmen had re-
acted to the Shakespearean stimulus. The independent Lessing had
made Shakespeare a rallying cry for the critical campaign against
neoclassicism, as well as an exemplar for practicing playwrights to
emulate.

Shakespeare could be looked upon as the calm at the center of the
Sturm und Drang—that tempestuous movement which produced so
many plays that sound like exaggerations of his. His most successful
emulator was Schiller, whose rendering of *Macbeth* is properly *geist-
lich*, with the witches fulfilling his notion of a Greek chorus, and the
Porter's drunken monologue deleted in favor of a solemn hymn to
the sunrise. Yet Shakespeare's chronicle plays were the inspirations
for the grandiose pageantry of *Maria Stuart* and the *Wallenstein* trilogy. What was lacking may have been hinted by—of all people—
Karl Marx, when he distinguished between Schillerizing and Shake-
spearizing: between mere ideological mouthpieces and completely
dramatized personalities, in brief, between propaganda and purer art.
Shakespeare's pre-eminence in the world's drama was securely established by the critic mainly responsible for the standard German translation, August Wilhelm Schlegel, in his Vienna lectures of 1808,
Vorlesungen über dramatische Kunst und Literatur, which seem to
have had more impact on Coleridge than the latter was willing to
acknowledge. The German and the English currents, in their reflux,
converged to shift the tide in France after the Revolution, and after
that retarded classicism which was temporarily upheld by Napoleon's
authoritarian tastes.

Now the word "romantic" is an anglicism. Its adoption into Continental languages ran parallel to the spreading cult of Shakespeare,
which, as it moved across Europe, brought out the latent nationalistic
self-realization of the literatures that responded to it. Significantly,
that word made its first French appearance in the prefatory discourse
to the first full-scale French translation of Shakespeare by Pierre
Letourneur in 1776. This was the occasion for the rear-guard action
expressing Voltaire's extreme protest, his letter to the French Academy. In a footnote contrasting *romantique* with the usual adjective
romanesque, and with its synonym *pittoresque,* Shakespeare's exponent defended his neologism on the grounds that it conveyed a more
emotional response to nature. Immediately afterward it was employed, still rather self-consciously, in a volume on the appreciation
of picturesque landscapes by the Marquis de Girardian, a friend of
Jean-Jacques Rousseau. Thence the archromanticist seems to have
picked up what was to become his shibboleth; for *romantique* was

naturalized into a context describing the Swiss landscape in the fifth of Rousseau's *Rêveries du promeneur solitaire,* written in 1777 but published posthumously.

During that same year, at the height of the American Revolution, the English critic Maurice Morgann took up Voltaire's challenge and predicted that Shakespeare would soon be enacted on the other side of the Appalachian Mountains. His voice would ring through riverboats and mining camps. But there is an inevitable lag between the emergence and the acceptance of revolutions in the arts. It was not until 1830, with the première of Hugo's *Hernani,* a drama which owed more to Shakespeare than to its French forerunners, that Romanticism made its triumphant arrival in the capital of its enemies. It took an English battering-ram to breach the wall of French classicism, as Sainte-Beuve would phrase it, before a native Romanticist could carry an audience. Hugo had tried and failed, with his pseudo-Shakespearean *Cromwell;* the preface was more telling than the play. That, in turn, had been preceded by Stendhal's manifesto, *Racine et Shakespeare,* which had borrowed some of its ammunition from Dr. Johnson's magistral defense. Stendhal, without paying much attention to either dramatist, had pitted them against each other as programmatic symbols of authority and autonomy, offering his compatriots the choice between obsolescence with Racine and modernity with Shakespeare.

The actual cross-fertilization occurred during the 1820's, when a celebrated English troupe of actors played Shakespeare at Paris, with aftereffects that are memorialized in the painting of Delacroix and the music of Berlioz, as well as in literature. Berlioz' frenzied courtship of the fascinating Irish actress, Henrietta Smithson, reverberates through his sequence of Shakespearean compositions. His operatic version of *Much Ado About Nothing* was tactfully rechristened *Béatrice et Bénédict* because the French title of Shakespeare's play might have been construed as a reflection upon his musical style: *Beaucoup de bruit sur rien* could be too pointed a comment on the orchestration of the new school. Shakespeare, then, could awaken fresh talent in France as he had been doing in Germany. Yet, though he was now welcomed, he was never quite at home in the garb prescribed for diplomatic visits. Desdemona's controversial handkerchief, scorned as a vulgarity by the purists, was replaced in Vigny's *More de Venise* with an innocuous scarf and an impeccable bracelet. Meanwhile the Germans, at the opposite pole, had become so acculturated that they fell into their provocative habit of talking about *unser Shakespeare.*

That usage might be warranted as a claim of spiritual kinship, so long as it could be advanced for other languages with their own possessive pronouns, and while the English "our" retains its priority—in other words, so long as Shakespeare transcends any one nationality by appealing to all. The German claim could be substantiated by a vast corpus of commentary, yes, but more appropriately by a living record of presentation in the theater. This could not have been accomplished without a translation which, while remarkably faithful to the original, has come to occupy an honored niche in German literature. The circumstance of using a text which dates back no more than one hundred and fifty years means, of course, that their Shakespeare is closer to them by some two hundred years than our Shakespeare is to us. Moreover, it is not for nothing that the two languages are structurally interrelated. When Juliet invokes Apollo's chariot, for instance, she speaks of "fiery-footed steeds," which does not sound quite the same as "flammenhufiger Gespann" or even "flame-hoofed team." Yet it comes close because Schlegel has managed to capture the compound epithet, where Salvatore Quasimodo is forced to string the words out in Italian: "cavalli dai piedi di fuoco."

As a little exercise in comparative stylistics, let us concentrate on a well-known and problematic line which distressed Pope and other English rigorists because it perpetrated a mixed metaphor: "Or to take arms against a sea of troubles." The German flows just as naturally, and somewhat more regularly: "Sich waffnen gegen eine See von Plagen." Here too the Russian of Pasternak's translation seems no less accurate, though perhaps more compressed. But the image could never accommodate itself to the rules of French logic and clarity. If Pope balked, you can imagine Voltaire's objections. He undertook to rethink the entire soliloquy, while conferring the dignity of alexandrines upon it:

> Demeure, il faut choisir et passer à l'instant
> De la vie à la mort et de l'être au néant.

Thus Hamlet's existential dichotomy is rounded out with a flourish more characteristic of Sartre; and, since an anticlerical is speaking, it will not surprise you that—among the other ills that flesh is heir to—Voltaire goes out of his way to drag in lying priests ("nos prêtres menteurs"). The impulse of French translators is to qualify Shakespeare's trope by neutralizing one component or the other, modifying "take arms" to "lutter" or "s'insurger" and "a sea of troubles" to "un monde de douleurs" or "la mer orageuse"—or else abstracting both, as in Letourneur's rendering: "se révoltant contre une multitude de maux."

Yet a more concretely literal rendering, in the most widely circulated French Shakespeare, that of the poet's son, François-Victor Hugo, sounds at once odd and prosaic: "s'armer contre une mer de douleurs." (Here we must blandly ignore the collocation of syllables, *mer de*, which Voltaire played upon for a scatological snicker.) As Hamlet goes on to remark, "There's the rub"—and the figure from bowling, for an unfavorable inclination of ground, slows down, if it does not stop, the translators. Again they try to generalize the dilemma: "the rub" becomes "l'obstacle" or "l'embarras." Others introduce metaphors of their own: a reef (Guizot), a gulf (Ménard), a question mark (Montégut). Dumas is unwontedly laconic and colorless: "Ah! tout est là!" In the second volume of the Pléiade Shakespeare, the editor, André Gide, prints eleven versions of the *être ou ne pas être* passage, but not his own, which takes the unexpected step of transporting the catachresis from warfare to horsemanship: "mettre frein à une marée de douleurs." In his previous translation of *Antony and Cleopatra*, Gide has been more resistant to the Shakespearean afflatus. There the succinct tribute of Enobarbus,

> Age cannot wither her nor custom stale
> Her infinite variety,

is decompressed and divided into two heavy commonplaces: "Les années passeront sans la flétrir. Son extrême diversité met au défi la lassitude." One is reminded of those Academicians who criticized an exuberant line from *Le Cid*, "Ses rides sur son front ont gravé ses exploits," by patiently instructing Corneille that, though wrinkles denote the passing of years, they cannot strictly be said to engrave exploits.

"There's the rub"—reverting with Gide to *Hamlet*—becomes "C'est là le hic." That is to say, a metaphor from sport is transposed to a bit of scholastic jargon. Since the *hic* is an abbreviation of the Latin *Hic est quaestio*, it is basically a repetition of Hamlet's "That is the question." But the transposition from an athletic to a bookish expression is revealing, as we shift from England to France. Every barrier of untranslatability in language is a genuine index of disparity in culture. Shakespeare seems to provoke a certain stylistic intransigence, even on the part of the flexible Gide, who does not brand Shakespeare a drunken savage as Voltaire did, but tells us that the reader undergoes "une sorte d'enivrement verbale." Though such poetic intoxication can be exhilarating, it deviates at its peril from sober prose. The contribution of *Hamlet*'s latest French translator, the gifted poet Yves Bonnefoy, has been to round out the cycle by utilizing in earnest what Voltaire had conceived as a reduction to absurdity and literally rendering our troublesome line: "ou de prendre les armes contre une mer de troubles." This willingness to adapt the French to Shakespeare, rather than to adapt Shakespeare to the French, sets the tone for the *Hamlet* of Yves Bonnefoy.

This would not be a viable strategy if the French convention were not changing at the hands of such poets as M. Bonnefoy. English poetry has an open diction, an *ouverture* which—in his critical comments—he opposes to the *fermeture*, the closed diction, of conventional French poetry. What has happened during the past half-century, as we might learn from comparing translations, has brought French literature closer to a Shakespearean openness of form. As it were, some spirit has been breathed into the letter. At all events, whatever we lose through these international transactions can be regained with interest whenever we return to the reading of Shakespeare at first hand. Yet that reading, even for natives of English, is not just an unimpeded projection from the page to the mind; it is rather a gradual unfolding, which varies from person to person and stage to stage in the amount of meaning it reveals. Since all comprehension is at best an approximation, we must pursue our object from our varying distances. And, since even Shakespeare's puns are " a lively feature of his work," they need not be written off when the translator is as resourceful as Mario Praz in his command of both languages involved (*Shakespeare, Il Castiglione et le facezie*).

To pinpoint the areas of probable misunderstanding is a valuable aid to potential understanding. Those refracted images disclose much about the cultures between which they mediate. The intervention of Shakespeare has acted as a touchstone for bringing out positive aspects of German romanticism and negative aspects of French classicism, although the Germans did not understand him as well as they thought and the French are coming to understand him better. The quality— or should it be the quiddity?—whatever confers on poetry its uniqueness is, by definition, untranslatable. The poem addressed by Hamlet to Ophelia pivots upon an ambiguity which is peculiar to English, the use of the verb "to doubt." Two accomplished and indefatigable linguists, Erika and Alexander Gerschenkron, have studied one hundred translations of this quatrain into sixteen languages. Their forthcoming article, "The Illogical Hamlet: A Note on Untranslatability," is a devastating chronicle of evasions, circumlocutions, misconstructions, and downright mistranslations, which leaves us wondering what can come out of a process wherein so much is lost, beyond the self-congratulation of those who may happen to have been born into Shakespeare's language—or, at least, our demotic dialect of it.

The answer, I would suppose, is that every reincarnation must assume its own autonomous form, though it has been brought to life by Shakespeare's inimitable touch. "Every historical period finds in him what it is looking for and what it wants to see." Such is the warrant, at any rate, for a widely heralded, currently published, and already influential book, *Shakespeare Our Contemporary* by Jan Kott. As a Pole, Professor Kott has honorably suffered under both the Nazi and Soviet regimes. That may explain why he does not want to see any meaning at all in history. Instead he looks for, and naturally finds, an anachronistic panorama of meaninglessness in Shakespeare's histories. He finds no humor in the comedies or anywhere else, while tragedy is displaced by grim grotesquerie, since moral choices must confront alternatives which are equally absurd in the world Professor Kott envisions. Accordingly, the book that Hamlet reads is not by Montaigne, as some scholars like to believe, but by Sartre, Camus, or Kafka; while *King Lear* is subtitled *Endgame* and updated for Samuel Beckett's Theater of the Absurd, where dialogue subsides into endless monologue, will power is smothered in inertia, and the stormy heath shrinks to the asphyxiating proportions of a pair of garbage cans.

Shakespeare, thus roughly handled and forcibly subpoenaed, bears witness to the anger, the cruelty, and the violence of our own times. Nevertheless, there are other contemporary interpreters to whom his lessons seem more optimistic. Writing to commemorate his quadricentennial in the Soviet literary journal, *Novy Mir*, the orientalist Nikolay Konrad accepts the tragic sense of history as a bond between Shakespeare and the Russian soul, with the implication that Stalin was cast as Macbeth or Richard III. But Professor Konrad sees the blood and terror as an expiation which clears the air for more humanistic perspectives. Meanwhile, the West German periodical *Akzente* has marked the jubilee with a curious article by that brilliant novelist Günter Grass, compendiously entitled "Pre- and Post-History of the Tragedy of Coriolanus from Livy and Plutarch through Shakespeare to Brecht and Me." What Herr Grass gets out of Shakespeare or reads into him—"herausglesen und hineingelesen," in his own phrase—is something more than a parody of the pedantic *Quellenforschung* conducted by German professors; it is an attack against Bertolt Brecht on charges of political opportunism, using techniques of burlesque which Brecht applied to other writers and taking its departure from his last production, a Marxist revision of Shakespeare's play.

Coriolanus, somehow one of the few plays by Shakespeare that never seem to get produced in Soviet Russia, is wryly characterized by Herr Grass as an ever green, and therefore sour, apple ("dies immergrüne, aber sauer Apfel"). Truly it seems to affect its audiences with the kind of social tension, the conflict of ideologies, the very class struggle it dramatizes. Riots broke out when Max Reinhardt produced it during the 1920's in Berlin, and a French cabinet fell when it was presented in the mid-thirties at the Comédie-Française. *Julius Caesar,* another one of Shakespeare's public inquiries into the hazards of Roman citizenship, has elicited similar repercussions from time to time, most pointedly when Orson Welles costumed it in Fascist uniforms. It was first translated into Japanese for liberal and patriotic reasons in 1884, the year of Japan's new constitution; but it was not acted until 1901, when a performance—Kabuki-style in Tokyo—seems to have been generally regarded as alluding to an explosive train of events touched off by the assassination of a reactionary politician. When a Swahili version of the same play was recently published by Julius K. Nyerere, the Premier of Tanzania, it was reported to have stressed the understandable moral that conspirators come to bad ends. The echoes must intensify to a crescendo, when a Tanzanian or a Japanese Cassius exclaims:

> How many ages hence
> Shall this our lofty scene be acted over
> In states unborn and accents yet unknown!

Carrying prophecy to the point of fulfillment, in purporting to look ahead, those lines hark back to Shakespeare himself, even while they look beyond him—and with him—to ancient Rome. Through them he takes his stand in our cultural firmament, encompassing so much of what has gone before, enkindling so much of what comes after, that we are bound to take our bearings from him. The dependence of latter-day writers upon his igniting spark was indicated and exemplified by Vladimir Nabokov, when he named his last English novel with an oblique allusion to *Timon of Athens:*

> The moon's an arrant thief,
> And her pale fire she snatches from the sun.

Most of us, as students, feel more at ease with the microcosm of Shakespeare's text than in the bedazzlement of such cosmic vistas. Yet comparative literature can help us to realize how much of our light is reflected from his radiance, how many of our luminaries can be viewed as his satellites. In short, it can teach us to reckon the larger magnitudes, to recognize the stars by discerning the constellations. As distinguished from the specific study of individual authors, it must place its stress on interrelationships rather than on objects in themselves. But a literary object owes its existence to a network of such relationships, not least to those that link it with ourselves.

Haskell M. Block

The Alleged Parallel of Metaphysical and Symbolist Poetry

At its best, the comparative approach to literature is concerned not only with questions of historical relationship, but with the interpretation and illumination of works of art, in themselves as well as in their interrelations. As a way of defining literary values, comparison moves hand in hand with analysis. Yet, comparison, by its very nature, implies contrast: differences as well as similarities. It is now a commonplace that comparative studies cannot be limited to strictly causal relationships. From the standpoint of theme, attitude, art form, or tradition, works widely separated in time and place may illuminate one another in vital and significant ways. This is not to say, however, that any work may be fruitfully compared with any other. The test of any comparison lies, I believe, in the degree to which our understanding and appreciation of the literature at hand is thereby enhanced. The natural tendency to magnify similarities and minimize differences may in fact result in serious falsification of literary history and critical judgment. Consideration of such falsifications may serve to point to some of the dangers in this approach and to ways in which they might be overcome.

The alleged parallel of metaphysical and symbolist poetry offers to my mind a classic example of gratuitous and arbitrary comparison. I would not deny for a moment the enormous and fruitful impact of the rediscovery of Donne and his contemporaries on English and American poetry in the 20th century, and it is easy to appreciate at least some of the motives underlying the claim that metaphysical and symbolist poetry are essentially similar and indeed identical. Before proceeding to direct examination of this view, it might be well to consider briefly how it came to develop.

This history of the parallel has been described in some detail, although incompletely, by Joseph E. Duncan in *The Revival of Metaphysical Poetry*.[1] To the best of my knowledge, the first statement of this relationship appears in an essay of Edmund Gosse, "The Poetry of John Donne," first published in *The New Review* in September, 1893, and reprinted the following year in *The Jacobean Poets.*[2] In explaining what he considers as Donne's revolution in English versification, Gosse declares: "To see what he aimed at doing, we have, I believe, to turn to what has been attempted in our own time by Mr. Robert Bridges, in some of his early experiments, and by the Symbolists in France." [3] 1893 is indeed an early date for this *rapprochement,* and it is no surprise that Gosse does not elaborate; from the context, it is clear that he has in mind Donne's mixed cadences and irregularities of accent rather than the themes, images, or attitudes in his poetry. Nevertheless, this brief suggestion provides the germ of one of the most consequential poetic theories of our time. Gosse did not hesitate to restate his view somewhat more extensively a few years later, in the second volume of his *Life and Letters of John Donne,* where he declares of the poet:

> He desired greatly to develop the orchestral possibilities of English verse, and I have remarked that the irregular lyrics of Mr. Robert Bridges and the endless experiments of the Symbolists in France are likely to be far more fruitful to us in trying to understand Donne's object, than any conventional repetition of the accepted rules of prosody.[4]

We should note in passing that Gosse did not exactly admire these "endless experiments" of the symbolists. For while he was one of the first critics to call the attention of the English public to Mallarmé's poetry, it can hardly be said that he did the French poet a service.[5]

The next significant assertion of the parallel is probably that of Herbert J. C. Grierson in his chapter on Donne in the fourth volume of the *Cambridge History of English Literature* (1910).[6] Grierson's essay is one of the pioneer scholarly discussions of Donne's poetic technique. Commenting on Donne's ingenuity and love of artifice, he declares that the poet is "one of those who, like Baudelaire, are 'naturally artificial; for them simplicity would be affectation.' " [7]

Perhaps in this slight and offhand remark lies the origin of T. S. Eliot's famous pronouncement.

It was apropos of Grierson's anthology, *Metaphysical Lyrics and Poems of the Seventeenth Century,* that Eliot wrote his essay of 1921, "The Metaphysical Poets." [8] We should recognize that Eliot is no happier here with the phrase, "metaphysical poetry," than are most 20th-century critics, yet he accepts the term in large measure in the sense in which it is used by Samuel Johnson in his essay on Cowley. For Eliot, the characteristic metaphysical device is "the elaboration (contrasted with the condensation) of a figure of speech to the farthest stage to which ingenuity can carry it." Donne's "brief words and sudden contrasts," his "telescoping of images and multiplied association" issue, in his best poetry, in "a direct sensuous apprehension of thought, or a re-creation of thought into feeling." I need not here take up the question of the "dissociation of sensibility" and the broad historical and cultural assumptions underlying Eliot's view of Donne. More to our purpose are his citations from Corbière and Laforgue, both of whom, we are told, "are nearer to the 'school of Donne' than any modern English poet." To this pair of French poets Eliot was soon afterward to add Baudelaire, akin to Donne in his mastery of surprise, in his "unity and order";[9] and then, in an essay of 1926, Mallarmé.

It is noteworthy that Eliot describes his brief "Note sur Mallarmé et Poe," published in the *Nouvelle Revue Française,* as a contribution to comparative literature. Explaining that he does not propose to decipher the enigmas of Mallarmé's poetry or to analyze his syntax or metrics, Eliot declares:

> Mais il y a un autre aspect du "problème" que je puis peut-être traiter avec plus de compétence, et qui n'est pas négligeable: ce qu'on pourrait appeler l'aspect de littérature comparée—je ne veux pas dire une vaine étude des origines et des influences, mais la définition du type du poète, établie par une comparaison avec d'autres manifestations de ce type dans d'autres langues et à d'autres époques.[10]

This classification of families of poets may very well have been set forth in the Clark Lectures delivered by Eliot at Trinity College, Cambridge, also in 1926. Eliot steadfastly maintained the privacy of these lectures, and they remain unpublished.[11] We have some notion, all the same, of Eliot's approach to his subject from the brief comments of Mario Praz, who states that Eliot spoke of three metaphysical periods in European poetry: medieval, baroque, and modern, with Jules Laforgue as the chief representative of the modern period.[12] It is this same formulation that we find in Eliot's remarks on Mallarmé.[13]

Mallarmé for Eliot in 1926 is part of a family of poets that includes Cavalcanti, Donne, and Poe, all of whom exemplify "le poète métaphysique." That is, they all make use of metaphysical speculation to refine and enlarge their power of sensibility and emotion. On the one hand, Eliot separates "la *poésie métaphysique*" from "la poésie philosophique." The latter is represented by Dante and Lucretius in a complete and systematic sense, or by Baudelaire on a simpler and more fragmentary scale. On the other hand, Eliot distinguishes the expansion of sensibility of the metaphysical poet from that of the *halluciné,* as in Rimbaud or Blake: "Il y a fort peu de *l'halluciné,*" Eliot declares, "chez Mallarmé." Hence, for the poet of *Hérodiade,* the world beyond the limits of the normal and everyday is simply an extension of the real world, "aggrandi et continué." In both Mallarmé and Donne, Eliot declares, "Nous sommes dans un monde où tout le matériel, toutes les données, nous sont parfaitement familières." The work of both poets, he insists, is rooted in common, elemental reality.

The essay of 1926 marks Eliot's fullest published statement of the metaphysical-symbolist parallel. His reexamination of the French symbolist tradition in his essay of 1948, "From Poe to Valéry," makes no attempt to establish the slightest analogy or affinity between Donne and Baudelaire or Mallarmé. Evidently by the end of the 1920's he had decided that his definition of "metaphysical" in the abstract, of what all "metaphysical" poets had in common, was "too general to be useful." [14] It is also apparent that as his interest in Dante and in Baudelaire developed, his interest in Donne declined.[15]

In his essay of 1921 on Andrew Marvell, Eliot did not hesitate to group Baudelaire with Donne and Laforgue, as poets who "may be considered the inventor of an attitude, a system of feeling or of morals." [16] By 1930, in large part under the impact of Charles Du Bos, his view of Baudelaire had developed considerably. In *The Criterion* in January of that year, he declared, "any adequate criticism of Baudelaire must inevitably lead the critic outside of literary criticism." [17] This is certainly the case in Eliot's famous essay on Baudelaire, a pronouncement of central importance for the understanding of Eliot's own development as both poet and critic; however, as a critique of Baudelaire, it is to my mind one-sided, partial, and essentially wrong.[18] René Galand in his perceptive study of the impact of Baudelaire on Eliot has rightly asked: "Is the Baudelaire whom Eliot sees the real one?" The same may be asked of the "metaphysical" Baudelaire described in Eliot's essays ten years earlier.

The parallel of metaphysical and symbolist poetry is as much the creation of Eliot's followers as of Eliot himself. By 1931 Eliot was ready to qualify his position sharply, and in his essay, "Donne in Our Time," he declared:

> . . . it is impossible for us or for anyone else ever to disentangle how much was genuine affinity, genuine appreciation, and how much was just a *reading into* poets like Donne our own sensibility, how much was "subjective." [19]

Yet, what for Eliot was literary strategy soon became literary history; hypothesis came to be asserted as fact.

George Williamson opens his discussion of *The Donne Tradition* (1930) by insisting on a parallel between Donne and Baudelaire in their common obsession with death: "Especially in its morbidity, Donne reminds us of Baudelaire, for his own poems brought to the dying Elizabethan age the sharper flavor of *Les Fleurs du Mal.*" Both poets, according to Williamson, are poets of decadence, both express a desire to escape from this world, "and both wrote poetry which surprises, shocks, and baffles expectation." [20] Mr. Williamson insists that Baudelaire's "Le Goût du Néant" helps us to understand Donne better, in view of their common pursuit of the strange and the perverse, their common fascination with ugliness and with death. Readers of Eliot's essays of 1921 and 1923 will recognize at once the source of the comparison. In *The Donne Tradition,* Eliot's suggestion is enlarged to the plane of generalization: Donne's imagery "can in fact be regarded as an early adventure into the field since exploited by the Symbolists." In both poets, Williamson insists, symbols function in the same way, whereby the emotion is "merged with the idea and both bound up with the scene which provokes them." [21] Donne's modernity, therefore, links him not only with Browning, Meredith, and Eliot, but with Baudelaire, Mallarmé, and Valéry in their common indirectness and intellectuality.[22]

Williamson's elaboration of Eliot's views has been shared by others. In his essay on "Donne's Relation to the Poetry of His Time," Mario Praz restates the definition of metaphysical poetry as the fusion of thought and feeling, and finds it "singularly akin" to Baudelaire's envelopment of philosophical thought in concrete sensation.[23] Praz, however, is concerned with an analogy in technique rather than with a broad statement of historical parallelism, and his remarks are not expanded.

By far the most extreme assertion of the identity of metaphysical and symbolist poetry may be found in Cleanth Brooks' *Modern Poetry and the Tradition* (1939). For Brooks, there is no essential difference between a definition of metaphysical poetry and of all poetry,[24] and the parallel between metaphysical and symbolist poetry is proof of this essential continuity. He finds that the "subtlety of the figurative language of the symbolist poets is analogous to that of the metaphysicals—and for the same reasons."[25] Brooks does not support this view by analyses of particular poems, metaphysical or symbolist, but it is characteristic of his flat identification that he can write of "symbolist-metaphysical poetry" as if the two terms were interchangeable.[26]

Evidently for Mr. Brooks, a "symbolist poet" is any poet who uses images and symbols in a complex and subtle way.[27]

It might be well to examine this view of symbolist poetry more carefully. Brooks' view of the symbolists is based essentially on Edmund Wilson's *Axel's Castle*. In particular, Brooks accepts at face value Wilson's distinction between two modes of symbolist poetry: the "conversational-ironic" and the "serious-aesthetic,"[28] a distinction, as we shall see, of doubtful validity. In this way, however, it is possible for Brooks to include Corbière and Laforgue among the symbolists. He insists most strongly on the metaphysical parallel for the "conversational-ironic" poets, but he does not hesitate to extend it to all poets in the symbolist tradition. Thus, W. B. Yeats demonstrates "the ultimate identity of metaphysical and symbolist poetry."[29] In *The Well Wrought Urn*, Brooks qualifies this view of Yeats considerably,[30] but in *Modern Poetry and the Tradition* he seems to hold that any poet who employs symbols or who describes feeling in an ironic or paradoxical way is perforce a symbolist. It would be better to speak of "symbolic" poetry in this broad, generalized sense if confusion is to be avoided, and perhaps this is what Brooks meant. It is difficult to escape the conclusion that his easy coalescence of metaphysical and symbolist poetry is arbitrary and extreme.

More recently as well, scholars investigating the impact of metaphysical poetry in our time have on occasion followed the example of Eliot, Williamson, and Brooks. Sona Raiziss in *The Metaphysical Passion* (1952) insists on the "strong resemblance between the symbolists and the English metaphysicals,"[31] and extends similarities in technique into an all-embracing formulation.[32] Thus, Eliot's "Gerontion" is described as a "symbolist-metaphysical poem."[33] For Sona Raiziss, as for Cleanth Brooks, the great glory of the symbolists seems to be their emulation of the metaphysicals. Joseph E. Duncan, in his recent study, follows this approach in writing of "the metaphysical poetry" of Yeats and Eliot,[34] although he is acutely aware of the limitations of the parallel—of the basic differences which offset incidental similarities.[35]

Even at the very outset, the parallelism did not go unchallenged. In a brief review of *The Donne Tradition* in 1931, Charles J. Sisson aptly remarked:

> I do not think that the study of Baudelaire is likely to help one to understand Donne. There is a profound difference between the men in the very real zest of Donne. The *Goût du Néant*, I feel, is something that would have been almost meaningless to him. . . .[36]

Similarly, it was with such views in mind that Merritt Y. Hughes in his essay, "Kidnapping Donne," argued against the tendency to make Donne's wit "a master key to literary history." [37] Sisson and Hughes intimated what later critics came to assert: that the dissonance, complex intellectuality, and bizarre figurative language of the metaphysical poets offer little direct illumination of the art of the symbolists.

Perhaps the sharpest distinction between metaphysical and symbolic poetry was drawn by Allen Tate in his essay, "Tension in Poetry" (1938). Following the view of John Crowe Ransom, he declares that "in metaphysical poetry the logical order is explicit; it must be coherent; the imagery by which it is sensuously embodied must have at least the appearance of logical determinism." [38] As a rationalist, the metaphysical poet "begins at or near the extensive or denoting end of the line." [39] The symbolist poet—which for Tate includes the romantic—proceeds in an exactly opposite manner: beginning with intensive and connotative or richly associative experience and moving toward the opposite end of the scale. Tate's distinction is unduly schematic, and his categories are so broad as to make virtually every modern poet a symbolist. He adds, however, that these approaches, while exclusive of one another, are not exhaustive. His refusal to accept the common parallelism and to explain one group of poets by means of the other marks a significant departure from the traditional formula in modern criticism.[40]

The last twenty years have witnessed a noticeable coolness in the celebration of the metaphysical poets by contemporary critics [41] and, at the same time, fewer instances of rash parallelism. Frank Kermode in *The Romantic Image* contends that what he calls Eliot's "Symbolist historiography" has seriously distorted our understanding of Donne and Milton and, indeed, of the whole course of literary history.[42] To my mind, Mr. Kermode is quite right in his view that "Donne is, to say the least, of doubtful value to the Symbolist theory," despite the tendency of Eliot and his followers to confound the two.

Attempts at redefining the character of metaphysical poetry have also worked to the disadvantage of the Eliot position. Leonard Unger has pointed out that while Donne occasionally uses a device or technique similar to that of the symbolists, such as implied metaphor,[43] figurative language in Donne is frequently explicit, marking a direct connection between the image or symbol and what it represents. Unger's analysis suggests that the common definitions of metaphysical poetry will not fit any particular poem when it is subjected to a close reading. The usual distinguishing qualities of metaphysical poetry—elaboration of conceits, irony, paradox, rich interplay of figurative language, dislocation of context, and the like—are all approximations rather than absolutes. Mr. Unger has shown convincingly that like "romantic" or "symbolist," "metaphysical" is an approximate term; nonetheless, it is here to stay and we should try to use it with what precision we can.

An altogether different approach to the definition of metaphysical poetry has been suggested by Joseph A. Mazzeo, who sees a poetic of correspondences as the key to the essential character of early 17th-century poetry.[44] Mazzeo is undoubtedly right in relating the poetics of Tesauro or Pallavicino to metaphysical figurative language, and his attack on the emblem theory of metaphysical poetry is convincing.[45] Nevertheless, Tesauro's "Imprese eroiche e Simboli figurati" point to fixed and concrete values, more denotative than suggestive. Mazzeo leaps to an identification of Renaissance and Baudelairean correspondences,[46] but it should be observed that, for the poets and theoreticians of the 17th century, correspondences aim at order and clarity rather than at vagueness and mystery, or at suggestiveness as an end in itself. As Joseph H. Summers has declared apropos of "The Poem as a Hieroglyph" in the works of George Herbert, "the meaning was precise and clear even if complex and subtle." [47]

This central difference is borne out by studies of the language of metaphysical poetry. Josephine Miles has called our attention to Donne's reliance on active verbs which serve to give body to intellectual argument, and she sees a sharp difference between the modern "substantial emphasis" and the metaphysical "active predication." [48] Donne's technique is essentially one of logical relation developed through a process of intellectual analysis at once vigorous and striking. It is a technique that, at its best, has contributed to the making of some of the finest poems in the English language, but it is remote indeed from the characteristic manner of the symbolist poets.

The symbolist movement extended approximately from 1850 to 1920, beginning in France and spreading throughout Western literature. Just as it would be incorrect to describe every European writer between 1800 and 1830 as a romantic, so it is equally wrong to hold that every French poet in the later 19th century was a symbolist. As a distinct literary period and style, the symbolist movement rests not on mere chronology but on assumptions and techniques that define the works of its adherents and link them in a common tradition. Essentially symbolist poetry is an art of suggestion, evocation, musicality, and mystery. Mallarmé's definition of poetry as "l'expression par le language humain ramené à son rythme essentiel, du sens mystérieux des aspects de l'existence . . ." [49] may serve as a key to the poetics of the movement. Increasingly, especially in France, Mallarmé has come to be viewed as the central figure and most typical exponent of symbolist poetry. Emile Verhaeren could write, as early as 1887, "A cette heure, il n'est qu'un vrai maître symboliste en France: Stéphane Mallarmé." [50] Similarly, in his masterful study of the poet, Albert Thibaudet declared, "Nul mieux que Mallarmé, par la nature de son génie et par le sens de son art, ne fut authentiquement un symboliste." [51] The existence of the symbolist movement, historically and aesthetically, is in no way dependent on the manifesto of 1886. The main line of symbolist poetics and poetry moves from Baudelaire to Marlarmé to Valéry. To be sure, there were other important symbolists: Villiers de l'Isle-Adam, Verlaine, Verhaeren, the young Maeterlinck, the young Claudel, the early André Gide—all within limits are a part of the symbolist movement. We may add lesser but no less characteristic figures: Régnier, Dujardin, Rodenbach, Mockel, Van Lerberghe, and others of kindred spirit. Despite marked individual differences, all of these writers shared Mallarmé's conviction that the object of the poet is to seize "les rapports, entre temps, rare ou multipliés; d'après quelque état intérieur." [52] Poetry is the expression or revelation of an "état d'âme." [53] In its evocation of dream, vision, and analogy it moves inward, toward the abstraction and solitude of inner life. Suggestiveness and musicality are the essential properties of the magic and mystery of poetic utterance, itself an embodiment of the mystery and wonder of the universe.

If we consider the poetry of Jules Laforgue from this standpoint, we can understand why Warren Ramsey has declared that Laforgue takes his place among the "initiators of the Symbolist movement, rather than with the true Symbolists." [54] Clearly, the unusual rhythmic and musical properties of symbolist poetry are absent in the work of Laforgue. Ramsey further asks if we may properly insist on a resemblance "between Laforgue's psychological notation and the conceit, the fancifully elaborated image of the English Metaphysicals." And he suggests that "offhand, there would seem to be little in common between the associationist, enthusiastic poet that was Laforgue and the imposer of rational design that was Donne." [55] Similarly, Martin Turnell has argued vigorously that Laforgue's psychological association is altogether different in organization from the intellectual coherence of the metaphysical conceit. "This difference," Turnell writes, "between Laforgue and the Metaphysical Poets is so vital that I must be forgiven for underlining it." [56]

The case of Rimbaud is analogous. Rimbaud was seized on by the young symbolists in 1886, largely owing to the efforts of Verlaine, yet his position as a symbolist poet is questionable, to say the least, if more than chronology is involved. André Dinar in *La Croisade symboliste* remarks, "Je confesse mon embarras devant le cas Rimbaud dans l'affaire du symbolisme." [57] At this distance and in view of post-symbolist literary developments, it is difficult indeed to group Rimbaud's poetry with that of Mallarmé and his followers. There are genuine and significant affinities in poetic theory, rising in large part out of Rimbaud's interest in magic and occultism, but these are over-shadowed by the poetics of *dérèglement*, as well as by Rimbaud's turbulent and explosive poetic style. Rimbaud is no more a symbolist than he is a metaphysical poet.[58]

Nevertheless, English and American critics, ever since Arthur Symons' *The Symbolist Movement in Literature*, have not hesitated to regard Rimbaud and Laforgue among the symbolist poets. Paul Verlaine's account of Tristan Corbière in *Les Poètes Maudits* may have had something to do with his inclusion in this group, yet Corbière is even farther from the center of the symbolist movement than either Rimbaud or Laforgue. One is obliged to conclude that what Edmund Wilson has called the "conversational-ironic" mode of symbolism does not deal with symbolist poetry at all.

The parallel between metaphysical and symbolist poetry rests not only on a casual reordering of literary history, but also on a radical elimination of the profound differences between the works of the principal metaphysical and symbolist poets. Assuredly, Donne was not a symbolist, and Mallarmé was not a metaphysical. A brief comparison of two poems distinctly related in subject matter may serve to support this view.

Donne's "The Dreame" is one of the better known poems of the *Songs and Sonnets*, part of a group of poems concerned with the joy of passionate experience. As such, however, it is relatively subdued. It is not nearly as ingenious a love poem as "The Good-Morrow" or "The Extasie," and it lacks such singular imagery as the comparison of the poet's beloved to the foot of a compass or to a hemisphere. Joan Bennett considers the poem unusual among Donne's love poems in its concentration on a single object.[59] In this sense, the poem is perhaps not wholly representative of Donne's art, yet it embodies many of his characteristic attitudes and devices.

Pierre Legouis has pointed out that the poem is a dramatic lyric, wherein a single character expresses himself freely, with the responses of his partner implied in the development of the poem.[60] This development mediates between the planes of past and present, dream and reality. While the poet was lying asleep, dreaming of the love of his beloved, she entered his room, waking him, and giving rise to the experience re-created in the poem. Dream and reality are thus inextricably bound together, as Donne suggests in the declaration, "It was a theame/ . . . much too strong for phantasie," that is, too vivid and overpowering to remain merely within the province of the imagination. The beloved is at once dream and reality, for in her presence she embodies the poet's vision. In his commentary, Grierson has called our attention to the abstract character of line seven: "Thou art so truth," in preference to the less metaphysical emendation: "Thou art so true." [61] The truth of the beloved is opposed to the falsity of dreams or fables or anything unreal. The conclusion of the first stanza issues, appropriately, in the poet's injunction: "Enter these armes." On the purely physical plane, the experience of the poem is at this point complete.

The subtlety of argument traditionally associated with Donne finds expression in the second stanza, wherein he provides an ingenious supernatural explanation of his beloved's entry into his room. She is like an angel in her loveliness, but her power to read his thoughts surpasses even that of angels. Grierson sees an analogy here to "the subtleties of scholastic theology," but Donne's avoidance of the profane is wholly for secular and private ends, even if set forth in religious terms. Louis L. Martz has described the effect as "witty blasphemy," wherein the poet deifies his mistress "by attributing her arrival in his bedroom to her Godlike power of reading his mind." [62] If angels lack this power, God does not.[63] For the poet, then, the beloved is like God.

The final stanza returns to the plane of physical passion, now viewed as a completed experience, and in the light of the celebration of the beloved in the preceding lines. The poet's assertion of the purity and spirituality of their love may be read as an appeal for its prolongation. The physical and spiritual are here fused; the poet is a torch, ready to be kindled or extinguished. With the departure of his love, he will return to the plane of dream, now inseparable from lived reality.

Mario Praz has pointed out the continental affiliations of the love-dream, wherein the poet experiences in a vision what he longs for in reality. Praz finds in Donne's poem a freshness lacking in earlier, similar poems, in that "The Dreame" is not simply "a rhetorical complaint to an absent beauty," [64] but a passionate expression of the presence of the beloved, actually before the poet's eyes. It is out of the vividness of this experience that the simplicity and directness of the language arises. Of course, we cannot be sure that Donne actually had this experience. J. B. Leishman remarks that, while he finds the poem dramatically convincing, "I think it is more likely to have been all dream than, as it professes to be, half dream and half fact." [65] This may be so, but the reality of the poem is insistent enough. As Leishman goes on to indicate, the diction "is precise and almost scientific." [66] The language may not be "strictly denotative," but it is indeed largely so, sharply restricted in association, vivid, concrete, and immediate.

Mallarmé's "Apparition" is also about the poet's dream of his beloved. It is described by Mallarmé's editors as probably his best-known poem.[67] Its relative clarity of syntax and imagery makes it far more readily accessible than the poems of Mallarmé's later style, and, in this sense, perhaps it is not altogether typical. As in the case of Donne, it is probably impossible to find a single poem that would embody all of the salient qualities of Mallarmé's art.

"Apparition" is an early poem, yet Mallarmé kept it for twenty years before releasing it for publication, possibly because of its unusual personal and sentimental quality. Just as Donne's poem may describe an experience with Ann More, so Mallarmé's may deal with an episode in his love for Marie Gherard. This is not of primary importance. There is, indeed, the likelihood that Mallarmé wrote the poem at the behest of Henri Cazalis, in homage to his friend's beloved.[68] In a letter of July, 1862, the poet declares of a poem promised to his friend: "Je ne veux pas faire cela d'inspiration: la turbulence du lyrisme serait indigne de cette chaste apparition que tu aimes." [69] Quite unlike Donne's "The Dreame," "Apparition" is not a turbulent poem at all; it is chaste, subdued, remote from the plane of sensory experience.

The use of the imperfect tense throughout the poem is a principal source of this remoteness. Whereas Donne's poem moves from present action to past recollection and then back again to the present, Mallarmé locates the experience of his poem wholly in the past, and, indeed, in three distinct phases of the past. First, there is the poet's solitary recollection of his beloved, which dominates the opening lines; then, there is the physical relation between the poet and his love, existing in a still more remote past; and finally, there is the evocation of the poet's childhood rising out of the dream-vision of his love. From the opening line, the atmosphere is one of melancholy: "s'attristait" is reinforced by "pleurs," "mourantes," and "sanglots," all suggesting a sense of pain and loss. The gap between the past and present is absolute. We should also note Mallarmé's use of synesthetic metaphor, as in "blancs sanglots," and the rich connotative implications of "l'azur des corolles," pointing, I believe, to the loss of the poet's identity with the realm of the absolute. The dream takes place on the anniversary of the beloved's first kiss; the capitalization of "Rêve" testifies to its absolute centrality in the poem.[70]   Dedicated to the total assimilation of the Dream, knowingly intoxicated by it, the poet identifies his dream-vision with his beloved, who reappeared as if in answer to the poet's self-abandonment to the allure of her image.   We know that this reappearance in lines 11–12 is fictive, the result of the intensity of the poet's dream; it is described in language that heightens the contrast between the pervading sadness and the gaiety and beauty of the beloved.   The final lines of the poem move from the plane of imagined reality to that of magic and supernatural revelation, whereby the image of the fairy, enchanting the sleep and, by implication, the destiny of the poet in his childhood, merges with the apparition of the loved one.

Even so casual a reading of "The Dreame" and "Apparition" will suggest not only a basic difference in the poets' attitudes toward love and the beloved, but more important for our purposes, antithetical renderings of the relation of dream to reality.   For Donne, the two are continuous; for Mallarmé, they are not.   Donne's dream leads outward, towards shared, physical experience; Mallarmé's leads inward, towards private and inner, spiritual experience.   Hence the relative concreteness and particularity of diction in Donne as opposed to the indefinite and suggestive language that dominates the poem of Mallarmé.   Donne's poem issues in a return to active participation in love; Mallarmé's recedes to the point of outer remoteness from any physical relationship.   Despite its relative accessibility, already in "Apparition" we may sense Mallarmé moving markedly away from his early, Baudelairean idiom, toward the technique he was to formulate in his revolutionary poetics: "Peindre, non la chose, mais l'effet qu'elle produit." [71]   The conceptualization of the concrete that was to develop in Mallarmé's later work from this doctrine of effects carries us far indeed from the witty intellectuality of Donne.

We may return with justifiable skepticism to T. S. Eliot's declaration of 1926 that in both Mallarmé and Donne "nous sommes dans un monde où tout le matériel, toutes les données, nous sont parfaitement familières." [72]   Mallarmé's sense of what Eliot describes as the real world is vastly different from that of Donne.   It is true that Donne uses symbols in his poetry, and we know that Mallarmé was profoundly interested in metaphysics, yet it would be reprehensible to call Donne a symbolist poet or Mallarmé a metaphysical poet, if these terms have any meaning at all.   Perhaps the history of the alleged parallel of metaphysical and symbolist poetry should inspire a reasonable caution in our use of such generalizations, even when speaking of their most illustrious and most typical representatives.   Perhaps especially so.

As Jean Cocteau has well remarked, apropos of Mallarmé: "Les grands poètes resistent par quelqu' endroit solide aux étiquettes qu'on leur impose." [73]

Comparison implies contrast; incidental similarity is not the same as basic identity. As part of the poetic strategy of certain poets of our time, the parallel we have considered may be altogether justifiable. Particularly in the United States, the impact of metaphysical upon modern poetry has been immense.[74] In retrospect, the parallel may charitably be viewed as an awkward attempt in the 1920's to justify the attractiveness and apparent modernity of the 17th-century poets.[75] However, from the standpoint of scholarship and criticism, the parallel offers an instructive lesson in the comparative study of literature.[76] Comparison must move hand in hand with analysis; it cannot be divorced from the aesthetic qualities of works of art in their uniqueness and radical particularity. As Mallarmé reminds us in a plea which comparatists fail to heed at their peril:

> Le poète puise en son Individualité, secrète et antérieure, plus que dans les circonstances même exaltant celle-ci, admirables, issues de loin ou simplement du dehors.[77]

NOTES

1. Joseph E. Duncan, *The Revival of Metaphysical Poetry* (Minneapolis, 1959), pp. 124–126.

2. See *The New Review*, 9 (1893), 236–247. The essay was reprinted in *Living Age* (Boston), 199 (1893), 429–436.

3. "The Poetry of John Donne," p. 244.

4. (London, 1899), *II*, 334.

5. See Bruce A. Morrissette, "Early English and American Critics of French Symbolism," *Studies in Honor of Frederick W. Shipley* (St. Louis, 1942), 164–165; and Ruth Z. Temple, *The Critic's Alchemy* (New York, 1953), 201–218.

6. Joseph E. Duncan, *op. cit.*, p. 124 and n. 29, finds a suggestion of the parallel in an anonymous article in *The Quarterly Review*, 192 (1900), 239–240. I am unable to share his view. Frank Kermode has claimed, in *The Romantic Image* (London, 1957), p. 149, that "Arthur Symons in fact developed the parallel to a considerable extent." Mr. Kermode offers no evidence for this view, and I find no support for it in *The Symbolist Movement in Literature* or in Symons' essay, "John Donne," *Fortnightly Review*, n.s. 72 (1899), 734–745. Symons was certainly capable of drawing the parallel or of extending the views of Gosse, but one may wonder if he actually did so.

7. Herbert J. C. Grierson, "John Donne," *The Cambridge History of Eng-*

lish Literature, ed. A. W. Ward and A. R. Weller (Cambridge, 1910), *IV,* 249.

8. First published in *The Times Literary Supplement,* October 20, 1921, pp. 669–670.

9. T. S. Eliot, "John Donne," *The Nation and the Athenaeum* (1923), 332.

10. T. S. Eliot, "Note sur Mallarmé et Poe," *Nouvelle Revue Française,* 27 (1926), 524.

11. See E. P. Bollier, "T. S. Eliot and John Donne: A Problem in Criticism," *Tulane Studies in English,* 9 (1959), 111, n. 23. For Eliot's definition of metaphysical poetry in the Clark Lectures, see Edward J. H. Greene, *T. S. Eliot et la France* (Paris, 1951), p. 88.

12. Mario Praz, "Donne's Relation to the Poetry of His Time," *A Garland for John Donne,* ed. Theodore Spencer (Cambridge, 1931), pp. 58–59. See also Mario Praz, "The Critical Importance of the Revived Interest in Seventeenth Century Metaphysical Poetry," *English Studies Today,* ed. C. I. Wrenn and G. Bullough (Oxford, 1951), p. 163.

13. It is interesting to note that Spanish critics have similarly insisted on a parallel between baroque and symbolist poetry. Thus, Guillermo de Torre declares that "Mallarmé es fundamentalmente un barroco," and sees between Góngora and Mallarmé "Secretas armonías y paralelismos a la distancia!" *Las Metamorfosis de Proteo* (Buenos Aires, 1956), pp. 188, 190. This view leads to a further parallelism of the baroque and the *avant-garde* that was an important part of the literary strategy of the 1920's in Spain. For an account of the history of the Góngora-Mallarmé parallel, see Alfonso Reyes, "De Góngora y de Mallarmé," *Obras Completas* (México, 1958), *VII,* 158–162.

14. Bollier, *op. cit.,* p. 112.

15. Duncan, *op. cit.,* p. 146.

16. T. S. Eliot, *Selected Essays* (London, 1946), p. 292.

17. Cited by René Galand, "T. S. Eliot and the Impact of Baudelaire," *Yale French Studies,* No. 6 (1950), 32–33.

18. Cf. Granville Hicks, "T. S. Eliot's Baudelaire," *The Nation,* 132 (1931), 20. Hicks argues that "Eliot's conception of Baudelaire underestimates the poet's significance, and is, in its way, quite as narrow as Symons's." I am grateful to Professor Wiliam T. Bandy for this reference.

19. Eliot, "Donne in Our Time," in Theodore Spencer (ed.), *op. cit.,* p. 6.

20. George Williamson, *The Donne Tradition* (Cambridge, 1930), p. 4.

21. *Ibid.,* pp. 242–243.

22. *Ibid.,* p. 246.

23. Praz, "Donne's Relation to the Poetry of His Time," p. 58. For a similar view, see Martin Turnell, *Baudelaire* (New York, 1953), pp. 290–296.

24. *Modern Poetry and the Tradition* (Chapel Hill, 1939), p. 39.

25. *Ibid.,* p. 59.

26. *Ibid.,* p. 237.

27. Brooks, "Shakespeare as a Symbolist Poet," *Yale Review*, n.s. 34 (1945), 642–665.

28. Cf. Edmund Wilson, *Axel's Castle* (New York, 1950), p. 96.

29. Brooks, *Modern Poetry and the Tradition*, p. 64.

30. (New York, 1959), p. 250.

31. (Philadelphia, 1952), p. 51.

32. *Ibid.*, pp. 30, 111, 179.

33. *Ibid.*, p. 179.

34. Duncan, *op. cit.*, p. 129.

35. *Ibid.*, p. 219, n. 36.

36. Review of Williamson, *The Donne Tradition*, in *The Modern Language Review*, 26 (1931), 233.

37. *University of California Publications in English*, 4 (1934), 67.

38. Allen Tate, *On the Limits of Poetry* (New York, 1948), p. 79.

39. *Ibid.*, p. 86.

40. It is important to note the similar reservations of John Crowe Ransom in "Eliot and the Metaphysicals," *Accent*, 1 (1940–1941), 152.

41. Duncan, *op. cit.*, p. 181.

42. Kermode, *op. cit.*, p. 146. A similar stress on the contrast between metaphysical and symbolist styles is convincingly set forth by F. M. Kuna, "T. S. Eliot's Dissociation of Sensibility and the Critics of Metaphysical Poetry," *Essays in Criticism*, 13 (1963), 241–252.

43. Leonard Unger, "Donne's Poetry and Modern Criticism," *The Man in the Name* (Minneapolis, 1956), p. 55.

44. See Joseph A. Mazzeo, "Metaphysical Poetry and the Poetic of Correspondence," *Journal of the History of Ideas*, 14 (1953), 221–234.

45. Mazzeo, "A Critique of Some Modern Theories of Metaphysical Poetry," *Modern Philology*, 50 (1952), 88–96.

46. "Metaphysical Poetry and the Poetic of Correspondence," p. 232.

47. *George Herbert* (London, 1954), p. 145.

48. "The Language of the Donne Tradition," *Kenyon Review*, 13 (1951), 46.

49. Letter of June 27, 1884, reprinted in Mallarmé, *Correspondance, 1871–1885* (Paris, 1965), p. 266.

50. Cf. Emile Verhaeren, *Impressions*, troisième série (Paris, 1928), p. 115.

51. *La Poésie de Stéphane Mallarmé* (Paris, 1926), p. 93.

52. Mallarmé, *Oeuvres complètes* (Paris, 1956), p. 647.

53. *Ibid.*, p. 869.

54. Warren Ramsey, *Jules Laforgue and the Ironic Inheritance* (New York, 1953), p. 5. The contrasts between Laforgue and the symbolists are emphasized by Marie-Jeanne Durry, *Jules Laforgue* (Paris, 1952), pp. 98–101.

55. Ramsey, *op. cit.*, p. 203.

56. G. M. Turnell, "The Poetry of Jules Laforgue," *Scrutiny*, 5 (1936), 143.

57. (Paris, 1943), p. 60.

58. For a spirited attack on the view of Rimbaud as a symbolist poet, see R. Etiemble, *Le mythe de Rimbaud: Structure du mythe* (Paris, 1952), pp. 63–104. M. Etiemble gratuitously extends his strictures to include symbolist poetry as well; his generalizations here are of very limited value, but his view of Rimbaud's relation to the symbolists is, I believe, essentially correct.

59. *Four Metaphysical Poets* (Cambridge, 1933), p. 19.

60. Pierre Legouis, *Donne the Craftsman* (Paris, 1928), pp. 75–77.

61. *The Poems of John Donne*, ed. Herbert J. C. Grierson (Oxford, 1912), *II*, 33.

62. *The Poetry of Meditation* (New Haven, 1954), p. 213. Pierre Legouis has cogently described the poet's entreaty as part of a dramatic action wherein "metaphysical subtleties reveal themselves as amorous blandishments." *Op. cit.*, p. 76.

63. Cf. Grierson (ed.), *op. cit.*, *II*, 34–35.

64. "Donne's Relation to the Poetry of His Time," p. 55.

65. *The Monarch of Wit* (London, 1951), p. 183.

66. *Ibid.*, p. 224.

67. Mallarmé, *Oeuvres complètes*, p. 1412.

68. *Ibid.*, pp. 1412–1413. Cf. Lawrence Joseph, "Mallarmé et son amie anglaise," *Revue d'Histoire Littéraire de la France*, 65 (1965), 457–478.

69. *Correspondance, 1862–1871* (Paris, 1959), p. 36.

70. For a different view, see Jean-Pierre Richard, *L'Univers imaginaire de Mallarmé* (Paris, 1961), p. 123.

71. *Correspondance, 1862–1871*, p. 137.

72. "Note sur Mallarmé et Poe," p. 526.

73. "Discours sur Mallarmé," *Fontaine*, 4 (1942), 90.

74. For an able summary of the impact of metaphysical techniques on modern American poetry, see William Van O'Connor, *Sense and Sensibility in Modern Poetry* (Chicago, 1948), pp. 81–92.

75. Cf. Arnold Stein, "Donne and the 1920's: A Problem in Historical Consciousness," *Journal of English Literary History*, 27 (1960), 16–29.

76. Frederick J. Hoffman has argued that the modern attachment to the metaphysicals is an expression of the cult of the object and the "reductive strategies of modern criticism." See *The Mortal No* (Princeton, 1964), p. 357.

77. *Oeuvres complètes*, p. 876.

APPENDIX

THE DREAME

Deare love, for nothing lesse than thee
Would I have broke this happy dreame,
   It was a theame
For reason, much too strong for phantasie,
Therefore thou wakd'st me wisely; yet
My Dreame thou brok'st not, but continued'st it,
Thou art so truth, that thoughts of thee suffice,
To make dreames truths; and fables histories;
Enter these armes, for since thou thoughtst it best,
Not to dreame all my dreame, let's act the rest.

As lightning, or a Tapers light,
Thine eyes, and not thy noise wak'd mee;
   Yet I thought thee
(For thou lovest truth) an Angell, at first sight,
But when I saw thou sawest my heart,
And knew'st my thoughts, beyond an Angels art,
When thou knew'st what I dreamt, when thou knew'st when
Excesse of joy would wake me, and cam'st then,
I must confesse, it could not chuse but bee
Prophane, to thinke thee any thing but thee.

Coming and staying show'd thee, thee,
But rising makes me doubt, that now,
   Thou art not thou.
That love is weake, where feare's as strong as hee;
'Tis not all spirit, pure, and brave,
If mixture it of *Feare, Shame, Honor,* have.
Perchance as torches which must ready bee,
Men light and put out, so thou deal'st with mee,
Thou cam'st to kindle, goest to come; Then I
Will dreame that hope againe, but else would die.

APPARITION

La lune s'attristait. Des séraphins en pleurs
Rêvant, l'archet aux doigts, dans le calme des fleurs
Vaporeuses, tiraient de mourantes violes
De blancs sanglots glissant sur l'azur des corolles.
—C'était le jour béni de ton premier baiser.
Ma songerie aimant à me martyriser

S'enivrait savamment du parfum de tristesse
Que même sans regret et sans déboire laisse
La cueillaison d'un Rêve au cœur qui l'a cueilli.
J'errais donc, l'oeil rivé sur le pavé vieilli
Quand avec du soleil aux cheveux, dans la rue
Et dans le soir, tu m'es en riant apparue
Et j'ai cru voir la fée au chapeau de clarté
Qui jadis sur mes beaux sommeils d'enfant gâté
Passait, laissant toujours de ses mains mal fermées
Neiger de blancs bouquets d'étoiles parfumées.

V | HISTORY OF IDEAS

Wolfgang Bernard Fleischmann

Christ and Epicurus

In his "Familiar Colloquy" entitled *Epicureus* ("The Epicurean"), a dialogue composed to the best of our knowledge in 1518, Erasmus of Rotterdam has his two interlocutors, Hedonius and Spudaeus, agree that:

> "If we will speak the truth none are greater Epicureans than those Christians that live a pious life. They come nearer to it than the Cynics, for they make their bodies lean with fasting, bewail their own weaknesses, either are poor or else make themselves so by their liberality to the poor, are oppressed by the powerful, and derided by the populace. And if pleasure be that which makes happy, I think this kind of life is as distant from pleasure as can well be." [1]

For the thought of an age in which, as Erasmus' Spudaeus points out earlier in the same dialogue, Epicureanism is of all pagan philosophic systems most "condemned by a universal consent," an equation of Christ and Epicurus as teachers of holy living may seem at first glance a totally unrepresentative vagary of Erasmus' mind. A tradition of critical attention both to the philosophic antecedents and to the influences upon later thought of the *Epicureus*, however, reveals that the dialogue is only one among several important Renaissance statements on the compatibility of Epicurean and Christian ethics.

More than a hundred years ago, Charles Nisard's work on what he called the gladiators of the republic of letters pointed to Lorenzo Valla's dialogue *De Voluptate* of about 1433 as a document in which a reconciliation of Christianity and Epicureanism was attempted on ethical grounds. As Nisard shows, Valla has the humanist Niccolò Niccoli, appearing in the guise of a participant in the dialogue, enunciate a doctrine of reconciliation on ethical grounds between Epicurean and Christian ways of life: "Sans donner raison au stoïcisme, il relève l'épicurisme vers les biens du ciel, dont il fait une description brillante et pleine d'enthousiasme." [2]

A brief but succinct study by B. J. H. M. Timmermans, published in the 1938 volume of *Neophilologus*, demonstrates that Erasmus' dialogue was indebted to Valla's, justly pointing out, however, that the

Epicureus demonstrates a far better reasoned understanding of classic Epicurean doctrines than the *De Voluptate:* Valla's Christian Epicureanism finds its resolution in the supreme sensual pleasures of the New Jerusalem; Erasmus', in the victory of spirit over flesh common to both doctrines.[3]

Responding for the most part to the main thesis of Thomas Mayo's *Epicurus in England* (published in 1934), to the effect that manifestations of Epicureanism in Restoration England owed their genesis well nigh solely to the 17th-century French Neo-Epicurean school of Gassendi and of his followers, Don Cameron Allen addresses himself to the earlier Epicurean thought of Valla and Erasmus, as this impinges upon the history of ideas in the European Renaissance, seen in a general and international way. Allen's key article on "The Rehabilitation of Epicurus and his Theory of Pleasure in the Early Renaissance," published in the 1944 volume of *Studies in Philology*, points to an understanding of the essential asceticism of Epicurean ethics reaching back to Boccaccio and Petrarch and making its way into the mainstream of humanist thought by way of Valla, Poggio Bracciolini, Francesco Filelfo, Marsilio Ficino, and Cristoforo Landino. "As the Renaissance moved northward," to quote Allen, "it is in the writings of Erasmus that one finds the first extended account" of Epicurus' character and doctrine of pleasure, in a sympathetic light. Vanini and Montaigne carry on a tradition of understanding commonalities on ethical grounds between Epicurean and Christian doctrines which, by the time this was established as a widespread philosophic point of view in 17th-century thought, was, Allen concludes, "more than three hundred years old." [4]

Walter Kaiser's book on the *Praisers of Folly: Erasmus, Rabelais, Shakespeare,* published in 1963, profits by its author's intensive scrutiny of studies on Renaissance Neo-Epicureanism by Saitta, Gentile, Garin, Kristeller, and Wind, as well as by his successful attempt at relating the *Epicureus* to Erasmus's major work, *The Praise of Folly*, in a meaningful way. The notion of Epicurus as Erasmus' "adorable prince of Christian philosophy," herald of a way of life at once ascetic and joyful, is, as Kaiser convincingly shows, integrally assimilated to the commanding Renaissance figures of Erasmus' *Stultitia*, Rabelais' Pantagruel, and Shakespeare's Falstaff, literary exemplifications of the wise, but optimistic, fool in Christ.[5]

Better critics than I have thus established not only the existence of an attempted reconciliation between Epicurean and Christian ethics within the history of Renaissance thought, but have further shown the concretization of these in the make-up of some eminent characters in 16th- and 17th-century literature. All of the critics mentioned here have, it should be added, been careful to point out that Renaissance Christian Epicureanism was an *avant-garde* phenomenon in relation to Gassendi's later, more massive revival of Epicurus, operating as it did against a background both of explicit antagonism from religious quarters and of popular disdain related to this. The general Renaissance image of an Epicurean was not that of the rational and reasonable Hedonius in Erasmus' *Epicureus*, but that of Ben Jonson's Sir Epicure Mammon, whose catalogue of lusts perhaps yields, to my mind, the best available synoptic statement of the attributes *vox populi* attributed to an Epicurean in the early 17th century.

> I will have all my beds blown up, not stuf't
> Down is too hard and then, mine oval room
> Fill'd with such pictures as Tiberius took
> From Elephantis, and dull Aretine
> But coldly imitated . . . My flatterers
> Shall be the pure and gravest of divines,
> That I can get for money. My mere fools,
> Eloquent burgesses, and then my poets.
> The same that writ so subtly of the fart,
> Whom I will entertain still for that subject. . .
> We will be brave, Puffe, now we have the med'cine
> My meat shall all come in, in Indian shells,
> Dishes of agat set in gold, and studded
> With emeralds, sapphires, hyacinths, and rubies.
> The tongues of carps, dormice, and camels' heels,
> Boil'd in the spirit of sol, and dissolv'd pearl,
> Apicius' diet, 'gainst the epilepsy:
> And I will eat these broths with spoons of amber,
> Headed with diamond and carbuncle. . . .[6]

In 1619, nine years after the performance of Jonson's *Alchemist*, it was possible for Julius Caesar Vanini, author of the *Amphitheatrum aeternae Providentiae Divino-magicum, Christiano-physicum, nec non Astrologo-catholicum, adversus veteres Philosophos, Atheos, Epicureos, Peripateticos, et Stoicos*, in which the pretended refutation of Epicurean thought was really an apology, as Don Cameron Allen points out, for Valla's kind of Christian Epicureanism, to be put to the stake for his beliefs.[7]

If Christian Epicureanism is thus shown as a minor aspect of early Renaissance intellectual history, and a somewhat subterranean one at that, documents relating to it tend still to be understood as representative of Renaissance concerns with Epicurean matters as a whole. Notably, the understanding of 15th- and 16th-century critical approaches to Lucretius' poem *De Rerum Natura*, the most massive and comprehensive exposition of Epicurean thought available in the age, tends to be colored by an awareness of Valla's or Erasmus' contemporaneous Christian apologies for Epicurus. As a result, Lucretius' poem and its limited but distinct popularity among an early Renaissance readership is assumed to be an integral part of Epicurean thinking prior to Gassendi's 17th-century apologia for Epicurus, which is, in turn, seen as being one for Lucretius, also. If I address myself once again to the notion of Valla's and Erasmus' Christian Epicureanism, it is for the purpose of showing that this represents an aspect of 15th- and 16th-century thought somewhat related to the contemporaneous *fortuna* of Lucretius' *De Rerum Natura*, but in the main distinct from it. A successful demonstration of two different early Renaissance traditions related to Epicurus—a Lucretian and a Christian Epicurean one (with the general and popular anti-Epicureanism mentioned above directed at both and making a third)—carries within it the possibility of clarifying later Neo-Epicurean developments in the history of ideas, in the light of possibly continuing separate Lucretian and Epicurean traditions.

As one looks back from the 15th century to the Middle Ages, two distinct descendancies on this order are definitely seen to exist. The medieval *fortunae* of Epicurus and Lucretius differ radically, in three essential ways: [8] By way of Diogenes Laertius' 3rd-century *Lives of Eminent Philosophers* and its early 14th-century Latin imitation by Walter Burley, a well-reasoned and sympathetic account of Epicurus' doctrine was continuously available to at least some learned medieval readers; Lucretius' poem, by contrast, went underground between the 9th and 15th centuries. The portrait of Epicurus, the man, painted by Diogenes Laertius, was that of a maligned ascetic, whose way of life (as distinct from his doctrine) could not but please a good Christian; St. Jerome's spurious late 4th-century account of Lucretius, the only biographical sketch of the poet available to medieval readers, shows him as driven to dementia and suicide by an overdose of aphrodisiac. There is sporadic evidence of some reasonably balanced and objective medieval thought about Epicurus; by contrast, all recorded medieval comment on Lucretius dates from the early Middle Ages only—none of this shows a comprehensive appreciation of the *De Rerum Natura* as a philosophic and poetic whole. Permit me to illustrate these three striking differences in somewhat greater detail:

Diogenes Laertius' *Lives*, with its tenth book containing a life of Epicurus, an account of his disciples, a register of his works, the letter to Herodotus with its detailed explanation of Epicurus' atomistic system, and a set of maxims, is not only surmised to have survived in Byzantium, but Western manuscripts of the Greek text date back to the beginning of the 13th century. Moreover, a Latin compendium of the *Lives*, taking over in the main Diogenes Laertius' biographical account of Epicurus and making a brief synopsis of his thought as accounted for by Diogenes, appeared in manuscript form at the beginning of the 14th century. The *Liber de Vita et Moribus Philosophorum*, for which Walter Burley, an English pupil of Duns Scotus and early fellow of Merton College, Oxford, is responsible, was widely enough circulated to be translated into Spanish before the end of the 14th century and was to serve, as we shall see later, as a highly popular epitome of Epicurus' thought available to early Renaissance readers both in Latin and in vernacular versions. By contrast, there is no evidence whatever that Lucretius' *De Rerum Natura* was available to public scrutiny between the 9th century—from which date both the earliest available manuscripts of the poem and the last echoes of its text in medieval Latin literature—and Poggio Bracciolini's "discovery" of Lucretius in 1417. For general statements about the poem, medieval readers relied on the 4th-century treatises *Adversus Nationes* by Arnobius and the *Divinæ Institutiones* by his pupil Lactantius, both of which present Lucretius and his Epicurean doctrines with polemical hostility.

St. Jerome's account of Lucretius as a voluptuary, whose imbibing of love philters is made to account both for his alleged suicide in the midst of insanity and for his poem as the product of lucid intervals, could scarcely encourage medieval acceptance of the *De Rerum Natura* as a respectable work of art. By contrast, Walter Burley takes over Diogenes Laertius' assertions that Epicurus—his doctrine of the soul's mortality and of his lacking Divine Providence nothwithstanding—lived frugally and in poverty. In Burley's version, doctrines actually emanating from Seneca, a moralist acceptable to the Middle Ages, are presented as Epicurus' own sayings: Thus meditations upon sin and pious thoughts upon death are made part of Epicurean doctrine. "Inicium [*sic*] salutis est," to quote Burley's chapter on Epicurus, "cognicio [*sic*] peccati et meditari mortem. Corrigi no vult qui peccare si nescit." [9]

The legend of Epicurus as a kind of pagan holy man, engendered by Diogenes Laertius and continued by Walter Burley, is most likely responsible for two important 14th-century statements on Epicurus, which Don Cameron Allen (without speculating upon their likely source) [10] has already noted: Boccaccio's allusion to the sobriety and asceticism of Epicurus, in the *Comento* on Dante's *Divine Comedy*, and Petrarch's identification of Stoic and Epicurean ethics in respect to the advocacy of poverty and fasting, in the *Senile Epistles*.

Over and above sporadic medieval sympathy for Epicurus traceable

to Diogenes Laertius' life, there is yet a second, not unsympathetic
view of Epicurean thought which found currency in the Middle Ages.
This is rabbinical, and found its most eminent precipitation in the
12th-century writings of Moses Maimonides. An article by Bergmann
on the usage of the name "Epicurean" in rabbinical writings, notably
in those of Maimonides, points to a general Jewish rejection of the
Epicurean, Hebraized into *apikoros,* on the grounds of religious un-
belief—never, by contrast, on those of ethical practices.[11]   Norman
De Witt, in his work on *Epicurus and his Philosophy*, holds the Jewish
refusal to accept Stoic and patristic allegations of sensual excess in
the gardens of Epicurus as an even stronger influence upon some relatively tolerant medieval views of the philosopher than Diogenes Laertius' eulogy of Epicurus' way of life.[12]

It should be stressed here, as a relevant factor, that neither the
Jewish tradition of vindicating Epicurus from charges of sensuality
nor the eulogy of Epicurus as an advocate of poverty and fasting, in
the tradition of Diogenes Laertius and Walter Burley, associated
Lucretius' name or work with the life and doctrines of Epicurus. What
critical praise of the *De Rerum Natura* was available to a medieval
reader came from Roman antiquity and was confined, for the cases of
Cicero, Ovid, Velleius Paterculus, Quintilian, Statius, and Pliny, to a
purely literary appreciation of the poem's excellence. Cicero's remark, in that letter to his brother Quintus singled out for possible
inauthenticity, to the effect that art, not intelligence, triumphed in
Lucretius' poem further detracted—if it was known in the Middle
Ages—from any appreciation the poem's intellectual parts might then
have gotten. The only indication that 9th-century scribes, at least,
felt duty bound to point to the philosophic content of Lucretius' poem
was their faithful transcription, reflected on every surviving manuscript, of explanatory headings, surmised to have originated in the
2nd century, which reflect an excellent understanding of Epicurean
philosophy. Yet these headings confine themselves, in the main, to
explicating Lucretian-Epicurean accounts for phenomena of nature,
rather than Epicurean ethics. Thus the very point of contact between
Diogenes Laertius' sympathetic account of these and of their exposition in Lucretius' poem, which might have alerted those few 9th-cen-
tury readers to whom both the *Lives* and the *De Rerum Natura* could
have conceivably been accessible physically and linguistically to a connection between them, was never established. If any but vague bel-
letristic praise of the *De Rerum Natura* survived the 9th century, it
was a recognition of Lucretius' poem as a scientific commentary literally upon the nature of things, by way of pale reflections of this aspect of the poem in Isidore of Seville's 7th-century treatise entitled *De*

Natura Rerum and Hrabanus Maurus' 9th-century one entitled *De Rerum Naturis*. It might thus be said that, at those early 15th-century moments when both Lucretius' poem and Diogenes Laertius' full account of Epicurus entered the mainstream of the Italian classical revival—the first, by way of Poggio's rediscovery of the *De Rerum Natura* in 1417, the second, by way of Ambrosius Traversarius Camaldulensis' full Latin translation of Diogenes Laertius' *Lives,* in 1431 [13] —the two documents were, by dint of medieval traditions preceding, very unequally equipped to withstand the onslaught of popular and clerical anti-Epicureanism: Burley's chapter on Epicurus, the excursions by Petrarch and Boccaccio upon his ethics, and what may have been known of rabbinical comment upon these had prepared the learned world to reject Epicurean doctrines concerned with the soul and with Divine Providence, but to accept their ethical content, indeed to make this compatible, as was accomplished both by Valla and by Erasmus, with Christian doctrine. For the case of Lucretius, however, a biography indicating both a licentious life and a sinful death, hostile patristic commentary, and—last, but not least—a polemically antireligious tone assumed in the *De Rerum Natura,* in distinction to Epicurus' more gently voiced objections, became stumbling blocks for Renaissance acceptance of the poem's full philosophic impact.

It may be said, rather, that 15th- and 16th-century interpreters of Lucretius resumed the stance of classical and early medieval ones. In the late 15th century, Pontanus, Politian, and Marullus initiated a tradition of praise for the stylistic beauties of the *De Rerum Natura* which, as Bernard Weinberg has amply shown in his history of Italian criticism in the Renaissance, became a commonplace in 16th-century treatises on poetry. Pontanus and Marrullus, again, strove faithfully to approximate Lucretius' methods of scientific argumentation and exposition within their own didactic verse, initiating a model for such 16th-century Neo-Lucretian poems as Scipione Capece's *De Principiis Rerum* of 1534 and Aonius Palearius' *De Immortalitate Animorum* of 1536. Both of these works demonstrate an acceptance of Lucretius' poem as a serious "scientific" account of the nature of things, coupled with an emphatic rejection of its philosophic implications. The one commentary upon Lucretius' text published prior to 1550, Johannes Baptista Pius' Bologna production of 1511, is frankly hostile to its poet. Petrus Crinitus' "Life of Lucretius," first published in his *De Poetis Latinis* of 1504 and reprinted in numerous uncommented 16th-century editions of the *De Rerum Natura,* does not even attribute stylistic excellence to the poem. Lucretius' verses are harsh and prose-like, "duriores . . . quasi orationi solutae similes," Crinitus asserts in a judgment which may have contributed to Lucretius' exclusion from

Renaissance classrooms where the impiety of the poet did not already guarantee this. Sixteenth-century vernacular imitations of Lucretius, Ronsard's and Du Bellay's in French, Spenser's in English, single out stylistically outstanding passages from the *De Rerum Natura*, notably the Invocation to Venus, for emulation, keeping distant from the philosophic content of the poem. In the main, then, what admirers Lucretius found in the 15th and 16th centuries were sympathetic to his powers as a poet and to his supposed insights into the workings of nature, but without tolerance for his Epicurean materialism.

Within the same span of time, the reception of Epicurus' own ethical doctrine, as associated with his biographical sketch, was on a vastly more sympathetic order. We count twenty-one editions of Lucretius published between the Brescia princeps of 1473 and the year 1600, including diplomatic reprints of commented and uncommented editions. No vernacular translations of the *De Rerum Natura* were published in that time. For the cast of Walter Burley's *Vita et Moribus Philosophorum* alone, Hermann Knust's critical edition of 1886 lists or refers to nineteen separate printings of the Latin version between 1467 and 1516, to which a published 15th-century Spanish translation, a German translation published in 1490 under the title of *Das Buch von dem Leben und Sitten der heydnischen Maister,* an Italian translation published at Venice in 1521, and a French paraphrase containing the chapter on Epicurus and published at Paris in 1536 as *La Mer des Histoires* must be added. Traversari's complete Latin translation of Diogenes Laertius had at least two printings before 1500, plus several in the century following. There are four editions of Diogenes Laertius' Greek text of the *Lives* recorded for the period 1533 to 1593. Thus a sympathetic account of Epicurus' asceticism, notably as accompanied by Burley's interpolations from Seneca, reached a larger and broader Renaissance audience than ever did the poem of Lucretius. The fact that this account was, at least down to the middle of the 16th century, entirely devoid of cross references to the *De Rerum Natura* and explicitly reconciled to Christian modes of living and dying through the efforts of Valla and Erasmus permitted the emergence of a Christian Epicureanism, a synthesis of attention to the good things on earth and in heaven, to occur. Whether Valla, Erasmus, and Rabelais were aware of Lucretius or not, they did not require the background of the *De Rerum Natura* for a formulation of Christian Epicureanism: Diogenes Laertius and Walter Burley were quite sufficient to the purpose. Indeed it may be said that Lucretius, if explicitly mentioned by Valla, Erasmus, and Rabelais, would have offered obstacles to the success—or even safety—of their doctrines in an overwhelmingly anti-Epicurean age. Thus the silence of their writings in regard to the *De Rerum Natura*, much marvelled at—particularly in the case of Erasmus—by scholars and critics,[14] may have been the result of a counsel of prudence.

At this point, I must confess to having made the Lucretian-Epicurean diptych somewhat too neat a pair of medieval-Renaissance traditions. Unluckily for a simple-minded historian of ideas like myself, any tradition contains great-minded and highly learned thinkers who see connections where the majority of scholars, critics, and readers do not. Thus in their 4th-century polemics, Arnobius and Lactantius, addressing themselves to Lucretius in a Latin reminiscent of their antagonist's poetry, were explicitly attacking the teachings of Epicurus as well. An early letter from Marsilio Ficino to Antonius Seraphicus, dated 1457, expresses notions about the compatibility of ethical tenets proposed specifically in the *De Rerum Natura* with Stoic and Christian doctrines. Of 16th-century commentators upon Lucretius' life and work, even Crinitus and Pius allow that parts of the *De Rerum Natura* dealing with the conduct of human affairs may incite to true virtue, an opinion repeated by at least four later 16th-century tractates on the art of poetry—Francesco Filippi Pedemonte's, Octavio Mirandula's, Tomaso Correa's, and Antonio Passerino's. Both Dionysius Lambinus and Obertus Gifanius, editors of commentaries to the *De Rerum Natura* published in 1563 and 1565 respectively, explicitly relate Epicurean ethics, as voiced by Lucretius, to Stoic and Christian doctrine. Gifanius' commentary carries the Greek text of Diogenes Laertius' "Life of Epicurus" by way of an appendix. John Calvin's spleen—knowledgeable weapon of a learned humanist turned sour—was vented upon Epicurus and Lucretius in like and equal measure. By contrast, Montaigne, great intellectual avant-gardist of the 16th-century, bases a reconciliation between Epicurean and Christian morality, effected in the *Essais*, both upon Diogenes Laertius and upon Lucretius. To Montaigne, as well as to Ficino, Lambinus, and Gifanius before him, I should presume to attribute as well-reasoned an understanding of the essential similarity between Lucretian and Epicurean ethical teachings as to any student of the question in centuries to follow.

Yet studying the cases of Valla, Erasmus, and Rabelais in the context of their Christian Epicureanism *sans* Lucretius has its values for the history of ideas, in spite of the proven presence of Renaissance contemporaries who were either less cautious in their published work or knew better than to argue Epicurean matters without invoking the *De Rerum Natura*. For 17th- and 18th-century thought continues to display instances of an Epicureanism at once reconciled with Christianity and separated, in the main, from Lucretius. Two of these deserve mention, in closing: The first is Pierre Gassendi's *Animad-versiones in Librum Decem Diogenis Laertii* and its companion volume, *De Vita et Moribus Epicurii*, both published at Leyden in 1647. The latter volume, on the life and death of Epicurus, was the subject of a number of vernacular popularizations and condensations in late 17th-and early 18th-century France and England—Jean François Sarasin's *Discours de Morale sur Epicure* (1651), translated into English in 1658 by Joseph Spence; Jacques Parrain, Baron des Coutures' *La Morale d'Epicure* (1685), translated into English by John Digby in 1712; and Jacques Du Rondel's *La Vie d'Epicure*, published at Paris in 1679, at Amsterdam (in Latin) between 1693 and 1698, and in English, translated by Digby, in 1712. What is striking both about Gassendi's *De Vita et Moribus Epicurii* itself, as well as about its various *vulgarisations*, is that, in the main, they follow Diogenes Laertius and Burley. The poem of Lucretius (for more authentic source for an exposition of Epicurean thought that it represents) is only sporadically and meagerly quoted. It may thus be said that the literature of the so-called 17th-century Epicurean revival, sparked by Gassendi, is essentially dependent upon Diogenes Laertius (whose tenth book is, incidentally, what Thomas Stanley calls his own chapter on Epicurus in the 17th-century *History of Philosophy*), rather than upon Lucretius, thus continuing the tradition of Valla and Erasmus not only in attempting, once again, to reconcile Epicurean and Christian ethics, but in remaining distant from the text of the *De Rerum Natura*.

The second, and more striking, instance of a continuation in the vein of Erasmus and Valla of Christian Epicureanism I should like to mention is John Locke's discussion of sensation in his *Essay Concerning Human Understanding* of 1689. Locke's sensationalism has been tied to Epicurean doctrine by Karl Borinski's work, *Die Antike in Poetik und Kunsttheorie* (1924), by Wilhelm Menzel's *Der Kampf gegen den Epikureismus in der französischen Literatur des 18. Jahrhunderts* (1931), and by De Witt's book on Epicurus, of 1954. Yet, try as one might, it is not possible to locate one explicit reference either to Epicurus or to Lucretius in all of Locke's essay. At the same time, as one reads statements like:

> Delight or uneasiness, one or other of them, join themselves to almost all our ideas, both of sensation and reflection; and there is scarce any affection of our senses from without, any retired thought of our mind within, which is not able to produce in us pleasure and pain.

or

> That we call good, which is apt to cause or increase pleasure, or diminish pain in us; or else to procure or preserve us the possession of any other good, or absence of any evil. . . .

it is clear that one is here dealing with a system of thought on sensations geared, like Epicurus', to see good in pleasure, evil in pain. Further, the system is tied to a Christian godhead. Since excess of pleasure leads to pain, and the want of pleasure to dissatisfaction with earthly objects, God, according to Locke, has given man both a system of moral balance and the occasion for turning from pleasure on earth

> "to seek [pleasure] in the enjoyment of Him with whom there is fulness of joy, and at whose right hand are pleasures for evermore."

Here we are back with Erasmus' lean and abstemious Epicureans as the best Christians, as well as with Valla's supreme sensual pleasure, as found in the New Jerusalem. Locke has adopted, without giving his sources or system a name, the tenets of Renaissance Christian Epicureanism as a basis of his own system of human sensation, made compatible—in spite of its pleasure–pain dynamic—with a Christian quest for the life beyond. Without following Borinski, Menzel, and De Witt in attributing to John Locke an authentic Epicureanism based upon meaningful confrontation with Epicurus' and Lucretius' own thought, I see Locke's sensationalism *cum* Christianity, with heaven posited as the highest sensual experience, as derivative of Renaissance Christian Epicureanism in Valla's and Erasmus tradition.[15]

Recognizing, with Norman de Witt,[16] the importance of Locke's thought for the foundation of American political philosophy, at the same time as its roots in Christian Epicureanism, one cannot but understand Thomas Jefferson's positing, in his introduction to the Declaration of Independence, a divine creator who had endowed men with the unalienable right to the pursuit of happiness as yet another intellectual heritage from Valla and Erasmus, at greater remove.

Considering the very real strains to which American civilization has been subjected through its members' continued belief that they are at once divinely created and statutorily entitled by their Creator to the pursuit of happiness on earth, one cannot help but wonder how much benefit we have derived from that portentous wedding of Christ and Epicurus, devised and codified by ingenious Renaissance minds. One might also dream that if it had been Lucretius, rather than Diogenes Laertius' Epicurus, who had been thus Christianized, the contradictions inherent in that transformation might at least have been tempered and mediated by a power which has been known both to resolve contradictions and to console the perplexed—the force of great poetry.

NOTES

1. Cf. Erasmus, *Whole Familiar Colloquies* (Glasgow, 1877), p. 401ff.
2. Charles Nisard, *Les Gladiateurs de la République des Lettres* (Paris, 1860), *I*, 282.
3. Cf. B. J. H. M. Timmermans, "Valla et Erasme, Défenseurs d'Epicure," *Neophilologus*, 23 (1938), 414–419.
4. Cf. Don Cameron Allen, "The Rehabilitation of Epicurus and his Theory of Pleasure in the Early Renaissance," *Studies in Philology*, 41 (1944), 1ff.
5. Cf. Walter Kaiser, *Praisers of Folly: Erasmus, Rabelais, Shakespeare* (Cambridge, Mass., 1963), especially pp. 63–83.
6. Ben Jonson, *The Alchemist*, ed. R. J. L. Kingsford (Cambridge, 1958), 26.
7. Allen, *op. cit.*, pp. 13–14.
8. On the medieval-Renaissance *fortuna* of Lucretius, cf. W. B. Fleischmann, "T. Lucretius Carus," *Catalogus Translationum et Commentariorum*, ed. P. O. Kristeller (forthcoming, Washington, D.C., 1967), vol. *II*. Unless otherwise indicated, all points here follow my own development in this article, with its attendant bibliographies; on Diogenes Laertius, cf. *Diogenes Laertius, Lives of Eminent Philosophers*, ed. R. D. Hicks, rev. ed. (Cambridge, Mass., and London, 1950), *I, IX–XXXVIII*, which absorbs all pertinent material previously published in relation to the *fortuna* of the *Lives;* on Walter Burley, cf. *Gualteri Burlaei: Liber de Vita et Moribus Philosophorum*, ed. Hermann Knust (Tübingen, 1886), pp. 396–420.
9. Knust (ed.), *op. cit.*, p. 276.
10. Allen, *op. cit.*, pp. 4–5.
11. J. Bergmann, "Das Schicksal eines Namens," *Monatsschrift für Geschichte und Wissenschaft des Judentums*, 81 (1937), 210–218.
12. Norman Wentworth De Witt, *Epicurus and his Philosophy* (Minneapolis, 1954), p. 355. A general *fortuna* for Epicurus is featured here, pp. 328–358, inaccurate for its total omission of Burley, but valuable for taking up Cicero's and Seneca's connections to the Epicurean tradition, which provide further evidence for a not unsympathetic view of Epicurus available to medieval readers.
13. Cf. "Traversari, Ambrogio," *Enciclopedia Italiana*, for a reliable and full account of this translation.
14. Cf., *inter alia*, Simone Fraisse, *L'Influence de Lucrèce en France au seizième siècle* (Paris, 1962), pp. 20–21.
15. On both the Neo-Epicurean revival and Locke, cf. W. B. Fleischmann, *Lucretius and English Literature, 1680–1740* (Paris, 1964), pp. 10–16, 169–171, 198–211.
16. Cf. De Witt, *op. cit.*, pp. 356–358, on Locke's Epicureanism and its intellectual descendancy in Jefferson's thought.

Index

A B C D E F G H I J   5 4 3 2 1 7 0 6 9 8